Working with the Professionals

to create the home you want

Working with the Professionals

to create the home you want

Andrew Pears
Consulting editor

Mike Lawrence

Paul Hymers

Jeff Howell

MARSHALL PUBLISHING • LONDON

A Marshall Edition
Conceived, edited, and designed by
Marshall Editions
The Orangery
161 New Bond Street
London W1Y 9PA

ISBN 1 84028 221 5

Originated in Singapore by Pica
Printed and bound in Portugal by Printer
Portuguesa

Project Editor Theresa Lane
Art Editors Fehmi Comert, Simon Wilder
Editors Sue Harper, Jackie Matthews
Photo Researcher Claire Taylor
Copy Editor Simon Gilham
Proof Reader Constance Novis
Editorial Assistant Emily Salter
Research Assistant Helen Taylor
Indexer Jill Dorman
Managing Art Editor Patrick Carpenter
Editorial Director Ellen Dupont
Art Director Dave Goodman
Editorial Coordinator Ros Highstead
Production Anna Pauletti
DTP editor Lesley Gilbert

Contents

Finding a contractor
(pp. 16–17)

Interior improvements
(pp. 34–35)

Redecorating rooms
(pp. 36–39)

Converting basements (pp. 88–91)

Improving your living room (pp. 54–55)

Converting lofts (pp. 84–87)

Creating a self-contained space (pp. 104–105)

Interior improvements (pp. 34–35)

Converting garages (pp. 92–93)

Introduction

Knowing where to start and how to proceed with home improvements can be a mind-boggling experience. Although some people love to do the work themselves, plenty of homeowners simply don't have the knowledge, skill, inclination or time to take on do-it-yourself home-improvement projects. *Working with the Professionals* is for those people. This book is divided into three main chapters: it explains how to hire and manage professionals to do your home improvements, what types of improvements can be made to your home and how your house works.

An expert can advise on the best way to achieve the maximum storage space in any room in your home, especially in the living room (above, top) and the kitchen (above).

Choosing a professional is not difficult once you know how to go about it. The first step is to decide on the scope of the work you want done so that you can select the right type of professional – for example, an architect for a major renovation or an extension, a designer who specializes in bathrooms for a bathroom refit, a contractor to oversee a standard basement conversion or a carpenter to replace your kitchen cupboards. If you have trouble choosing colours and deciding on an overall plan for your home improvements, some of these professionals, such as an architect or designer, will be able to present the best available options based on both your budget and tastes.

One area that professional designers seldom overlook is the small details – for example, the handles on these kitchen units.

Your task doesn't stop with choosing a professional – you must also think about getting estimates, creating budgets, signing contracts and developing plans that will meet planning permission and Building Regulations, as well as how to work with the professionals on a day-to-day basis once the work proceeds.

Understanding what's involved beforehand will make the whole process flow more smoothly. Unfortunately, disputes do sometimes occur and, if you find yourself in this situation, you should know the best way of resolving it.

Knowing what options are available will make it easier for you to decide how to improve your home. This book explains how the experts can make home improvements, both inside and outside a house. They may be decorative, such as replacing a floor covering, or practical – for example, adding to your house's existing wiring. Whether you want to create a large open-plan room from two small adjoining rooms, convert your garage or update your bathroom, you'll learn about the materials that you can choose from, whom you should hire, how the work should proceed and when you should inspect the work.

An architect goes through years of education and training to ensure that your home renovation is practical, safe, and attractive.

Working with the experts will inevitably involve discussing technical details that can be confusing. To help you understand the terminology and, in general, how your house works, you need to learn about the sections of the house that the experts will be renovating. This information will help ensure that you recognize good workmanship. It will also explain why the experts have to make changes in certain ways; for example, why a load-bearing wall cannot be knocked down without first strengthening the support for the structure above it. Finally, a reference section with forms and contracts, a glossary and a list of resources rounds off all you need to know in order to work with the professionals.

A designer who specializes in bathrooms (top) or kitchens (bottom) will know the latest – and best – materials available to provide you with an original room that will meet your tastes.

1

Choosing and managing the professionals

The easiest part of renovating your home is making the decision to change certain features that you don't like or find inadequate. Determining what you do want and who should make the improvements, however, can be a baffling experience. This chapter will explain what the professionals do, how to get them to do what is best for you and your home, and how to ensure that you don't incur any financial or legal problems along the way.

A desirable, innovative living space can be yours if you hire an architect who will design the renovation and choose materials to suit your tastes.

1 Architects and surveyors

Like doctors and lawyers, architects are licensed professionals. Their qualifications include five to seven years of studying architectural design, building practice and related subjects such as mathematics and physical sciences.

Traditionally, the way to organize major home improvements has been to engage an architect, surveyor or engineer to take charge of the project. In recent years, this has become less common, perhaps because of the extra costs of professional fees, the growing trend towards self-build work and also because of a lack of understanding of the professionals' role.

Some caution may be justified. For some jobs, a reliable and experienced builder will be adequate without the additional expense of an architect. However, if the work you are proposing is major – for example, an extension or conversion – you should definitely consider engaging the services of an architect or surveyor.

Getting professional advice

Professionally trained architects or surveyors will belong to the Royal Institute of British Architects (RIBA) or the Royal Institute of Chartered Surveyors (RICS; see pp. 168–171). You must make sure that the person you choose has these letters after his or her name. This means that they must work to the standards set by the professional bodies and are answerable to them. The fees that they charge for their professional assistance are also set by these professional bodies. The fee should be set against the fact that the architect could help you save money in some areas and avoid making costly mistakes in others. They should be able to advise you which of your ideas are feasible and which are impossible, or which are only possible at considerable expense.

For example, a number of home-improvement schemes will involve the creation or relocation of bathrooms and kitchens. Bathrooms and kitchens differ from other living areas because of the need for hot and cold water supplies and drainage. In some parts of a house these provisions can be made easily, but in others, pumped water systems or even structural alterations may be required to accommodate the changes. A good architect or surveyor should be able to advise you of these possibilities or restrictions at an early stage in the design process, so that no time is wasted in trying to plan changes where they are not possible.

Another popular improvement scheme is to plan for the removal of an internal partition wall to alter the room layout of a home.

The architect works with the homeowners at all stages to ensure they will be happy with the final results.

Ask yourself

- Do you need an architect? The answer is yes if your project is large or complicated such as building an extension. For simple improvements, such as installing a new window or kitchen sink, the answer is no.

- Do you know of a reliable architect? If not, ask your friends, family and neighbours for one they would recommend.

- Have you interviewed and hired an architect before? If the answer is no, compile a list of questions to ask and write down the answers. Use these notes to compare candidates.

Sometimes this can be a simple matter, but occasionally an internal wall will be structural – that is, it will be supporting the load of a floor or roof above – and its removal will entail costly structural work. Again, the advice of a professional, in this case often a structural engineer, may be useful to point out the problems and suggest alternative solutions.

Choosing a professional

The important point to bear in mind when choosing an architect or surveyor is that they will have differing experience, ideas and areas of specialization. Some concentrate on the sympathetic restoration and conservation of historic buildings, using traditional concepts and materials;

Adding an extension to the house and creating an open-plan arrangement between the old and new sections is best left to an architect, whose education and training should ensure the structural integrity of the house.

some are more interested in modern design, using the latest materials and following the latest fashions; while others prefer to merge the two, attempting to adapt older buildings into modern living spaces.

Traditionally, architects were responsible for designing buildings and supervising the construction process from start to finish. Surveyors were responsible for the inspection and maintenance of existing buildings. Today, these role distinctions have become slightly blurred, with some surveyors taking on design work, especially for extensions and renovations to older properties.

It is important to choose a chartered building surveyor, whose expertise will include structural building work, rather than a general practice surveyor, who will be more concerned with property valuations and other estate agency-type work. Contact the Royal Institute of Chartered Surveyors (RICS) for a list of local qualified building surveyors.

Making a short list

Compile a list of likely architects, then contact them to describe your project and ask if they are available to take it on. If they are, ask them to send you information about their firm, including their qualifications and experience with projects like yours. Interview your chosen short list and ask what the architect sees as the important challenges of your project, how he or she will approach it, what services are provided and what fees are charged. Ask to see their portfolio.

How to get what you want

The first thing is to be clear about what you want and what you are aiming for in any particular space. You can ask the architect or surveyor to come up with ideas but it is easier and less time-consuming if you have thought it out first. Many aspects of design will depend on whether the space is to be used for entertaining, for work or for relaxation.

You will then need to find someone who understands your aspirations and ideas and your budget and who is willing to work with you to achieve your dream home. The first step is to contact a number of different professionals and discuss your ideas with them. Explain what you want. After all, it is your home and you are paying for the advice. On the other hand, it is always worth listening to what architects and surveyors have to say and considering their suggestions before you make up your own mind.

Interior designers and specialists

As a rule, designers take on smaller, simpler and more specific projects than architects. They often provide exactly the right service for homeowners who don't need an architect's comprehensive (and more expensive) expertise.

A skilled interior designer can use his or her experience to bring the best out of a living space. As with architects and surveyors, you need to select a talented professional, someone who will work with you to produce the home that you really want.

Interior design encompasses creating a new look for the fabric of the building – the walls, floors, ceilings, doors and windows – and matching this with decoration and furnishings. It presents a wide range of possibilities, depending on the original state of the building, the amount of structural alteration that is necessary or permissible and, of course, the amount of money that is available for fittings, decorating and furniture.

Some of the best interior designers are those who are able to achieve the most with the least intervention. For example, it would be difficult and wasteful to try to replicate a totally modern interior in a Victorian ter-raced house and, similarly, there is little point pretending that a 1980s flat with two bedrooms is actually a 16th-century coaching inn with exposed timber beams and bulls-eye leaded window panes. A skilled designer will advise against such options and suggest more achievable objectives to match the clients' aspirations.

Lighting designers and electricians

One of the most important specialists to consult at an early stage in the planning of any building work is a competent lighting designer. Experienced electricians often have a good eye for lighting and are able to suggest options that produce similar effects for a fraction of the cost.

Lighting is important for setting the mood of a room, as well as providing the means to work and live efficiently and safely. With care, it is possible to have a range of lighting effects within a room that can be chosen and changed to suit the occasion. Kitchens, for example, need good light on the work surfaces for food preparation – which is often best achieved with below-unit lighting – and also a strong central light to illuminate cooking, washing and cleaning activities. However, if the kitchen also doubles as a dining area, then a retractable light over the table, adjustable with a dimmer switch, can provide soft romantic mood lighting. All of this requires extensive planning and wiring at an early stage in the project to avoid disruption to fittings and decoration later on.

Other specialists that you may wish to consult might include a window

designer (fenestration engineer), structural engineer, kitchen and bathroom installer, or heating and air-conditioning engineer. Kitchen and bathroom designers, for example, can not only design beautiful rooms for you but will also have a wide knowledge of available fixtures and appliances and be able to suggest ways of

Don't forget !

• A designer may charge fees based on hourly rates, area of the proposed work or a flat fee. He or she should include an initial and subsequent design consultation and a site visit, leading to preliminary sketches and final drawings.

• Contracts with designers vary in format and terms. Be sure you understand and agree on the contents before signing, and keep your copy to check on the work when it is finished.

- Does the designer have a speciality? For example, does he or she develop designs with mostly ethnic elements or in a farmhouse style? Or does he or she specialize in bathrooms, kitchens, loft conversions or other type of living space?

- Does the designer have a recognized qualification such as a City and Guilds certificate? Is he or she affiliated to any professional body?

- Can the designer provide references from recent customers?

- How does the designer charge for the work involved?

making these spaces more accessible for elderly or disabled users.

If you or a member of your family works at home, it may be worthwhile consulting an interior designer to construct your optimum office space with appropriate lighting and storage.

Choosing a designer

There is no professional regulatory body for designers as there is for architects. A number of professional bodies do exist, for example, the Chartered Society of Designers (CSD) and the Institute of Professional Designers (IPD; see pp. 168–171) but these societies or institutes do not oversee professional qualifications or

act as regulatory bodies. Qualifications for interior designers include City and Guilds certificates, diplomas or degrees in Design from art and design colleges or – for example, in the case of lighting specialists – the appropriate technical qualifications.

However, the best way to select a designer is by word of mouth. Ask friends, neighbours and colleagues for recommendations, especially if they have had work done that is similar to what you want. Next, try to look at some of their work or ask to look at their portfolio of completed projects. You will want someone you can trust and with whom you can establish a good rapport.

The designer and homeowner have agreed on a Mexican theme for this kitchen. The paint colours chosen for the walls are based on typical Mexican colours, and the pottery above the cupboards complements the colour scheme.

The chunky cupboards are reminiscent of old-world Mexico. The designer has chosen handles and hinges that are contemporary in style, yet they easily blend in with the cupboards.

The designer has taken great steps to obtain this Mexican theme, but the kitchen must also be practical. The kitchen island functions as a work surface and includes the stove and burners for cooking.

1 Planning and Building Regulations

A building project beyond simple repair and maintenance will require permission from your local authority's planning department. Many conversion projects also require inspection to ensure the work is safe.

The control of the erection of new buildings and the extension or alteration of existing buildings is usually exercised by the local authority or council, through their planning and building control departments.

Planning permission

Each local authority will have a local plan, which details the authority's policy towards developments within its area of jurisdiction. For example, certain areas will be designated as suitable for housing, for industrial or commercial development or for mixed residential/industrial use. Development within these areas is likely to be tightly controlled, so there is little chance of getting permission to build a family home in the centre of an industrial estate, for example.

However, if you are applying for permission to rebuild or extend an existing home, then the situation is more relaxed. In fact, small exten-sions, up to 70 cubic metres (2472 cu ft) or 15 percent of the original volume, whichever is the greater, to detached or semi-detached houses may not require planning permission at all. Nevertheless, different local author-ities follow different rules, and it may be necessary to seek permission if the proposed extension will extend beyond the existing building line, will be taller than 3.5 metres (11.5 ft) or will include windows that may overlook a neigh-bouring property.

Changing the use of a building – such as converting a barn or outhouse into some type of living accommoda-tion – may also require permission. Planning regulations become more stringent in conservation areas and in National Parks or if you live in a listed building. In these cases, the knowledge and skill of a local architect can be especially valuable.

It is never worth taking a chance with planning permission. If you go ahead with building work and find out later that you have broken one of the rules, then the consequences can be severe, invariably resulting in com-pulsory demolition.

The best approach is to consult the planning officer at the earliest possible stage and ask what is likely to be permissible. Application for planning permission is usually a relatively simple process. You, or your architect, have to fill in a form and accompany it with drawings (which may be simple sketches) of the proposed work. If planning officials are treated with courtesy and asked for their advice and guidance at every stage, it is unlikely that you will experience too many difficulties.

Building Regulations approval

The responsibility for enforcing Building Regulations rests with the building control department of your local authority. These regulations mainly deal with the structure of the building (drainage, foundations and new openings), moisture control (damp-proof courses, vapour barriers, insulation and mechanical air extrac-tion) and safety (fire doors, staircase design, windows and doors).

Building control officers will initially check and approve plans but they will also visit the site to check on the compliance with the regulations. It is not their job to check the quality of work so they will not pass any judgement on this aspect unless it was done so badly that the structure is unsafe. The quality of the brickwork, carpentry or plastering, for example, is dependent upon the skill of the builders and your own diligence, or that of your architect or surveyor who is supervising the job.

This extension required permission before work could begin. At various stages of the construction, an inspector visited the site to ensure the work met with the regulations set by the local planning authority.

Other rules and regulations

One important aspect of planning regulations relates to the party wall between your property and your neighbour's. Any building work carried out on that wall or on the boundary between the properties or within 3–6 metres (9.8–19.7 ft) of this boundary (depending on the depth of the excavation) will need a party wall award, which is an agreement between you and your neighbour.

The provision of gas and electricity supplies and, to a lesser extent, the supply of mains water to a property are also subject to regulations. Water supply is usually provided by a local company, which will connect your house to their supply at the nearest available point. For town and city dwellers this is usually underneath the pavement at the front of the property. In the country you may have to take responsibility for a longer length of service pipe. The pipe that brings water into your house must be buried at least 750 mm (29.5 ins) deep, so that it does not freeze up. If your proposed building work includes the provision or rerouting of an incoming water supply pipe, then you should contact your water company at an early stage in the planning process.

Electricity and gas supplies and appliances, because of the dangers that they can pose, should only be installed and serviced by trained and qualified personnel. This means employing certified members of particular trade associations. Gas-fired heating systems and appliances should be fitted by a member of the Council of Registered Gas Installers (CORGI) and electrical work should only be undertaken under the supervision of a member of the National Inspection Council for Electrical Installation Contractors (NICEIC; see pp. 168–171).

1 Finding a contractor

When the time comes to start your building work – after the planning is completed and all the permissions are obtained – you will need to find suitable and reliable contractors and subcontractors.

If your building project is large or complex you may use an architect or surveyor, who may supervise the entire progress of the job. If you are not using an architect, you need to decide whether to employ a contractor to oversee the job. He or she will give you an estimate for the whole of the work and will subcontract parts of it to skilled tradespeople. Otherwise you yourself will have to look for builders, joiners, electricians or plumbers.

Quality mark scheme

People often assume that there must be some kind of register of competent trained construction firms. However, this is not the case and anyone can call themselves a builder and advertise for work. The govern-

ment has launched a "Quality Mark Scheme" for builders working in the domestic sector, but membership of the scheme is voluntary and it is not yet clear what effect, if any, it will have on standards. One problem with a voluntary scheme is that small firms or sole traders, although they may be competent and reliable builders, might be put off by the paperwork and administration involved, as well as the cost of the membership fees. Another problem is that less reputable firms may join the scheme simply in order to give themselves credibility and use the membership in their advertising.

Builders' qualifications

The best way to find reputable workpeople is to choose a firm whose directors or owners have professional qualifications. Do not be afraid to ask them. The Construction Industry Training Board is responsible for the training standards in the industry. Individual tradespeople may have a City and Guilds qualification, a National Vocational Qualification (NVQ) or a skills certificate. In Britain the best building firms will be members of the Chartered Building Company scheme and their directors will be Fellows or Members of the Chartered Institute of Building, with the letters FCIOB or MCIOB after their names (see pp. 168–171).

A common piece of advice is to use builders who are members of trade associations, but homeowners should be aware that membership of these associations is open to anyone who can pay the annual subscrip-

tion fee. Few builders' trade associations require applicants to produce evidence of training or qualifications and these associations exist for the benefit of their members.

The two exceptions to this are the associations that control fitters of gas appliances and electricians. Gas and electrical work must only be undertaken by trained and registered

Ask yourself

- Does the size of your project warrant hiring a contractor? The answer is yes if you need to hire more than four people.

- Has the contractor been in business for at least four years? Can he or she provide references from satisfied customers?

- Does a potential contractor have adequate insurance to protect you in the case of any accident, shoddy work or breach of contract?

- Does the contractor have experience working on projects similar to yours?

In a home renovation where a wall is knocked down and replaced by floor-to-ceiling windows, the contractor will be responsible for hiring and overseeing a number of other professional tradespeople.

professionals. If you choose a company from the Yellow Pages or other advertising, look for the CORGI and NICEIC logos (see p. 15).

Historic buildings

If you are looking for a builder to work on a building of particular historical interest, it may be worth seeking advice from an organization that takes an interest in these things. For example, the Society for the Protection of Ancient Buildings (SPAB) has lists of contractors skilled in the use of traditional techniques and materials to restore older properties. Other organizations specializing in the conservation of buildings of a particular period are the Georgian Society and the Twentieth Century Society. Builders located through organizations such as these are familiar with the structure and materials specific to the period in which the house was built and have contacts with other suitable tradespeople.

Asking advice

If your building project entails the services of an architect or surveyor, then you will be able to take their advice on tradespeople to employ. In the absence of a supervising architect or surveyor, the usual advice given to people looking for a reliable builder is to seek recommendations from friends and neighbours who have recently had work done. They may not, of course, be able to judge the quality of work done but you can ask them at least about the builders' punctuality, reliability and tidiness.

• Did the professional turn up on time in the morning?

• Did he or she turn up every day, or was jobs being juggled so there were days when work didn't proceed?

• Did he or she do everything that had been promised?

• Did he or she clean up the work site at the end of every day?

Some areas have neighbourhood associations that pool information and experience about useful local facilities. You may also make enquiries at your local council's building control department, which normally has a list of approved builders to tender for work at various price levels. These last resources will at least provide a

Facts & figures

When having work carried out on your property you should also consider the insurance angle. Ask your contractor whether they have an "All Risks Policy", which will cover for both damage to your property and accidents to people.

You should also notify your household insurance company that building work is being carried out.

useful constraint on your builder as he or she will wish to remain on the neighbourhood or council list.

Asking the right questions

For many jobs, householders will have to employ a local builder located through an advertisement in a local shop window, newspaper, the yellow pages or a local trade directory. In this case, the only way to check on the builder's credentials is to question them.

Ask about their experience and qualifications, how many years he or she has been in the trade, and for details of other work completed by them in the area. Ask whether he or she has done work similar to that which you are planning. The builder may have a portfolio of work or, better still, may be able to arrange for you to see work done in another house in the neighbourhood.

Ask the builder when he or she will be able to start and for an estimate of when the job will be finished. For building work that will involve more than one trade – for example a new kitchen, which will need plumbing, wiring and carpentry – it is important to know whether all the work will be done by your builder or his or her employees, or if subcontractors will be brought in to do specialized tasks.

1 Inviting quotations

If you decide to invite several different building firms to tender for your work, you need to know how to compare their estimates so that you know that you will get the best work at the best price.

The normal procedure is for your architect to ask three reputable building contractors to tender for the work. If you are not using an architect or surveyor, it is still advisable to follow the same procedure yourself by getting three quotes or estimates.

Inviting quotes

The architect should produce detailed drawings of the "before" and "after" state of the property (generally titled "existing" and "proposed") with an accompanying written list of the operations to be carried out, referred to as a specification, or "spec" for short. A larger job will also have a "bill of quantities", which is a precise list of materials and labour operations involved in the job, drawn up from the plans by a quantity surveyor. The bill of quantities is used by the builder to estimate the price.

These documents are sent out to the three (or more) contractors, who are invited to submit a fixed price for the work, together with evidence of their bona fide business status and possession of suitable insurance cover. You and your architect have to then decide which tender is the most promising. Note that this does not necessarily mean choosing the lowest price, but can also depend upon a builder's track record and their reputation for quality and reliability.

Comparing quotes

It is important to realize that you will not be able to compare these estimates unless they are for exactly the same job. Suppose you are planning a small lean-to conservatory for the back of your house, and you call in three local

builders and simply ask them how much they would charge to build a conservatory on that site. You are quite likely to be given three wildly varying estimates. One builder may be envisaging dwarf brick walls, with a suitable concrete foundation, while another may be thinking of building with glass panels straight on top of the existing patio slab. One may be thinking of double-glazed PVC windows, but another is planning for traditional single-glazed timber windows. Similarly, the provisions for drainage may vary from a new back-inlet gulley to feed rainwater from the roof directly into the drainage system to simply letting the roof water discharge straight onto the ground.

All these factors are variable, and all are reasons why the cheapest price may not represent the best value. It is important to discuss all the options and ensure that the builders' written

quotes specify exactly what they are planning to provide for the money (see pp.164–165).

Checklist for a quote

Points to consider include:
- Drainage and water disposal
- Heating (and can your boiler cope with the added demand)
- Lighting (can the existing consumer unit cope)
- Decoration – for example, what type of paint and how many coats
- Rubbish – specify who is responsible for clearing up and how often
- Timescale – always get a timetable
- Lead-in period – how long will it be before they start the job
- Payment terms
- VAT
- Defects period and guarantees
- Contractors' work area and storage
- Insurance of the work
- Health and safety

Don't forget

Make sure estimates include as much information as possible:

- Contractor's qualifications and proof of their insurance status, plus a health and safety assessment of the works.
- Fees for permits, building control and utilities if appropriate.
- Allowance for demolition, clean-up and debris removal.
- Allowance for site work, including levelling, tree removal and landscaping.
- Allowance for project construction (including itemized costs and allowances for all work and materials and a statement of who pays for telephone calls and the water and electricity used).
- Allowance for finish and decoration work (also itemized as described above) and a contingency allowance for unforeseen works.

Costs of materials

A critical factor that affects the price of building work is the cost of materials. Bricks, for example, can range in price from around £150 to over £400 per 1000 bricks, depending upon type, quality and appearance. Building work should ideally use bricks matching the originals. For old Victorian houses, it may be necessary to use second-hand or "reclaimed" bricks, available from demolition contractors or architectural salvage companies. (In fact, if you have had to seek planning permission for your work, the local authority may have specified "second-hand bricks to match originals".) The cost and quality of second-hand bricks can vary, so make sure your builder will be able to obtain a suitable supply and that his or her price is for that type of brick. You can ask to see a sample.

Another example of wide variation in cost is electrical fittings. Wall-mounted electrical power sockets can vary in price by up to 200 percent, depending upon type and quality. The better quality ones, carrying a British Standards Specification "kitemark", will cost more, but they have a proven safety record and will probably last longer. So, if electrical work is involved in your building project, make sure that your builder has specified the type and make of the materials he or she intends to use.

When examining a bid, you should always scrutinize it for all the details. The bid for this bathroom included work and materials supplied by a plumber, electrician, carpenter and tiler. Plumbing fittings vary widely in price and quality.

Ask yourself

- Do the quantities and quality of materials differ between bids?

- Do the materials differ from those indicated on the drawings or specification?

- Are any steps or materials left out, intentionally or by mistake?

- What about the prices quoted for materials or products. Are they accurate and reasonable?

After you have hired a contractor for your project, the next steps are to negotiate and draw up a formal contract. The contract binds both the contractor and you to fulfill all aspects of the agreement and it should be drawn up carefully.

A contract is a legally binding business agreement between the two parties who have signed it once they have agreed upon the supply of goods or services, the standard of work and the price. Most contracts that we enter into in the course of our everyday lives are informal or verbal, but they are still legally binding.

For example, you are entering into a contract when you buy something, however small, in a shop. You have paid the asking price and the shopkeeper has provided you with goods, which are expected to perform satisfactorily according to their description. Building work is the same in law as any other commercial transaction. In practice, many small building jobs are undertaken without a written contract, but remember that there is always an implied contract. Most of these jobs work out satisfactorily for both the client and the builder, but on the odd occasions when disputes arise, the lack of a contract can prove to be a major problem.

Do I need a contract?

In view of the many variables involved in building work and the possibility of the disputes that can arise between householders and builders, a suitable contract can solve or prevent a lot of problems. The most common causes of disputes are, from the builder's point of view, when the client has asked for additional work or changes to the original plan after the job has started, and from the client's side, when the builder takes longer to finish the job than agreed.

At its simplest, a contract may consist of no more than a one-page letter, describing the work to be done, the agreed price and the agreed completion date. There are, however, certain conditions that must apply for the document to be legal. These are that both parties must have accepted the agreement; they must both be at least 18 years of age and of sound mind; the work and conditions set out in the contract must be practically achievable; and both parties must derive benefit from the contract – that is, one party will have the renovation

Before signing a contract, make sure it includes details of all the work involved in the project, as well as who is responsible for doing the work. This kitchen renovation required coordinating a plumber, electrician, flooring expert and carpenter to install the new materials.

done for them and the other will receive money for the work.

Building contracts are between the client – who, for the purposes of the contract is known as the employer – and the builder, who is known as the contractor. Each of these parties may be a single person or a group of persons; however, if it is a group of persons such as a company, one individual signs the contract on behalf of the company.

A homeowner's contract

The Joint Contracts Tribunal (JCT) (see pp. 168–171) has recently drawn up a new building contract form aimed at making transactions between builders and homeowners more understandable and to help prevent dis-

agreements. These forms are available from high street retailers. They are simple in outline and language but detail exactly what the contractor and the customer are obliged to deliver in terms of prices, payments and time-scale. They also allow for variations from the original plans to be agreed upon as the work progresses. If your project is anything other than a very simple job, it is recommended that you use one of these contracts.

Letters of agreement

On a simpler level, a contract in the form of a letter of agreement between yourself and the builder will serve as a suitable legally binding document. The letter should include details of the name and address of yourself and the builder, the address of the property to be worked on and a full description of the work to be carried out, including the use of specific brands or types of materials to be used if relevant. If there are any drawings or specifications that have been used in the course of negotiations, these should be numbered, photocopied and attached to the letter, which should refer to them by number.

The letter should contain details of the contract price agreed between yourself and the builder, and an agreed start and finish date. It may also include provisos such as that the agreed contract price will only apply as long as work commences within one month of the agreement, and details of any agreed damages for running over the agreed completion date. Also important are rates for additional work, insurance details, health and safety arrangements and VAT provision. The letter should be signed by both the client and the builder and it should be countersigned by an independent witness.

For a sample letter of agreement and contract to use as a model, see pp. 164–167. Remember that you can change the phrasing of the letter or contract to suit your project.

Don't forget !

Depending on the complexity of your project, here are key items to look for in any contract:

- The contractor's name and business address
- Provision for obtaining all the necessary permissions
- A binding estimate of costs
- Plans and specifications
- The project start date, the interim deadlines and the formal completion date
- Provision for alterations to the plans or project after the contract has been signed
- Provision for removing or saving old building materials
- Specification of any work to be done by the homeowner
- Details of what facilities on the premises may be used by the contractor
- Provision for clean-up and site restoration
- Complete price for the job
- Payment schedule
- Warranties by the contractor to remedy defects in materials and workmanship (this extends to their subcontractors)
- Conditions under which the contract can be terminated
- Hold-back clause (withholds a portion of the contract price until the job is completed to homeowner's satisfaction)
- Arbitration clause (agreement to submit disputes to arbitration)
- Acceptance clauses (describes responsibilities of signatories)
- Places for signature by the homeowner and the contractor

Creating a budget

Deciding to have building work done on your home is perhaps the easiest step. Making decisions on how much money to spend on it – and making sure that the money is spent efficiently – is more difficult.

Budgeting for your building work must be thought out from the beginning. The worst scenario is to have to call a halt with an unfinished project. Building is not an exact science, and where alterations, extensions or repairs are taking place on an existing home, it is not uncommon for unexpected difficulties to arise during the course of the work. It is quite common in any type of building operation for the job to cost more and take longer than the original estimates, and it would be no bad thing to budget on a 25 percent increase in costs over the estimates. If the extra costs amount to less than this, then rejoice, and put the saved contingency money towards your next project – or a well-earned holiday.

If you have engaged an architect or surveyor to design, plan and manage your building project for you, then the finances will have been involved in his or her calculations right from the start. If the work is very extensive, the architect may even suggest employing a quantity surveyor to do the costing.

Which estimate to choose

If you are organizing the work yourself, and you seek estimates from three contractors, then they should all come in at within 10 percent of each other. If one is much higher than the others, it may be that the contractor doesn't actually need the work, but would consider it if you agreed to an inflated price. However, if one estimate is much lower than the others, then it may be that either the contractor is short of work (ask why), or that he or she has made a mistake in the calculations, which means that he or she

The renovation on this kitchen included installing ventilation for the cooker (which was moved to the island), new cupboards, lighting and flooring, and a new window.

may get halfway through the job and then realize that it can't be completed for the price. For these reasons, the middle quote can often be the most accurate, and the most promising.

Facts & figures

Before hiring a contractor or worker make sure you are clear about whether or not VAT is included in the pricing of both the materials and the services. Some "approved alterations" to listed buildings are zero rated and some smaller firms may not be registered for VAT. You should ask for VAT registration details and check with your local VAT office if necessary.

Budgeting is made easier by considering the following points:

- Avoid changes of plan
- Keep an up-to-date record of expenditure
- Avoid false economies in cheap fittings, shoddy materials or unknown workpeople
- Do not suppose that, if you decide to do some of the work yourself, it will therefore cost nothing.

The "black market"

You may well find a builder prepared to offer you a reduced price for paying in cash, rather than by cheque. The builder is suggesting this option so that he or she can avoid paying tax to the Inland Revenue, National Insurance contributions to the Department of Social Security or VAT, all of which are illegal manoeuvres. You would be unwise to involve yourself in any such dealings. Also, you will not get any relevant documentation with cash transactions, so if there should be any disputes as the work progresses, you may find it difficult to prove how much you have paid and for what. Always avoid cash payments, and make sure your builder supplies you with invoices and receipts for all payments made.

However, a low quote may be from a contractor starting up and trying to build up a client base (see pp. 164–165).

Making savings

The cost of building work is often roughly equal for labour and materials, and it may be possible to get work done more cheaply by economizing on either of these factors, or both. However, be wary of the "cheap" job option – if it is done to a poor standard, it may cost you more to have it put right.

There are potential savings to be made in the price of materials, especially by phoning around different suppliers and comparing prices. It is sometimes possible to negotiate large discounts by playing off one supplier against another, but this depends upon the size of your order and how busy the suppliers are. Unless the materials are covered by the builders' guarantee, you can also buy materials in advance of your building project if you see cheap special offers advertised. However, remember that tradespeople often get trade discounts, so using a professional to buy materials may be the better option.

For smaller jobs

An easy way of finding out how much a particular building project should cost is to look at a selection of ready-made solutions. If you are thinking of a new kitchen or conservatory, for example, you can write in or phone up for details from advertisers in the local press or Yellow Pages. This will give you some basic idea of what is available for the price. However, take into account that different manufacturers will describe things in different ways, and it is important to be clear about exact dimensions and the type and quality of materials used.

Having got a rough idea of the sort of price that you could expect to pay for an off-the-peg building product, you can call around local builders or specialist tradesmen to ask what sort of prices they might ask for producing and installing a similar product. Asking for customized changes to suit your needs could affect the price.

This kitchen refit was less expensive than the one shown to the left. The cupboards are more basic and fewer were needed for the smaller room, and the cooker is in the same position as the old one, so the utilities did not need to be moved.

Deciding on the order of work

The sequence of operations involved in any building project can be vital in getting the job completed on time, within the budget and to a professional standard – so it is important that your contractor carries out the work in a specific order.

To understand how the various construction tasks follow each other, it may be helpful to consider how a traditional brick-built new home may be constructed by a professional building contractor. Not all of these operations will apply to your project, but some of them certainly will, and if you are employing professional builders, then they will expect things to follow a similar pattern.

Site preparation

First in any construction project will come site clearance, including the demolition of any existing buildings and removing landscaping features such as walls, fences, paths and patios.

Any materials from the demolition which are to be saved or recycled will have to be separated, cleaned off and stored in a suitable location. For maximum efficiency, it is important that materials on site – whether new or recycled – should not be moved more than once. This means storing them in an area where they will not get in the way of any other operations later on. A good contractor will also time the deliveries of any new materials to arrive only when they're needed. Materials storage may be provided by temporary requisition of the garage or garden shed, or in a cleared area of the garden, where materials can be stacked and covered over with polyethylene sheeting to protect them from the weather.

The next stage comes under the general term "groundworks", and includes levelling the site, removing topsoil, preparing the sub-base for paths, drives and patio areas, and digging trenches for foundations and the service pipes (water, gas, electricity and telecommunication cables).

Building the shell

The concrete can now be poured for the foundations, followed by the building of brick walls up to ground floor level and the laying of a damp-proof course in the brickwork. The next part of the building, the construction of the walls, the upper floors and the roof, is known as the shell or superstructure and, for most people, is the most recognizable part of the construction process. However, even when the roof is on, the building is nowhere near completion, and the fitting-out of the interior can take as long, or longer, than the construction of the shell.

Door and window frames may be installed as the shell proceeds, or they may be fitted by carpenters afterwards in openings left for the purpose. Internal plumbing pipes and electrical wiring will next be fitted, and then the walls and ceilings will be plastered or dry-lined with plasterboard.

Smaller works

The construction of a conservatory or small extension to an existing house may actually proceed along similar

Home extension progress chart

ORDER OF WORK	NUMBER OF WEEKS											
	1	2	3	4	5	6	7	8	9	10	11	12
Demolition and site preparation	■											
Foundation excavation		■										
Foundation concrete			■									
Walls to damp-proof course (dpc)				■								
Oversite preparation				■								
Ground floor structure					■							
Drainage work					■							
Walls to roof						■						
Roof structure							■					
Roof coverings							■					
Windows/doors								■				
Break through								■				
Electrical 1st fix									■			
Plumbing 1st fix									■			
Plastering										■		
Joinery										■		
Rainwater goods											■	
Electrical 2nd fix											■	
Plumbing 2nd fix											■	
Drains testing											■	
Decorating												■

A combination dining room and sunroom was gained by building an extension over part of an under-used garden. The site had to be cleared of an old concrete patio and steps before building work could begin.

lines to the above, with groundworks, foundations and services pipes, followed by the shell. Other building tasks will be simpler and the order of work will still be similar, but it is important to remember that the final finishes – that is, the plastering and decoration – should only take place after all the other work has been completed. There is often a strong temptation to get a building job "tidied up" by calling in the plasterers and decorators, especially if you are living in the house at the time and are fed up with the dust and disruption. But there is really no point in producing a nice finished surface if it then has to be spoiled by the electrician cutting into it to install another cable somewhere.

For a smaller job, such as refitting a new kitchen or bathroom, the "site clearance" operation will, naturally,

be much simpler but may still involve a small amount of demolition (such as removing a disused chimney breast or internal partition walls), the hacking-off of damaged areas of plaster or the removal of outdated plumbing and electrical systems.

First and second fix

The sequence of operations described above is slightly complicated by the fact that several trades – carpenters, electricians and plumbers – have to separate their work into two distinct phases, which occur before plastering and after plastering. These are known as "first fix" and "second fix". For example, the first fix for an electrician is laying cables and fitting galvanized steel back boxes to take light switches and power points. After the plasterer has finished his work, covering the

cables and leaving the wall surfaces flush with the back boxes, then the electrician will return for the second fix, which means fitting the switches and sockets and connecting the cables to the electricity supply.

Similarly, after the basic carpentry of studding walls or joists has been done, the carpenter will return when the plastering is finished to attach mouldings such as skirting boards and picture rails and to construct fitted furnishings such as hanging space in the bedrooms or kitchen cupboards.

The end of the job

The timescale of building work is always deceptive because the major demolition and construction work appears to progress quickly – big changes appear in a short space of time – whereas fixing mouldings, water-proofing around bathroom fittings, grouting tiles and general "finishing" take much longer and you may think no progress is being made. At this stage, it is inevitable that some time will be lost as plaster cures and wood finishes and paint dry.

In addition, although you should have made sure that the builders clean up as they go, insofar as it is possible, you will certainly need several cleaning sessions after they have gone as the "dust settles".

Living with contractors

Most of the worst building stories concern the tribulations of trying to carry on a normal life while having building work done at home. With a large-scale project, it is often not unreasonable to decide to stay somewhere else for a few days.

Living with building work can be very difficult. If you or members of your family are usually at home during the day it may be better to schedule the work to coincide with a holiday. However, this is not always possible and many building jobs will have to take place while the house is occupied, so a certain level of inconvenience will have to be expected and endured. You should discuss this issue with your builder to ensure that disruption is kept to a minimum. The contract that you draw up with them should include these issues (see pp. 20–21).

Certain construction projects take place entirely outside the living area – for example building a new garage, an extension or a conservatory – and these should involve only minor intrusion into the home. But there will still, unavoidably, be noise, dust and the possible obstruction of access.

Noise

The builders should make it clear what their working hours will be and agree that they will not work outside these hours without permission. Some builders like to start work early, especially in the summer months. If you or your neighbours are likely to be disturbed by this then make this clear to the builders from the outset. Similarly, many builders like to listen to a radio while they work. If this disturbs you or the neighbours, especially if anyone is studying or working at home, ask for the volume to be kept low – most builders are rasonable. Disagreements often arise because of misunderstandings, so make your expectations clear right from the start.

Dust

There will always be a certain amount of dust or mess involved in building work, and a conscientious contractor will do his or her best to ensure that this does not intrude into the living areas. Where dust is unavoidable – as when an internal partition wall or ceiling is taken down – then the builder should seal off the area from the rest of the property by securely taped polyethylene sheeting over doors and windows. Carpets and other floor coverings are best removed or at least covered with linen dust sheets. Dust levels can be kept low by regular vacuum cleaning and by sprinkling water onto concrete or timber floors before sweeping up.

Avoiding obstruction

Maintaining safe and unobstructed access to the property during building work is important, especially for children, elderly people and the disabled. Builders should be instructed to do their best not to block access with materials and to keep the area clean and free of litter and debris. Disputes with neighbours can sometimes result from builders' vehicles blocking driveways or taking up parking space in city streets.

Deliveries of materials can be difficult for builders in congested areas. If an important delivery is scheduled a polite notice can be left somewhere visible asking neighbours or people who regularly park there to leave room for this.

Utilities

Builders may need access to certain facilities and this should be agreed beforehand. They may need to use your telephone occasionally and you may arrange that they use your bathroom and kitchen. In addition they will need water, and this is best provided via an outside tap. Otherwise, they will have to come into the kitchen or bathroom with muddy boots to fill buckets. It may be worth having an outside tap fitted as part of the work; you will always find it useful in the future.

Electricity can be provided externally by the fitting of a special weather-proof external power point; this will avoid the builders having to trail extension cables out through windows or doors. Finally, you should be clear about any security risks while the house is open and agree with your builders about who is responsible for the necessary precautions.

Complete renovation of a kitchen or bathroom may mean making other arrangements for eating and bathing until the work is finished.

Ask yourself

- What hours does the contractor plan to do the work?

- How does the contractor plan to keep dust and construction debris to a minimum?

- Has the contractor made plans for the work in such a way that access to your home will not be blocked?

Don't forget ❗

- Write into the contract any agreed-upon policies that will help keep interruptions to a minimum.

- Try to limit excessive noise by workers during the day to avoid disturbing family members or neighbours working at home.

- Try to interfere as little as possible with your workpeople.

1 Handling disputes

Getting construction work done on your home sounds like a relatively simple process. A building contractor does the work for which you pay. But, unfortunately, in real life construction is a complicated job.

Every building project and the relationship between the contractor and the homeowner is different. Even the best contract cannot allow for every detail or every eventuality. The best way to avoid problems is to communicate on a daily basis with your tradespeople. However, unavoidably, disputes do sometimes arise. Most disputes occur over variations in agreed upon work, costs or estimates, and variations in schedules or timing. Unacceptable quality of work is a close third.

Avoiding disputes

No matter how good your relationship with the building contractor is at the beginning of the job, there is always the possiblity that things will sour before the end, so the existence of a suitable contract and the supervision of an independent professional, such as an architect or surveyor, are always the best routes to follow. An official JCT contract (see p. 21), accompanied by the relevant drawings and specifications for the job, will lessen the risk of disputes, as everything should be set out in black-and-white and signed by both parties. If you have such a contract, the RIBA and the RICS both provide an adjudication service at a fixed price to assist either party in the dispute (see pp. 168–171).

Building projects are very stressful. Whenever a problem arises, try to keep calm and be reasonable with all the parties concerned. Remember that the builders will want to avoid the problem as much as you do. They have their reputation at stake and also cannot afford any delays in finishing your work and starting a new job.

The more involved a renovation is, the more likely it is that problems will arise. You can avoid confrontation with the professionals by going over all the details thoroughly during the early stages and throughout the project.

Changes of plan

If you have a less formal relationship with your builder, then try to avoid disputes by keeping a close eye on work as it progresses. This is particularly important if you request changes in the work as the job goes on. Suppose you are having a new kitchen installed and, while the new room is being fashioned from the old, you decide that it would be a nice idea to incorporate an extra light – for example, an adjustable-height downlighter over the dining table controlled by a dimmer switch. You mention this to the builder who agrees to the idea. You may assume that because he has agreed, he intends to install the extra items as part of his overall package, with no extra cost.

However, at the end of the job you are shocked to receive an invoice that has had £300 added to it for the extra work. The builder claims that he has had to call an electrician in for an extra half-day's work; had to spend time on the telephone ordering the parts, and that the extra task has delayed his already tight schedule by another day. This in turn has cost him money by delaying his progress on another job. The contractor's claims may be spurious, or he may feel that that this is genuinely what the extra work has cost him. In either event, the misunderstanding could have been avoided at the outset. Whenever you request a variation in the original agreed specification, make sure that you ask how much extra the work will cost, and also get something to that effect in writing.

Legal arbitration

If a dispute cannot be resolved by discussion and common sense, you can suggest arbitration by the RIBA or, if the amount of money involved is relatively small, you may be able to settle it by the Small Claims procedure. This is cheaper and quicker than engaging a solicitor and going to the county court (see box below).

However, you may in the end have to engage a solicitor to act on your behalf. The solicitor will also probably suggest using an arbitration service, designed to resolve disputes of this nature without the expense and stress of using the county court system. Once your builder knows that you are seeking legal advice, he or she may propose compromise terms of his or her own, which you would do well to consider before incurring further legal costs. In all events, remember that you should always keep any documentation relating to your work right from the beginning, as it may be vital in proving your case.

Bankruptcy

The worst thing that can happen is that your builder goes bankrupt halfway through your job. If this happens, then you must quickly take the

following step. If the builder has a set of keys to your property, then change all the locks. This may sound dramatic, but the builder may owe money to employees, subcontractors or builders' merchants, who could try to recoup their losses by helping themselves to what they see as "their" property, in the form of tools or materials left in your home. If any of them try this, then you should explain that, whatever the rights and wrongs of the situation, the builder has supplied the materials to you, that they are not allowed to enter your property without your permission and that any problem they have should be referred to the liquidator.

Thankfully, most building jobs proceed perfectly satisfactorily and disputes are rare, so do not be alarmed by this "worst case scenario". However, the best advice is always to guard against such events by having a proper signed contract with your builder or contractor from the start.

Alternative choices   !

If your dispute is for less than £5000, you can follow the Small Claims procedure. You have to obtain a form from the local County Court with the details of your case. A fee is payable up to a maximum of 10 percent of the claim. You should have copies of all the written communications between you and your builder, and if relevant, photographs of the problem area. Your claim will be registered and you will be given a date for a hearing. Usually this is less formal than a County Court, for example, the party sits around a table. You may take a representative with you or not. For larger claims you will have to go to the County Court and will need the help of a solicitor.

At the end of a building project, anxiety can set in for both the homeowner and the contractor. The latter, who generally has the experience of many similar jobs to draw on, may declare the work substantially finished, but you may not agree.

If your home improvement project has been supervised by an architect or surveyor, they will have made regular visits to check on the progress of the job and to authorize stage payments to the contractor by signing interim certificates. (Interim certificates are, in effect, written confirmation that the work has been completed satisfactorily up to an agreed-upon stage.)

Snagging

When a project is nearing completion, the architect will usually make a site inspection and note any defects or "snags". This process is therefore known as snagging. The snagging process should be followed for all jobs, even those that you are supervising yourself. Common defects to watch out for include cracked or imperfect plaster finishes, missing screws from electrical fittings, incorrectly sloping guttering and uneven flooring. You should always check that doors and windows open and close properly – including the satisfactory functioning of keys and locks – and that all lights and electrical power points are working. Electrical work should ideally have been undertaken by an NICEIC qualified electrical contractor and, if this is not the case, then an NICEIC inspector should be called in to inspect the work before final payment is made.

Any plumbing or central heating work should be thoroughly checked. Make sure that toilets flush properly, and leave bath and basin taps running for a few minutes to see that the water runs away to waste satisfactorily. Any gas appliance, such as a central heating boiler, gas fire or cooker, should be installed only by a CORGI registered gas fitter or engineer. These

Rules & regulations

• During the building work, 5 percent of the agreed fee is held back from the contractor.

• When the snagging process is completed, a certificate of practical completion is issued and half of the retention of 5 percent is then due to be paid.

• This is followed by a defects period, which may be between 3 months and a year.

• At the end of this period, a Final Certificate is issued and the remaining money (2.5 percent of the total) is then due.

tradespeople will have their work checked on a regular basis by CORGI inspectors, but there is no requirement for an inspector to visit every job.

The completion certificate

At the completion of snagging, the architect will issue a certificate of practical completion. This marks the start of the defects period. For a small uncomplicated contract, this can be either 3 or 6 months, but sometimes where there are major new services, the defects period will be 12 months to allow the services to run for a full season. It also allows the release of half the retention money under a JCT contract. While the works are being carried out a 5 percent retention sum is withheld from the contractor. This

This extension and deck was inspected as soon as it was finished to ensure that there were no defects in the installation of the deck flooring and rails, the roof, the windows and the lighting.

meant he or she was paid the amount certified by the architect less 5 percent. At practical completion, half this retention is paid.

Finally, it releases the contractor from any further liability to Liquidated and Ascertained Damages (LADs) the agreed amount the contractor has to pay if the work overruns the agreed contract period for reasons that are solely due to the contractor.

Building Control inspection

If your building project includes operations that fall under the control of the Building Regulations, then there will have to be a final inspection by a Building Control Officer from the local authority. However, operations that require Building Regulations approval are fewer than many people realize. New buildings and extensions must comply with the Building Regulations, as must existing buildings undergoing a change of use – for example an agricultural barn being converted into a home. Other than that, contractors are obliged to notify the Building Control Department of the local authority when they are fitting heat-producing appliances or fitting or altering drainage systems. Most other work does not need intervention from a local authority.

After completion

The six month retention period is a time for satisfying yourself that the job has been completed to your satisfaction, according to the original plans and specifications, and for allowing any previously unnoticed defects to come to light.

The most common defects that may occur in the six months after

When to inspect ❗

1

- As the renovation progresses, inspect the project for general quality of workmanship, but also keep an eye open for the finishing details.

- After the tradespeople clear the work site, thoroughly check all the details. Make a list of any missing items and incomplete or unacceptable work.

- Once the project has been "substantially finished", you should look through all your paperwork to ensure that you have all the documentation necessary, including any certificates and warranties.

completion are all associated with drying shrinkage. Concrete, mortar and plaster are all mixed with water, and any excess will slowly evaporate over weeks, causing hairline cracks to develop. Usually cracks of this nature are not serious, and they are best left until the property is next decorated, when they will have stabilized and can be filled with a proprietory filler. If you insist that your builder fills them after the six month retention period you may find that they open up again.

Timber, too, often has a high moisture content when it is first used and can shrink later, especially when the central heating is turned on after the summer.

The defect period is also the time when final measurements and calculations of the contract price are decided, taking into account any extras and variations agreed upon during the course of the work. At the end of this period, the architect will make a final inspection and snagging list. Once these works are completed, he or she will issue a Final Certificate that allows the release of the final retention to be paid to the contractor.

How the experts can improve your home

2

Whether you've just moved into a new house or have been in your home for a few years, there are bound to be ways that you want to improve it. Home improvements can be simple – perhaps just a new coat of paint on the walls. However, the more ambitious homeowner may want to add or knock down walls, convert a basement or loft, build on an extension, or upgrade the wiring or heating. Whatever the changes are, the experts are often the best people to do the work for you.

Incorporating new details into a room – such as the wall-mounted lighting fixtures, the borders framing the walls and the patio door in this living room – are best achieved with professional help.

2 Interior improvements

The typical modern home has rooms designed for a vast array of activities, from an eat-in kitchen to a living room with an entertainment centre to a home office. These various activities need different furniture, equipment, and other belongings, so interior improvements must be carefully planned to be practical, as well as to provide ample storage space.

However, for most people the home is also a special retreat. It is equally important to develop a style that will enhance its appearance and comfort, as well as reflect your personal taste. A professional can help you decide on a plan that incorporates all of these elements, creating a home that meets the needs of each member of the family.

Having a well-equipped and tastefully decorated kitchen (far left) adds to the pleasure of preparing meals for the family. An open-plan area comprising of a dining room and living room (left) creates a feeling of spaciousness that cannot be experienced in two separate rooms.

Redecorating rooms

Despite the popularity of do-it-yourself – and home decorating in particular – there are many people who either do not want to do the job themselves, or else feel that their skills are not polished enough to allow them to achieve the finish they want.

It is usually true that you will get a much more finished job from a professional decorator and they will also be able to suggest exciting decorating options that you may not consider yourself.

You first have to think about the scale of the work you want a professional decorator to do for you. You may have a room that simply needs freshening up with a coat of new emulsion paint on the walls and ceilings, and perhaps a change of colour for the woodwork. A more ambitious scheme could involve stripping the existing wallpaper and hanging something new, perhaps with the addition of a textured ceiling and a decorative feature such as coving or a dado or picture rail. Most extensive of all is a complete indoor makeover – new decorations throughout the house, perhaps following a move to a new property, or simply as a serious update to a house you have occupied but not had redecorated for some years.

Colour scheming

If you have a clear idea of what colours of paint and wallpaper patterns you want to use, briefing your decorator could not be simpler. All you have to do is give him or her the specification and let him or her do the estimating and purchasing.

If you are unsure about colours and patterns, a good decorator should be happy to give you advice. He or she may try out a range of wall and woodwork paint colours in your home, using tester pots, and bring you wallpaper samples to try in place. Inspect colours in both natural and artificial light, and take your time to decide what looks best. If you do not like the final results and want them changed, the mistake will be expensive to rectify.

Technical advice

Apart from getting help in making the right choice of colour scheme, you may also need professional advice about choosing the best types of decorating materials. For example, if you have small children you

A large room can handle strong colours such as the green used on these walls. To prevent the colour from becoming overpowering, white is used on the ceilings and wood trim, as well as in the curtains and bed linen.

Rules & regulations

- Remember that paints can be toxic. The toxicity is (mostly) intentional in that fungicides or preservatives are added to paints, for example, for rooms exposed to moisture such as bathrooms and kitchens. Do not use these paints in areas where they are not needed. The content is specified on the tin.

- Woodwork that might be chewed by toddlers or pets should be coated with a nontoxic product.

- The house must be well ventilated while the work is going on.

DIY jargon !

VOC An abbreviation for volatile organic compounds, these are carbon-based chemicals similar to those found in petrol. They are used as solvents in paints and are now regarded as harmful if inhaled regularly or in large quantities. Traditional gloss and semi-gloss paints, and clear finishes, have very high VOC levels – however, in water-based paints the VOC levels are much lower.

Neutral colours provide a calm setting for this living room. The designer has used various shades of white and beige to create the effect. Natural materials such as the rattan furniture also have a calming affect.

will want walls decorated with materials that are tough, stain-resistant and easy to keep clean. In kitchens and bathrooms you should be considering surfaces that are hygienic and waterproof and that help to discourage condensation and the formation of mould.

You may have had problems in the past with your decorations such as paint readily flaking off surfaces or stains penetrating and discolouring surfaces from within the walls. A professional decorator will be able to guide you on products and suggest solutions to previous problems so they do not recur.

Choosing materials

Materials for interior decorating fall into several categories: paint for walls and ceilings, paint for wood and metal, clear finishes and stains for wood, wallcoverings of various types, tiles for walls, and tiles and sheet materials for floors. Paint and wallcoverings are summarized here; see pp. 38–39 for information on wallcoverings and wall tiles and pp. 40–43 for details about different floor coverings.

Emulsion paint is the standard choice for internal walls and ceilings. Paint from the best-selling brands is relatively cheap, but designer colours from specialist paintmakers can be surprisingly expensive. Emulsion paint is water-based, quick-drying and has a low VOC content (see box, above left). The finish is either nonreflective (matt) or slightly shiny (satin or silk). Generally, the shinier the paint surface, the more resistant it will be to dirt. Be sure to tell your decorator which you want.

Gloss or satin paint is the traditional finish applied to wood and metal surfaces. Until recent years these paints have always been solvent-based, with a high VOC content. However, the trend is now towards using water-based paints for wood and metal, and the latest formulations are just as durable as their solvent-based relations. When specifying the finish you want, remember that a high gloss will highlight any imperfections in the surface, whereas a satin (eggshell) finish will be more forgiving.

Clear finishes for wood can be applied to existing woodwork, either as a new layer over an existing clear finish or as a new finish on stripped or replacement woodwork. Varnishes are basically paint without the pigments, and like paint, they can be solvent or water-based. The finish may be a high-gloss or a softer satin look. Both give a durable and easy-to-clean finish. If you want to colour the wood grain but not obscure it, an all-in-one coloured sealer will give a medium depth of colour, while a wood stain followed by clear varnish will give a stronger effect.

Remember that if you strip doors in your house, you must seal the grain with some sort of finish as soon as possible; otherwise, the door may dry out and warp so that it no longer fits the doorway.

Selecting a wallcovering !

There is an almost endless variety of wallcovering patterns but the types of covering available can be categorized in several groups.

PAPER WALLPAPER
pros: Least expensive type of wallcovering; vinyl-coated type is easy to strip
cons: Tears easily

VINYL WALLCOVERING
pros: Easy to wipe clean; solid-vinyl type is available for high moisture areas
cons: Expensive

EXPANDED VINYL WALLCOVERING
pros: Good for uneven walls; moderately expensive
cons: Medium durability

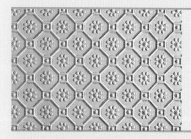

WALLCOVERING WITH RAISED PATTERN
pros: Hides uneven wall surfaces, especially on plaster walls; durable; can be painted
cons: Needs expert installation

SILK WALLCOVERING
pros: Some types have intricate patterns with better detail than paper or vinyl wallcoverings
cons: Very expensive; requires professional installation

The professional makeover

The best way to get the results you want may be to employ an interior designer who will visit your home, discuss your intentions and take note of the existing furniture, soft furnishings and decorative features that are to be incorporated in the new colour scheme. The designer will prepare sketches, colour cards and sample fabric swatches for you to see. Final designs (or a computer-generated print-out) will then be provided for your approval. An interior designer will have access to manufacturers' catalogues and trade suppliers and so will be able to draw on a huge database to find the products you want in the colours and patterns you like.

Choosing wallcoverings

Wallcoverings fall into two main groups: products to be painted over and products with a printed design. The first group includes cheap and cheerful woodchip paper and the various types of relief wallpaper with a raised surface pattern. The latter may be made from paper (often called Anaglypta, and the least expensive), cotton fibres, solid vinyl on a paper backing and Lincrusta (the most expensive and durable). All are good at hiding surface defects, and become more durable the more often they are painted. Printed wallcoverings may be just paper (fragile and easily stained), washable wallpaper (printed paper with a clear surface coating that can be wiped clean) or vinyl (printed plastic with a paper backing, and capable of being scrubbed if soiled). There is a wide range of prices, especially in designer printed wallpapers

Wallcoverings with a subtle pattern add colour to a room and provide a background for furnishings.

Tiled surfaces are waterproof and easy to clean, making them an ideal choice for bathrooms and kitchens.

Unusual paint effects can be created with special techniques that are best achieved by a skilled professional.

and luxury vinyls such as flock effects. Speciality wallcoverings include materials such as silk, suede, woolstrands and grasscloths. They are relatively expensive, so they are usually hung for effect in small feature areas such as alcoves or on chimney breasts.

Ceramic tiles

The walls of kitchens, bathrooms and cloakrooms are most often covered with ceramic tiles. They come in a huge range of colours and designs. Because of their small size, they are very easy to use, although tiling a large area and grouting (filling) the joints between the tiles can be time-consuming. Tiled surfaces are waterproof, easy to clean and immensely hard-wearing. Their only drawbacks are that they can create condensation in steamy rooms, due to their cold surface, and they are relatively expensive compared with other decorative materials. Wall tiles are generally about 4 mm (¹⁄₆ in) thick, and come in a number of standard sizes. The current trend is to use larger tiles which are quicker to fix and grout; rectangular 200 x 100 mm (8 x 4 in) and 200 x 150 mm (8 x 6 in) sizes are both common, although smaller

squares are still widely available. There is also a wide range of border and motif tiles for decorating tiled walls. Special durable ceramic tiles may be used for floors and are also available to use for splashbacks behind basins and work surfaces.

When work starts

Your decorator's first job will be to move the furniture – either out of the room or into the centre, where it will be covered with dust sheets, as will the floor. Any wall or ceiling fittings such as shelves and lights will be taken down and their positions marked so they can be replaced later on. If any surfaces are not being decorated they will be masked off. You should remove valuable items, take down curtains and blinds and disconnect home entertainment equipment yourself before work starts.

If the decorator is merely redecorating with paint, he or she will wash down the surfaces and make good any defects before starting to paint. For paperhanging, he or she may have to strip existing wallpaper or treat currently painted walls with a coat of size before hanging a new wallcovering. The decorator will paint or paper the ceiling first if this

is being redecorated, and will then tackle woodwork and fittings such as radiators followed by the walls. The stripping and preparation may well reveal defects in the old plaster or a damp patch, so be prepared for extra work at this stage.

When to inspect !

- It is best to inspect the work at the end of each day, after the decorator has left.

- Check newly painted surfaces for any signs of runs, bits of bristle or debris in the surface film, incomplete coverage and any other imperfections.

- With wallcoverings, look for lifting seams and poorly trimmed ends and for large blisters that are often the result of incomplete pasting. Don't panic if you discover a rash of small blisters; these disappear as the paper dries out, leaving a completely flat surface.

- Don't be afraid to point out faults to your decorator and ask for them to be fixed. Any faults not put right now will only annoy you in the future.

Replacing floor coverings

All floor coverings have a finite life and there comes a time when you will need replacements. But you need not simply choose another carpet or vinyl – there are many more alternatives now available.

With the increased range of floor coverings available, you may consider employing an interior designer to advise you. Many of these finishes are best left to be done by professional fitters.

Performance matters

A professional installer can ensure that the floor covering is laid properly. There are problems specific to various materials. For example, fitted carpets have to be laid under slight tension, with the edges anchored over toothed gripper strips fitted around the perimeter of the room. Without this tension, the carpet will stretch slightly underfoot and will be rucked up by furniture being moved over it. Getting the tension right involves hooking one edge of the carpet onto its gripper strip and then using a special tool called a knee kicker to stretch it,

first down the length of the room to the opposite gripper strip, and then out to the side walls.

Laying sheet vinyl also needs a professional hand if it is to be laid and fitted well. The sheet has to be accurately trimmed to fit snugly at the perimeter walls and to fit neatly around any floor-level fittings such as washbasin pedestals and WC

pans in the bathroom. The vinyl then has to be stuck down around the edges and at door openings with flooring adhesive or double-sided tape to prevent it curling.

While cork and vinyl tiles can be laid by the amateur, it is wise to leave laying ceramic and quarry tiles to the experts. The subfloor needs careful preparation, especially if it is

DIY jargon ❗

Gripper strip A narrow strip of plywood with short nails punched through it with all the points angled toward one edge of the strip. They anchor the edges of fitted carpet once it has been laid and stretched. They are nailed to wood floors and glued to solid ones with adhesive. Strips are installed around the room at a distance of just less than the thickness of the carpet from the skirting, with their teeth facing the wall. Special all-metal strips are installed at doorways.

the suspended timber type, to ensure that any movement which could crack the tiles is kept to a minimum. The tiles themselves must be evenly bedded in the appropriate adhesive, and the joints filled once the adhesive has set. So long as the job is done properly, the resulting floor should last a lifetime.

Saving time and money

Professional installation also saves time. Laying any new floor covering involves completely clearing the room, so the faster the job is completed, the more quickly the room can be put back into use. Professional fitting also guarantees that there will not be any expensive

mistakes, such as cutting sheet materials in the wrong place or suffering from tiles lifting and timber floors warping.

New flooring often alters the floor height in a room so you may have to have the doors removed, trimmed and rehung. Always be clear about who is doing this.

Choosing materials

Floor coverings come in small units or in rolls. Unit materials include ceramic floor tiles, cork and vinyl tiles and various types of decorative wood flooring in tiles and planks.

• Ceramic floor tiles are thicker than wall tiles and may be glazed over a plain colour or a printed design, or unglazed – these are better known as quarry tiles. Both are extremely durable but cold underfoot. They come in a variety of square, rectangular and interlocking shapes.

• Cork tiles are thin squares of compressed cork tree bark and are stuck down to the floor to create a surface that is warm and resilient underfoot. Cheaper tiles need sealing once laid, but more expensive types are sold presealed.

• Vinyl tiles are squares of solid plastic with an adhesive backing. Cheaper types are usually plain colours or simple printed patterns. More expensive types may imitate other floor coverings such as parquet, brick or mosaics. They make a durable floor that is easily cleaned.

• Decorative timber floors come in two main forms and in a wide variety of wood types. Planks are either solid or laminated strips with tongued-and-groove edges, which interlock to form a flat and stable decorative surface. Strips can be pinned down or held together by a

A durable, exquisite slate floor should last the life of a kitchen. They are available in both regular and irregular shapes.

Ask yourself ❓ ②

• What type of room will the floor covering be in? For example, you should avoid carpet for floors that may get wet such as in kitchens and bathrooms.

• How often do people walk in and out of a room? Rooms that are used a lot should have a durable floor covering. If you use carpet, select a durable one.

• Is the room well-lit or dark? Dark carpets will hide stains but light colours can make a small room seem larger.

system of hidden clips. The resulting floor is attractive, hard-wearing and easy to keep clean. Tiles are made by bonding small fingers of wood (usually presealed) to a fabric backing to make panels 300 or 450 mm (approximately 12 or 18 in) square. These can be loose-laid or adhered to the floor surface.

• Carpets come in a great range of colours and designs. They offer a floor surface that is warm and luxurious underfoot and hard-wearing if you pick the appropriate grade for areas that will get heavy traffic. Their biggest drawback is that they can harbour dust and house mites, both potential causes of allergic reactions in sensitive people. Most carpet nowadays is 4 m (approximately 13 ft) wide and is sold by the linear metre.

• Sheet vinyl is available in a wide range of designs. It is a relatively inexpensive flooring, providing a surface that is waterproof, hard-wearing and comfortable underfoot, especially if a cushioned type is chosen. It comes in rolls 2, 3 and 4 m (approximately 6½, 10 and 13 ft) wide, enabling you to have a seamless floor covering in all but the largest of rooms.

Selecting a floor covering !

Before choosing one of the variety of floor coverings available, consider which material best suits the usage of the room.

CERAMIC FLOOR TILES
pros: Durable; water resistance makes them a good choice for kitchens and bathrooms
cons: Cold and noisy to walk on

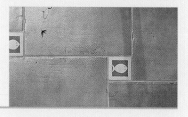

VINYL TILES
pros: Inexpensive; easy to lay
cons: Prone to lifting at edges

SHEET VINYL
pros: Inexpensive; some have a backing to make them warm and soft
cons: Can be slippery when wet; susceptible to damage

CARPET
pros: Comfortable; quiet; suitable for most rooms
cons: Harbours allergens; better quality ones are expensive

SISAL
pros: Warm, natural appearance; hardwearing
cons: May need to be woven with wool to make it softer, but this increases the price

WOOD FLOORING
pros: Natural beauty; ages gracefully; solid types can be refinished
cons: Can be noisy to walk on

When work starts

Rooms where new floor coverings are being laid have first of all to be cleared of all floor-standing furniture and fittings. You should find out before work starts whether your installer expects you to do this or whether he or she will do so on the day. You may need to be prepared to help with this.

The next step is to remove the old floor covering. The fitter will free an old carpet from its gripper strips and roll it up, then lift and remove the old underlay. It is a false economy to retain this, as crumbly old underlay will cause the carpet to wear prematurely. The gripper strips will probably also need replacing.

Sheet vinyl will be cut into strips and pulled up. Cork and vinyl tiles will almost certainly be left in place if they are securely stuck down, unless they were laid on floorboards over a hardboard underlay that can be prised free in sheets. Ceramic and quarry tiles either have to be broken away one by one – a job that can be extremely labour-intensive and costly – or else covered with a thin latex cement screed if there are no problems with raising the floor level slightly before the new floor covering is laid.

If any sheet material is cut up on the floor before removal, the decorator will probably use a knife that will score the floorboards unless you specifically ask him not to. If you later decide to strip the floor, these score marks are difficult, if not impossible, to remove.

Preparing the floor

When the old coverings have been removed, any defects in the floorboards or solid floor are revealed and will need seeing to before the

A floor with plain tiles can be enhanced by setting them off with inset tiles that fit in the corners.

A wooden floor can be left unstained but sealed with varnish, or it can be stained.

Laying floor tiles

Ceramic and quarry tiles have to be set out so that the edge border of cut tiles is the same width along opposite walls. The tiler will find the centre of the room, plan the layout and fix guide battens to the floor in one corner of the room to provide an accurately positioned starting point. If the tiles are going on a timber floor, he or she will put down an underlay of water-resistant plywood to provide a stable surface for the tiles. The tiler will then lay whole tiles section by section ending by the door, and leave the floor to harden overnight before returning to cut and fit the border tiles and grout (fill) the joints. Even if your house is new it is unlikely that the floors are exactly square, so some of these tiles will have to be tapered. If unsealed quarry tiles are laid, the last job will be to seal them.

new floor covering can be laid. Your fitter may be able to deal with minor problems, but for serious defects in the floorboards – such as long splits or short wobbly pieces – you may need a carpenter.

When old linoleum or vinyl is stripped off solid floors, it often reveals patches of crumbled damp concrete. Depending on the extent of this, you may need to call in a builder to dig out the bad patches and skim over the floor. Defects in the subfloor must be repaired or they will damage your new floor covering and shorten its life.

Laying carpets and sheet vinyl

The fitter will check that the floorboards are secure, nail down any that are loose and punch in any nails that have worked upwards and could damage the new floor covering. He or she will seal a concrete floor to stop dust rising through the carpet or to improve the adhesion of sheet vinyl or floor tiles. Some flooring materials will require a thin plywood or hardboard substrate to provide an even base. This is best laid by the fitter.

Laying carpet involves putting down new underlay with the butt joints between strips taped to keep them in place while the carpet is laid. This is cut roughly to size and then trimmed and fitted to each wall of the room in turn.

On stairs, gripper strips have to be nailed to the back of each tread and the bottom of each riser and short pieces may also be nailed to the sides of each tread. Joins in the carpet can be hidden at the back of a tread. Short lengths of underlay can then be stuck or stapled to each tread and the riser below it. Stair carpet is fitted to one edge of the staircase and then trimmed.

Sheet vinyl is laid in a similar way, being rough cut to begin with and then trimmed to fit and adhered down at the edges, seams and thresholds. The one exception is when it is being fitted in a bathroom or cloakroom, where the sheet has to fit closely round basin pedestals and WC pans. In this case the fitter will probably make a paper template of the whole floor and then scribe the perimeter and obstacle outlines onto the sheet before cutting it out and dropping it into place.

When to inspect

- When the job is finished, make sure that carpet edges are neatly tucked into the gap between the gripper strips and the skirting board, and that any seams are well matched and securely bonded to the carpet tape beneath.

- Check that sheet vinyl is perfectly trimmed all around, with no overcuts visible, that it is lying flat and that it is securely fastened beneath threshold strips at doorways.

- Inspect ceramic and quarry tiles by laying a straightedge across the surface to check that all the tiles are level, and check that all the grout lines are evenly filled.

- Where appropriate, check that doors have been shortened enough at the bottom to clear a new floor level comfortably.

Refitting a kitchen

Having a new fitted kitchen is one of the most popular home improvements, but it can be expensive. However, a well-designed layout makes the kitchen work far more efficiently, and it is also a good investment when you decide to sell your house.

Ask yourself

- Is the kitchen where your family and friends socialize?

- How active are you in the kitchen – do you use it mostly to heat convenience foods or are you a gourmet cook who requires plenty of work space?

- Do you use mostly fresh food, canned food or frozen food? This will affect your storage space – more cupboards, a larger freezer or plenty of vegetable storage space.

- Where should essential elements be placed? Are they within easy reach of your work area or near other items you tend to use with them?

Cupboards provide storage for everything from crockery to dry goods such as cereals. Baking trays and tins are best stored near the oven, and glass and china are easier to put away stored near the sink. Doors and drawer fronts may be solid wood or veneered with wood or plastic and can be stained or painted. Glass doors are an option on wall cupboards if you want to display the contents.

The wall behind the worktop where you prepare food and where it meets the hob and the sink should be made of a durable material to withstand food spills and water splashes. Ceramic tiles are an ideal choice.

In a large kitchen, an island provides additional storage and work surface. Some islands have a protruding edge, which allows people to sit around it to eat an informal meal.

Ceramic floor tiles made for heavy-traffic areas are ideal in kitchens because they won't be stained by dropped food or spills. However, they can be noisy to walk on and cold to bare feet in the winter. Other materials to consider include laminated wood flooring or vinyl – but make sure that the vinyl is stain-resistant.

Cosmetic changes

If the potential cost of a complete refit of your kitchen is too high, but it works well and simply looking a little old-fashioned, you could consider giving it a facelift. Kitchen units are generally constructed of plastic-faced chipboard or medium-density fibreboard (MDF) and they can be expected to last for years if they were properly installed in the first place. Because they are made in a small range of standard sizes, you can probably simply have new matching doors and drawer fronts fitted. Worn or damaged interior shelves and drawers can also be replaced. The work will probably take only a few days.

The complete refit

The most common kitchen refit involves stripping out everything and starting again from scratch. This is the option to choose if your kitchen is badly laid out or full of equipment that is seriously out of date and does not measure up to modern standards. Professional kitchen installers will provide a complete package deal, including new fitted appliances. They start by planning the layout of the new kitchen and selecting the type and arrangement of the kitchen units.

The planning will probably be done using a computer programme, which also allows you to see how the room will look from various angles and lets you refine the plan on screen until you are completely satisfied.

Extending the kitchen

Many older homes were built with kitchens that were designed solely for cooking in, and no amount of clever planning will get around the problem of finding space for all of today's kitchen appliances or for eating meals in the room if you want to. The only solution is to enlarge the kitchen, either by adding an extension if you have room or by borrowing floor space from adjoining rooms. For example, many older houses have a pantry or scullery next to the kitchen, which could have its dividing walls removed to create some extra space. Another possibility is to knock through the wall into the adjacent dining room to turn the two rooms into a large kitchen-dining room.

Using another room

The last resort is to tear out what you have and install a complete new kitchen in another room. For example, the dining room could become the kitchen and vice versa. You could even use a front living room as the kitchen, and knock through the existing kitchen and adjacent room to create a large living space across the back of the house. The greatest difficulty with this lies in rerouting services. Plumbing and wiring should be reasonably easy, but getting rid of waste water from the sink, washing machine and dishwasher may be difficult if the drains are at the back of the house. You may need to have a small-bore pumped waste disposal system installed to carry the waste water to the back of the house.

DIY jargon

Carcase The wood, metal or plastic "skeleton" frame of a kitchen unit or cupboard, to which the decorative surface and door is attached.

Carousel Storage device installed in a cupboard that pivots from a central point, giving more efficient access to the cupboard's contents. It is useful in cupboards placed in a corner, where items are normally difficult to retrieve.

Plastic laminate A material used for work surfaces, it consists of a core (a less attractive, inexpensive material) covered with a decorative veneer, or thin top layer.

Refitting a kitchen

The basic shape

The layout of your new kitchen will be determined primarily by the shape of the room. If it is rectangular and narrow, you will probably have to arrange all the units and appliances along one wall. A larger rectangle with doors at opposite ends is usually fitted out as a galley kitchen, with units and appliances against the two long walls. The main drawback to this shape is that it may be a through traffic route, so it may be worth considering providing an alternative exit from the house to the garden so that wall and floor units can be fitted across the end wall.

In a more square room, an L-shaped kitchen with units against adjacent walls is often a practical layout and may even leave space for a dining table.

The classic kitchen layout is the U-shape, with units and worktops ranged against three walls and with one key appliance in each section – usually the sink beneath the window, the cooker to one side and the refrigerator to the other. This arrangement is ideal for large kitchens,

where one side of the U can be used as a breakfast bar with storage beneath the worktop.

The final possibility in a large kitchen is to have the units around the walls and a central island. The island could be either a cupboard unit housing the oven and hob, with an extractor hood above it, or a dining table and chairs. The table could also serve as the main work surface for food preparation.

Thinking about appliances

You should think about which appliances you need and where they should be sited. For example, sinks are usually best fitted against an outside wall, ideally beneath a window. They are available in many different bowl, drainer and tap configurations. It is also worth considering having a waste disposal unit fitted beneath the sink.

Cooking equipment can be either a free-standing appliance or a built-in oven and hob. These can be together or separate, and can even use different fuels – perhaps a gas hob and an electric oven. You can have the oven and grill sited in a tall

Alternative choices !

As you start to plan your kitchen refit, don't be completely seduced by the temptations of glossy brochures. You may not need a fully fitted and customized kitchen with new state-of-the-art appliances, dazzling work surfaces and a barrage of cupboards. Alternatives to think about include:

- Storing china, glass and silverware in the dining room or in a shallow dresser instead of in standard kitchen cupboards.
- Using a table instead of the worktop or an island to prepare food.
- Moving laundry appliances to a utility room or large bathroom.
- Moving a freezer to the garage, especially if it is a large chest type.
- Concentrating units along one wall to allow more floor space.

Facts & figures

Kitchen base units are now manufactured in standard 600 and 1200 mm (approximately 24 and 48 in) wide modules, although suppliers will tailor-make units for awkward room sizes. They are a standard 900 mm (approximately 36 in) high with some adjustment possible from the legs. If your kitchen has an uneven floor or walls, the installer will be able to add shims or build out walls to bring all surfaces flush.

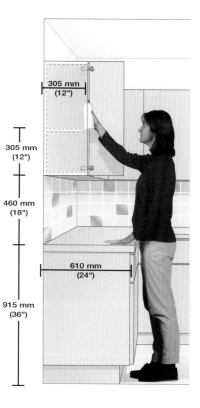

The worktop should be at a comfortable height for preparing foods; the wall-hung cupboards should be high enough to provide space for working below, yet be within reach to store items in them.

unit to avoid awkward bending and stooping while cooking. A unit such as this is usually best sited at one end of a worktop or in a corner. If you have a microwave this will also need to be sited on a part of the work surface, preferably near the rest of the cooking area.

Some large electrical appliances used in a kitchen need only a power supply, others need water and waste connections. Fridges and freezers can be sited anywhere. Tumble driers need a ducted vent to the outside air. Washing machines, dishwashers and washer/driers need to be against an outside wall or close to one to keep the waste pipe runs short. Dishwashers are best sited close to the sink for easy connection to its outlet trap. A tumble drier may be stacked on top of a washing machine to save space.

Choosing units

Dimensions of base units are given in the box opposite. Wall units are based on a module 300 mm (12 in) wide, but again tailor-made units are available in most ranges. The unit height may be 600, 800 or 900 mm (approximately 24, 31½ or 36 in) high, the last two giving valuable extra storage space.

The main choice of materials for kitchen units is between natural timber and man-made boards. Wood doors may be solid or veneered, and can be varnished, stained or given a decorative paint finish such as a colour wash.

You can have glazed doors on wall units where you want to display the contents. Man-made board doors are either painted with a hard gloss or finished with hard-wearing plastic laminates. Worktops are generally of thick chipboard or MDF, faced with laminates in a wide range of designs, but some suppliers also offer solid wood worktops in timbers such as beech, which can provide a warm natural look.

In addition to determining what will fit in the room, also consider the positioning of the appliances, cupboards and other features to make working in the kitchen easier.

If your kitchen is rectangular and narrow, all the cupboards and appliances must be along one wall. There will be very little work space, so consider investing in ways to increase it such as installing a pull-out chopping block that fits into a drawer.

The U-shaped kitchen has cupboards and worktops arranged against three walls, with one key appliance in each section – usually the sink and dishwasher beneath the window, the cooker to one side and the refrigerator to the other. The sink or the cooker can sometimes be incorporated into a kitchen island.

Selecting a work surface !

There is a variety of worktop materials to choose from, and some of these come in a great range of colours and patterns.

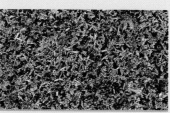

GRANITE
pros: Natural, durable, heat resistant; can be cut to desired shape
cons: Needs expert installation

STAINLESS STEEL
pros: Hygienic; modern look
cons: Costly; prone to scratching

SYNTHETIC STONE
pros: Tough, beautiful, durable
cons: Costly; needs expert installation

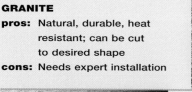

PLASTIC LAMINATE
pros: Inexpensive; comes in a variety of colours and patterns
cons: Prone to scratching

SOLID WOOD
pros: Beautiful, natural material
cons: Hot pots and pans can leave marks; ultraviolet light can change colour of wood

CERAMIC TILE
pros: Beautiful; durable
cons: Grout is prone to staining and mould

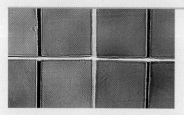

When work starts

The first job is to disconnect all power, water and waste connections to the various appliances. Any that are being refitted will be set aside. The workers will then take down the wall units, release and remove the worktops and strip out all the base units to leave an empty shell.

The next step is to make the alterations to the services. Electric supplies to a separate oven and hob may have to be extended from the existing cooker supply point. Extra power points are likely to be needed, both above and below the worktop level. It is usual to provide a single unswitched socket outlet in each recess containing a large appliance such as the refrigerator or washing machine, and to control it from a double-pole switch above the worktop so it can be isolated easily for repairs. Specific lighting fixtures will probably be needed for the work surface and changes also made to the main room lighting.

Plumbing pipework and waste pipes may also need altering if the sink, washing machine and dishwasher are being installed in different locations. Any supply pipework against outside walls should be insulated, and all pipes leading to taps and water-using appliances should have small isolating valves in easy-to-reach locations so that the water supply can be turned off easily for maintenance or replacement. All this work will be carried out before any of the units are installed.

Installation sequence

Installing the base units can now begin. Each carcase will be set in place, working outwards from the corners, and will be accurately

Wicker baskets fitting under the worktops are suitable for storing fresh fruit and vegetables.

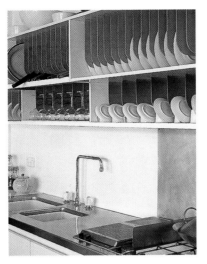

Racks are ideal for displaying china. Each piece has its own place, making it easier to store items.

Wire baskets for keeping vegetables and boxes for storing herbs and spices are a feature of these shelves.

levelled before being fixed to the wall. Neighbouring units are then screwed together as the run extends to ensure total stability.

When the base units are all in place, the worktops are cut to length and secured from below with screws and brackets. Joining runs at right angles is done with a precision jig and power saw to produce a neat mitre at the intersection – this is one job best left to the professionals. The joints should be fully bonded with adhesive to ensure that no water can penetrate.

Cut-outs are made for an inset sink and hob at this stage, and the cut edges of the worktop must also be sealed to prevent water penetration. Then the sink or hob is fitted on a flexible sealing gasket, and the junction between the sink and the worktop is further sealed with silicone mastic. The hob will be connected to its power or gas supply next, and any necessary wiring added to supply the automatic ignition. The built-in oven and grill is connected up and slotted into its unit.

Next the wall units are hung. They are mounted on strong steel brackets, which allow a degree of adjustment so the carcases can be accurately aligned and adjacent units screwed together.

The plumber will connect up the supply and waste pipes to the sink, while the electrician is completing alterations to the lighting, fitting fixed appliances such as cooker hoods and waste disposal units and slotting in floor-standing appliances. The carpenter will assemble and fit the drawers, as well as hang and adjust the doors. Then he or she will cut and fit plinths below the base units and cornices or other trims to the wall units. Final decoration may include tiling splashbacks, painting walls and laying new floor coverings. Meanwhile, the finishing touches such as sealing worktops to walls will be applied, and everything will be tested before the refitted kitchen is completed and ready for use.

Rules and regulations

Any alterations to existing waste water disposal provision must meet the requirements of the Building Regulations and any new wiring work should comply with the requirements of the IEE Wiring Regulations in England and Wales and must do so in Scotland.

Make sure that you get copies of all instruction manuals and appliance guarantees from your contractor and also ask for a drawing of the new service runs and layout.

When to inspect !

- Inspect the progress at the end of each day, especially work that will be concealed such as wiring and plumbing.

- When the cupboards are in position, check that each is secured both to the wall and to adjacent units.

- Use a spirit level to check that worktops are horizontal, both along their length and from front to back.

- Finally, check that doors and drawers are accurately lined up, and that they open and shut easily.

Refitting a bathroom

The bathroom needs not be purely functional but can be a room that is pleasing to be in, with decorative schemes of its own. The possibilities of upgrading bathroom fittings, layout and decor have expanded greatly in recent times.

The changing attitude to this once neglected room is seen in new homes – now often built with two or even three bath or shower rooms – reflecting the fact that people expect more than the traditional bath, basin and WC crammed into one of the smallest rooms in the house. However, there are several ways in which you can set about upgrading what you have at present.

The existing room

The most obvious improvement you can make is to replace the bathroom suite with a different colour or style. The bath will probably still be a standard rectangular one, but you could swap the existing pedestal basin for one set in a vanity unit (or vice versa), and choose a WC suite with a slimline cistern. The taps can also be upgraded to ceramic-disc types, which open and close within a quarter-turn of the handle. There is now a wide choice of sleek mono-bloc basin taps and bath taps that also function as shower mixers.

If you and your family all prefer showers, you will save space by sacrificing the traditional bathtub for a shower cubicle. The alternative is to install a shower over the bath – a dual-purpose arrangement that works well unless you have small children or elderly people in the household, where their safety may rule this out.

Modern bathroom designers often place emphasis on materials and the best use of space, making a once mundane room a room of luxury.

Changing the layout

Assuming that you decide to retain the bath, you may be able to rearrange the room layout to make it work better. For example, the bath could be placed against another wall, or a corner bath could be installed, freeing more floor space for other equipment. Swapping the positions of the basin and WC may make better use of space. The door could be rehung so it is hinged the other way around or so that it opens outwards rather than inwards – this can free up more floor space within the room.

This sort of rearrangement is where a professional bathroom

Ask yourself ?

- Are you happy with your bathroom layout, but find the decor dated? A simple solution is to change the fittings and repaint the room.

- Are you always bumping into things in your bathroom? By rearranging the components, you may create more space.

- Does it seem that there is always someone else in the bathroom when you want to use it? Consider adding another bathroom to your home.

designer may be useful. A designer will be able to offer you a wider range of options, and he or she will probably use computer programmes to juggle the various ingredients for the best fit and the optimum use of space. Although each bathroom fitting needs a certain amount of space around it, these activity zones can overlap because you will be using only one fitting at a time.

With the designer's help, you may find that you have room for additional fittings such as a bidet or two side-by-side basins, which allows two people to wash at the same time in the morning rush hour. You may also gain room for a heated towel rail, either electric or connected to the central heating system.

Extending the bathroom

If your existing bathroom is simply too small for what you want, then it is time to consider enlarging the room. For example, if you have a bathroom and WC that are separate but adjacent, you could remove the dividing wall and then replan the room within the enlarged floor area, although this is not to be recommended unless there is a second WC in the house.

The next possibility is to take space from a bedroom next to the bathroom, if this is a rarely used spare room. For this type of reconstruction you will need a builder, who can advise on the structural implications of the alterations as well as carrying out the work. The new partitioning required will have to be timber or metal framed, since it is unlikely that it will be over a load-bearing part of the building, and it will need cladding with a moisture-resistant material.

Different rooms

The last option is to create a second bathroom in an existing but little-used bedroom. How feasible this is depends mainly on the position of

DIY jargon

Monobloc tap A unit where the hot and cold taps come from the same fitting.

Soil stack A vertical pipe through which the waste from plumbing fittings, such as basins, bathtubs and toilets, travels to the drain.

the house soil stack to which all the waste pipes from the fittings will be connected. However, a pumped waste macerator unit can be used to carry waste water through small-bore pipes to a distant stack, so the problem is not insurmountable. You will also need to consider the capacity of your existing boiler and hot water supply.

Choosing materials

The most common materials are ceramic ware for washbasins, bidets, shower trays and WCs, and moulded glass fibre (often called GRP, short for glass-reinforced plastic) for baths. GRP baths tend to flex and need adequate bracing. Other plastics such as acrylics are used for inset basins and cheaper baths, and sometimes for WC cisterns. Enamelled steel or cast iron baths are another option, but are generally much more expensive than plastic ones. Shower cubicles have either plastic or toughened safety glass panels. Tiles and flooring can be replaced to tone in with the new suite and there is also a vast range of taps, mixers, showers and shower heads, plugs and wastes in a multitude of finishes. Make sure that you know whether your plumbing is mains pressure or open vented when choosing taps. Visit a good showroom, and always allow plenty of time for delivery – some items may not be available for several weeks.

Refitting a bathroom

When work starts

A simple change of bathroom suite can be done by a plumber in no more than a day and the makeover finished by a decorator or tiler. If you are having the room completely refitted by a firm of bathroom specialists, they will carry out all the necessary work including new decorations and floor coverings.

Once the plumber has turned off the water supplies to the various fittings, he or she will flush the WC and scoop out and mop up any water remaining in the cistern and pan. He or she will disconnect the cistern from the pan, undo its wall fittings and lift it off. Then the plumber will unscrew the pan fittings, disconnect it from the soil pipe and remove it. Removing the basin and bath is next. After removing the bath panels the supply pipes can be cleanly cut through with a hacksaw. It is easier to fit a short tail of pipe to the new bath taps and connect that to the existing pipes than to reattach the existing tap connectors in the restricted space at the end of the bath. The same technique may be used for the basin.

Another reason for cutting through existing supply pipes is that a small in-line isolating valve can then be fitted to each one. This is now a requirement of the water bye-laws and enables taps and ballvalves to be shut off individually, making repair or emergency work on them much easier.

Always choose a paint that has been formulated for a bathroom.

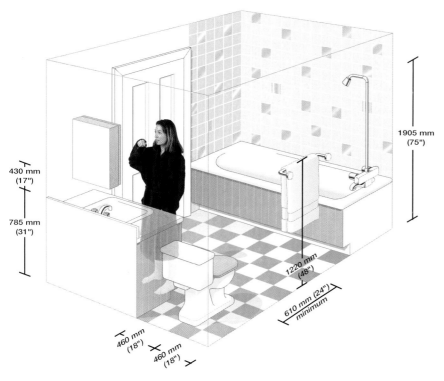

A bathroom should be planned with enough space for leg room at a toilet, with the mirror, the showerhead and towel racks at comfortable heights.

430 mm (17")
785 mm (31")
1905 mm (75")
1220 mm (48")
610 mm (24") minimum
460 mm (18")
460 mm (18")

Installation sequence

Once all the old fittings are removed from the room, the plumber will fit the new WC first if it is the only one in the house, so the facility is restored as quickly as possible. After positioning the new pan, connecting it to the soil pipe with a flexible push-fit connector and screwing it to the floor, he or she will prepare the cistern by installing its siphon and flush mechanism. Then the cistern is secured to the apron at the rear of the pan, fixed to the wall and the supply and the overflow pipes are connected.

Fitting the new bath and basin requires less work. The plumber will fit the new taps and their pipe tails, the waste outlet and the trap first, then manoeuvre the bath into place, get it level on its cradle and fix this to the floor. Reconnecting the supply and waste pipes is the final job. If the basin has a pedestal, this is positioned first and the basin placed

Two basins in the bathroom will reduce a large family's waiting time for morning washing. A heated towel rack will supply warm towels in winter.

Ceramic tiles can be used to finish the sides of a bathtub.

on top. Then the basin is screwed to the wall and the pedestal to the floor before the supply and waste pipes are reconnected. If the basin is inset into a vanity unit, the plumber will make the cut-out for it in the worktop, then clip it in place on its sealing gasket before moving the whole unit into position ready to be reconnected to the water supply.

A bidet will need new supply pipes run from the cold water tank and hot water cylinder if it has an ascending spray. This will mean lifting floorboards and gaining access to the loft to run in the necessary pipes. Otherwise, the supplies can be branched, or teed, off the existing bathroom supplies, which is a less disruptive job. Its waste pipe will probably be connected to the existing bath or basin waste pipe.

Adding a separate shower cubicle will require connecting new pipes to the shower unit. Ideally, the pipes should be concealed beneath the plaster of solid walls or within the structure of a partition wall. If this is not feasible, the pipes may have to

be surface-mounted. A towel rail can be connected to the hot water system so that it can be used in summer. An electric rail will need its own isolation switch outside the room.

With all the new fittings installed, the water supply will be restored so a check can be made to ensure that everything works and that there are no leaks.

Bathroom redesign

If you are having a radical redesign by a firm of bathroom specialists rather than a simple changeover, the same sequence will still be followed to strip the room of its fittings. As soon as that has been done, the team will carry out any alterations to the supply and waste pipes that are necessary to enable them to reach repositioned fittings, and they will also add any wiring that may be needed for shower or spa bath pumps and new lighting.

If the package includes redecoration they will also strip existing decorations before starting to install the new bathroom fittings. Once

everything is in place, tiling and decorating will be carried out, new lights and wiring accessories will be installed and a new floor will be laid to complete the job.

When to inspect !

- Look for neat workmanship; check fittings, hardware and surfaces for signs of damage such as scratched chrome or chipped porcelain.

- Make sure every fitting is secure by gripping it and attempting to move it.

- Check that silicone sealant has been used to waterproof areas between fittings and walls.

- Check overflow pipework to the WC, basin, bath and shower.

- When the job is finished, wipe a paper towel around all plumbing connections and look for signs of a leak on the paper. If you find any, contact the installer.

Improving your living room

Your living room is where you spend most of your waking hours at home. It is the room where all the family meet and is also the main room your visitors see, so you have plenty of reasons to want it to look its best.

Living rooms, perhaps more than any other room, tend to grow by accumulation – a new suite one year, new curtains the next – and to have elements that are difficult to blend together – the TV unit, the music centre, the coffee table. Calling in the professionals may be the best way to achieve the look you want.

Who to hire
Which professionals you employ will depend on the scale of the work. You may need decorators to tackle the walls, ceiling and woodwork; flooring contractors to lay carpet or a natural timber floor; soft

furnishings experts to hang new curtains or blinds, or furniture fitters to install off-the-shelf or tailor-made storage and display units. If you want a complete makeover, you may be better off calling in a firm of interior designers to coordinate the entire operation, subcontracting individual stages of the work to different specialists.

Redecorating the room
The living room is one area of the home where you may decide to choose more expensive materials and effects. You may want one of

the many modern decorative paint effects such as ragging, colour-washing or stencilling on your walls, and executing these well on a large scale can be difficult for the amateur. Similarly, exotic wall-coverings such as silks and grass-cloths can transform a room and give it a luxurious look, but they are expensive and can be ruined if hung by an inexperienced paperhanger. The quality of a professional's work will more than outweigh the extra expense for his or her labour (See pp. 36–39 for more details.)

Replacing floor coverings
In choosing floor coverings for living rooms, the relatively heavy use of the room should always be considered. Cheap foam-backed carpet or printed and laminated wood flooring will simply not withstand wear. Contract-quality carpets and solid wood or natural veneer floor coverings are comparatively expensive but hard-wearing. Professional installation will both produce a good finish and ensure that expensive materials are not wasted. (See pp. 40–43 for further details on floorings.)

Soft furnishings
Providing new curtains, blinds and other window decorations can also be expensive in living rooms. There is probably more than one window and one of them may be a large opening such as a bay or bow window or a French window or patio door. Here, professional advice will help you to select suitable materials,

A professional painter added just enough texture to these walls to make them warm and inviting. They complement the furniture and other furnishings recommended by an interior designer.

Ample storage space has been provided with these custom-built units. Wooden flooring was installed around the carpet to make a feature of the units. Ceiling spotlights provide plenty of light in the room.

ments. It also allows for a tidy installation when it comes to hiding all the wiring work that is a unavoidable part of today's home entertainment equipment. The display units can feature integral lighting to show off your treasures, and a mix of low and high-level units will make the best use of available floor space. Professional suppliers can provide as efficient a use of space as you would expect in a fully fitted kitchen or bedroom.

When work starts

If your living room is being given a complete makeover, you can expect it to be out of commission for a week or more. Work will proceed more quickly if most of the existing furniture and fittings can be removed, especially fragile music systems, allowing old decorations and floor coverings to be removed more easily and minimizing any damage to your possessions.

The contractors will tackle the redecorating first, and will then install any fitted furniture that is required. There is little point in wasting expensive floor coverings underneath storage units, which will in any case stand level and square better on a solid floor. Then the new floor coverings will be laid, curtains and other window dressings will be hung and finishing touches such as new door furniture and electrical accessories will be installed to complete the job.

pick the correct types of curtain track and achieve a coordinated effect throughout the room.

Storage and display

The living room is not only the home entertainment centre of the house but is also the family's showcase of treasures. Coping with these twin requirements means that the room needs some carefully planned storage and display units, especially to cater for the never-ending explosion in home entertainment equipment in recent years.

You have two choices in providing these units. The first is to buy free-standing furniture, probably from a coordinated range so that all the pieces are in the same style and

finish, and to arrange it within the available space. However, it is often difficult to make optimum use of floor space in this way. Fully fitted furniture can make better use of corners and alcoves, and can be tailored to your precise require-

Furnishings

An enormous difference can be made in your living room as soon as you recognize that the traditional idea of the central three-piece suite with all the other furniture cramped around it is not the only option. You can have one luxurious sofa and floor cushions or shop around for individual chairs that you like. Many houseowners like the wicker suites sold for conservatories that can have summery floral cushions.

If you want to coordinate your upholstery with your carpets and curtains, most big furniture stores will supply fabric samples that you can take home.

Getting more bedroom space

One of the most pressing demands in many homes is for extra bedroom space, usually because of a new addition to the family or the need to give growing children space of their own – or you may want a larger bedroom to gain privacy for yourself.

If you are unable to make more space by moving to a bigger house, converting your loft space (see pp. 84–87) or building a home extension (pp. 98–103) – which are all potentially very expensive options – you will have to work within the floor space you have.

Partitioning rooms

If you live in an older property with larger bedrooms than are usual today, you may be able to divide one room into two to create an extra bedroom. Such an alteration may sound like a simple proposition, but it needs careful planning and sound execution if it is to be a success.

You can get help in the planning from an architect or a building surveyor. He or she will be able to find solutions to the two main problems of partitioning rooms: providing access to both rooms and ensuring that each room has adequate natural light, ventilation and, preferably, sound-proofing.

It is rarely satisfactory to provide access to one room through another, so some form of corridor will be needed between door for the existing room and the entrance to the new room. This will eat up valuable floor space but, if properly planned, can be kept to a minimum.

Light and ventilation requirements can also pose problems. If the existing room has only one window,

An interior designer will not only help you decide on the layout for the bedroom but also assist in coordinating fabrics and patterns.

this cannot be shared. Each room must have an openable window and also background "trickle" ventilation. This means either creating a new window opening and building a window to match the rest of the house or replacing the existing window with two smaller windows, with a column of masonry between that coincides with the position of the new partition wall.

Once these main problems have been solved, your expert will also have to consider the necessary changes to the heating, lighting and power points. He or she will be able to ensure that the proposed changes will meet the requirements of the Building Regulations and will be responsible for notifying your local authority that this is the case.

Creating the partition is a job for a builder (if new window openings have to be created) or a carpenter, since it involves building a timber framework, lining it with sound-proofing insulation – this is essential between bedrooms – and cladding it with plasterboard on both sides. Extra work may be needed to strengthen the floor if the wall runs

Alternative choices !

Another source of bedroom space is converting a room designed for another purpose – for example, a little-used dining room in an older house, or a downstairs den in a newer split-level. This is only viable if you really can spare the space and if the location of the room truly enables it to function as a bedroom, with access to a bathroom and with a certain amount of privacy. Beware of converting below-ground basement areas into sleeping quarters; even if there are windows, such spaces may not be permissible for use as bedrooms by the terms of your local Building Regulations.

parallel with the room's floor joists, since all the load would otherwise be carried by just one or two joists (see pp.136–137). Again, your expert will advise you on the best solution to this problem. There are usually no problems with a partition wall at right angles to the joists.

Changing the layout

If you live in a relatively modern house with all the upstairs rooms divided by timber-framed walls, you could consider a more radical solution: replanning the entire floor layout. None of the walls is load-bearing because the roof is carried entirely by trussed rafters spanning the external walls. The walls can therefore be removed and new walls built to subdivide the floor space differently. However, the conversion involves massive upheaval of half the house as the whole floor has to be stripped of furniture and fittings. This is a job best done while you take a holiday.

If this sounds a feasible option, then again consult an architect or surveyor to ensure that the best possible use is made of the floor space available.

Using another room

Extra bedroom space can be made from an under-used downstairs living room. This is only viable if you really can spare the space – for example, by eating meals in the

lounge or the kitchen if the dining room is converted, or by giving up a study and redistributing its contents elsewhere in the house. If this change of use is possible, the converted room would suit a teenager better than a young child, or could be occupied by the parents to free a bedroom upstairs for a child's use. The room could do double duty as a day room if it is fitted with a sofa bed.

Rooms to spare

If you have more bedrooms than you need, there is little point in furnishing them all as bedrooms unless you regularly have people to stay. You could instead turn one room into a hobby or work room, a photographic darkroom or a music room (but beware the extra weight of a large piano).

If you work at home, the extra room could make an ideal home office (see pp. 60–61). And if you really wanted to splash out, you could knock two adjacent bedrooms together to form a spacious master bedroom suite. The extra space will provide a separate dressing area and perhaps an en-suite bathroom, as well as create more room in the main sleeping area in the bargain.

Refitting bedrooms

Cupboards and wardrobes with built-in shelves, racks and other features make the best use of storage space in the bedroom. In larger bedrooms, you can install free-standing units or extend the size of the existing storage space.

In the relatively cramped rooms in many modern homes, fitted furniture is the best answer for storage in the bedroom. The advice of a specialist bedroom designer will ensure that you get as much room for storing clothes and other items as possible, all neatly concealed behind matching doors.

Assessing your needs
Your present collection of clothes will give you a rough idea of the amount of storage space you need. The first priority is hanging space, and here fitted cupboards can be much better than traditional wardrobes with their single hanging rail. In your new arrangement you can have one rail for full-length items such as coats and dresses, and a lower rail or two, with one above the other, for shorter item such as jackets, shirts and trousers.

Divide your clothes into two groups, long and short, and measure how much rail space each group needs. Be generous – clothes get creased if they are crammed closely together, and if you are having a bedroom refit it is worth making allowance for new items to be added in the future.

Next, look at what you currently store in drawers or on shelves. A handy way of measuring how much you have is to stack items in piles about 450 mm (18 in) square and total their height. This will give the designers an idea of your needs when designing your fitted furniture. Don't forget accessories such as shoes, boots, hats and ties; also remember that the bedroom is often used for storing bulky items such as suitcases. You can use the large spaces on top of the full-length hanging units to keep suitcases or rucksacks out of the way.

Planning the units
Most fitted bedroom furniture, like kitchen units, is based on a modular design – units in a range of standard widths and heights that are mixed and matched to give you the storage space you need. Some top-of-the-range firms will make units to measure, but these will be expensive and will take longer to deliver than using standard units. However, in an awkward-shaped room this may

Items have been organized by size to make the best use of the fitted space, which includes double hanging rails, drawers and shelves.

When to inspect !

- There is really little point in inspecting the job until it is finished. When it is, check every surface for any signs of damage.

- Make sure that all fittings and hinges are secure and that drawers, sliding baskets and doors operate smoothly.

- If you find any faults or defects, notify the installer immediately so they can be fixed promptly.

available, such as pull-out hanging rails (ideal for shirts and blouses), tie and belt rails and shoe racks.

The panels and doors may either have a factory painted finish or a plastic surface, although doors can also be decorated with a variety of special paint effects. Louvre doors are a good idea for clothes storage as they allow the air to circulate.

When work starts

The installers will want the bedroom cleared of as much furniture as possible before starting the work, perhaps including the bed. Find out in advance whether they will do this. Since the storage units usually have a bottom shelf resting on a shallow plinth, they will stand better on bare floorboards – carpets may have to be trimmed back to allow for this.

The individual units will almost certainly arrive in flat-pack form, hence the need for maximum clear floor space in the room for their assembly. Each will be put together, set in place after any necessary trimming to fit around skirting boards and secured against the wall with brackets. Adjacent units will also be fixed together with cabinet connectors for maximum stability.

Once the run of units is completed, the various internal fittings will be installed and their operation checked. Plinths and ceiling trims will be added next, then the doors will be fitted and aligned to complete the installation.

Free-standing wardrobe units can be repositioned if you becomed bored with the current arrangement of the furniture in the bedroom, or they can be moved to make space for new furnishings.

be the best solution if you want to avoid space-wasting infill panels.

Depending on the size and layout of your bedroom, you may want units along just one wall or prefer them running around a corner. If the only available wall has the bed against it, the designers may offer a bridging unit over the bed, but this is awkward to reach and is best kept for rarely used items such as hats or winter woollens. Units look best if they reach ceiling height, making full use of all the available space and also avoiding dust traps on top.

In older houses, where the chimney breast alcoves are being used, the alcoves will probably not be deep enough from front to back for hanging space. Remember that the space you need is slightly more than the width of a coathanger to

prevent shoulders of jackets getting rubbed. This means building the units out into the room and putting dummy doors across the chimney breast. Depending on the depth of the alcoves, there could be limited storage space on shallow shelves behind these doors or just a large dressing mirror. Remember also that the walls will probably not be vertical or square, so the carpenter will need to use extra trim pieces to fill the irregular spaces or, better still, he may build the cupboards on the spot to fit your space.

In each section of the units, hanging space at different levels is the main component, but open shelves and pull-out baskets will make up a sizeable part of the arrangement. Your designers will also have other interior fittings

Saving floor space

Most cupboards and wardrobe units along a wall have hinged doors to each section. If floor space is tight, installing bi-fold or sliding doors may be a sensible way to gaining more space. It's a simple procedure for a carpenter to replace the doors.

Working from home is a way of life for more people as telecommuting becomes more common. You will have to create space that allows you to work uninterrupted and that has room for all the furniture, storage and equipment you'll need.

Depending on the size and layout of your house, there are several options for creating an office. The obvious one is to use a spare or underused room – perhaps a bedroom or a dining room – unless the house already has a study. The dining room option will be possible only if part of the kitchen can be used for eating or if there is room for a table in the living room. The office can still function as a dining room on special occasions if the table is kept as a work surface that can be easily cleared.

Converting space

Unused loft space is the next option, and this has the advantage that it does not encroach on the existing living area (unless you need to install a staircase). Loft conversions almost always require professional help (see pp. 84–87). Apart from creating access, the job will probably involve strengthening ceiling joists, installing windows or skylights that can do double duty as a fire escape, putting in a floor, and building wall and ceiling frames and insulating and cladding them with plasterboard. You will also need electrical supply and heating units extended to the area and telephone lines, and of course, you will need Building Regulations approval and possibly planning permission.

Another option is to convert an integral or attached garage. Creating access to an existing garage is usually realitively easy, as is extending electrical and heating supplies. Again, professional help will ensure a speedy and efficient conversion (see pp. 92–93). It will usually start with dampproofing and insulating the garage floor, replacing the garage door with windows or a sliding glass door and if one does not exist, making a doorway into the house. The job may need Building Regulations approval.

(see pp. 84–87)
(see pp. 92–93)

Rules & regulations

Turning part of your home into an office is regarded as a change of use as far as planning permission is concerned. You should, therefore, contact your local authority before even starting to plan the conversion and apply for permission if they say it is required.

However, many authorities take a fairly relaxed view of office work being carried out at home, and they may not require permission to be sought as long as a buisness is not seen to be operating from a private house. Unless you store and sell things, or receive lots of callers and deliveries that annoy the neighbours, they will probably be happy with the situation as it is.

485 mm (19") maximum

700 mm (28")

Your work table and chair should be adjusted so that your arms can be at a 90° angle and your back straight, with your feet resting flat on the ground.

A home office is best created in a secluded part of the house, where other family members are less likely to interrupt.

Ask yourself

- Will you be working at home part time or full time? A part-time office can be tucked into a corner; a full-time office should be secluded.

- Does the area chosen for your home office have sufficient lighting for work and enough electrical outlets for telecommunications equipment? You may need to hire an electrician to upgrade the electricity.

- Will your home office have room for office equipment, such as computers and telephones, for work resources, such as files and books, and for stationery and other office supplies?

New construction

If you have no space suitable for converting to an office, consider building an extension (see pp. 98–103) or a garden structure (see pp. 106–107).

A garden office is ideal, and many suppliers of prefabricated outbuildings provide structures suitable for all-year use. Most offer an erection service that includes providing a base, but you will need to employ a professional electrician to provide a separate new circuit to the buiding. You are not allowed to run extensions to it from your house circuits. Or you could employ a builder to create a purpose-built masonry office. Either way, the work will need planning permission, as an office is not part of the residential use of the house. However, it will be exempt from Building Regulations

approval unless it exceeds 30 sq m (100 sq ft) in floor area.

Building a small single-storey extension will be viable only if you have space for it at the side or back of the house. If you do, call in an architect or builder to prepare plans for you to submit to the local authority. The extension will have to meet planning permission and Building Regulation requirements.

Furnishing an office

There are a number of specialist companies who offer a home office design and installation service. This includes providing built-in work surfaces, filing and other storage space, plus the provision of telecommunication services. Always opt for a separate business line, and add a second line if you use a computer that needs links to other computers or the Internet, so phone and fax messages are not blocked when the computer is on-line.

Creating a utility/laundry room

If you have the space, a utility room is a useful alternative to having the laundry equipment in the kitchen. It can also provide valuable space for such large items as freezers, as well as for extra storage.

In most homes, the kitchen is expected to hold far too much equipment as we introduce more and bigger appliances into our lives. Laundry equipment, a large freezer and cleaning equipment may be competing for space designed for cooking and perhaps eating.

Creating a separate utility room could free kitchen space for a dishwasher, extra storage or a dining area, especially if you are refitting your kitchen anyway (see pp. 44–49). If you have enough space, the utility room could also be used for a freezer, and for storing brooms and mops, as well as an ironing board.

Options for change

Whether you can create a utility room depends on the room layout and facilities you have. If you have a large kitchen, it may be possible to partition off an area and create a separate room for the laundry and/or other equipment. It need not be a large area, especially if you take advantage of the fact that you can often stack a tumbledrier on top of a washing machine.

If you have a separate larder area – a common feature in many older homes – you may be able to use this as your utility room. Again you will have to stack the appliances, but the

arrangement will enable you to move all your food storage into the kitchen and concentrate all your laundry activities in one compact space.

In houses that have basements, this often seems the most obvious place for a utility room. However, this is not always the best choice and is a good case for advice from a professional before you make the decision. Basements are often not well ventilated, and if this is the case in yours, it will already be damp. Adding machines that need electricity and produce a certain amount of damp air themselves may not be a good thing for the general fabric of your house or in the long run for the machines themselves.

Another option is to convert part of an integral or attached garage to act as a utility room. If you can afford to sacrifice a minimum of 1 sq m (3 sq ft) at the back of the garage and your house drains are at the back of the

By keeping the washing machine and dryer side-by-side, you'll have room for storage space above the appliances. A laundry area doesn't have to be in a separate room – for example, you can partition it off a large kitchen.

Rules & regulations

You will need Building Regulations approval to make alterations to your house's underground drainage system, so make sure your builder or plumber gives the local authority the necessary notification.

Make sure that your installers allow for adequate ventilation. Laundry appliances give out lots of hot air and steam that can condense and cause damp problems in your walls. The Building Regulations may require that you install an electric fan.

You can use sliding or bifold doors to hide a washing machine and dryer. Stacking the appliances may be an option in a confined space.

house, this is an option that does not take any space within the house itself.

The last possibility you could consider is siting the utility room upstairs. As with the ground floor options already mentioned, you do not need a large area for the appliances, and you may be able to partition off part of a large bathroom or a bedroom next to it to create the space you require. The one drawback with this arrangement is the noise a washing machine makes when standing on a suspended timber floor. It certainly will not suit you if you always do your laundry late at night, since it will disturb sleeping children in a way that a washing machine situated downstairs will not.

In all these cases, but especially this last, you should install the machines on some kind of tray as a first defence against leaks.

Providing services

Getting water supplies to the site of your new utility room will not be a problem. The biggest difficulty in all these cases is the need to connect the washing machine waste outlet to the existing waste water drainage set-up. So long as the new utility area is next to an external wall, it should be possible to take the new waste pipe out through the wall close to the machine and then to run it on the outside of the house to the gully that takes the kitchen waste water. In a newer house with an internal soil stack, the waste pipe can be taken to that so long as the utility area is not too remote from the stack.

Your new utility area will also need power supplies for the appliances and lighting to allow you to use it, so your existing circuits will have to be extended. This should not pose any problem unless the existing wiring in your house is old.

Who to employ

The expert help you need for this job depends on which option you choose. You will need a builder to put up any partition walls, and a plumber and electrician (whom the builder will subcontract) to carry out the necessary work on the services. If you are simply using a larder to create your utility room, the plumber will be able to knock the necessary holes through for the pipework but you should employ an electrician as well.

In any room where there will be water and steam in the air it is very important that the electrical wiring complies with regulations. Generally, it is better to hire a proper electrician rather than accept if the plumber offers to do the wiring as well. If the utility room is not just a small annexe to the kitchen or garage, it also needs to be well lit.

Even if you are not providing trays to stand the washing machine on, you may want to stand appliances such as a freezer on a wooden plinth. A carpenter can construct this easily and may also find room for some shelving or drying space for you.

If the work is included in a complete kitchen refit, the installers carrying out that work will be able to include the utility room in the alterations, making wiring and plumbing runs more logical.

Depending on your budget, you may want to employ a decorator to finish off. It is best to create an airy light space and you may consider tiling all or part of the walls or using washable (that is, water-proof) paint or wall lining material. You should pay attention to the flooring materials also. The room will get heavy use and may be better with a quarry tile floor or vinyl floor covering.

When work starts

Depending on the scale of the changes, the professionals' first job will be to make the utility room space ready, creating partition walls and a doorway if necessary or stripping out an existing larder. Then water supply pipes will be extended to the area and terminated in isolating valves to which the washing machine hoses will be connected. The waste pipe will be run to an outside gully or internal soil stack. A ventilation opening to the outside will be made to take the exhaust from the tumble drier and will be fitted with an external weather-proof grille. Finally, the alterations to the electrics will be carried out, and you may wish to finish off with some basic decorating.

DIY jargon

Partition wall Also referred to as a stud partition, this is a timber-framed wall that separates two rooms or areas. It does not provide support for the ceiling above it.

Soil stack Or soil-and-vent stack, in a single-stack system (see pp.154–155), this vertical pipe transfers waste from sinks, lavatories, washing machines and other fittings to the underground drains.

2

A staircase is a complex structure, and in an older house it will probably have been tailor-made and assembled on site by a carpenter. Older staircases and newer models can often be improved with new decoration.

In older houses, the staircase was custom-made to fit the space. But houses built since the First World War usually have a prefabricated staircase, which was made to match standard ceiling heights and to fit the dimensions that met with the Building Regulations requirements at the time the house was built.

Unless your staircase has been attacked by dry rot or woodworm, you are unlikely to need to replace it. However, wear and tear can produce a variety of faults and these demand the attention of an experienced carpenter with good knowledge of staircase construction.

Structural work

The most common problem needing attention is creaky treads. The treads and risers fit into slots cut into the strings (the sloping side members of the flight), and are held there by slim timber wedges (see pp. 144–145). These wedges can work loose over time, allowing the treads to move slightly as the flight is used and to grate against the strings.

The treads may have been damaged, usually by careless movement of furniture, resulting in cracks across the treads or even split nosings – the projections at the front of each tread.

The balustrade – the handrail and the decorative balusters fixed between it and the staircase string – may have loose or broken components. This can be a serious safety problem, because the balustrade could give way if someone stumbled against it, so it needs expert attention to put it right straightaway.

Lastly, you may have a sound but old-fashioned balustrade that you simply want to replace with a more modern design.

When work starts

Repair work to the staircase treads and risers generally requires access to the underside of the flight. This is no problem if there is a storage cupboard beneath it, since the flight will probably have been left exposed. However, if the underside has been panelled in – with lath-

A new staircase can be made into an attractive feature of a hallway. The traditional style of this staircase was enhanced by designing it with curved steps and treads, which creates a flared effect.

and-plaster in an older home or plasterboard in a newer one – this will have to be removed first.

The carpenter's next job is to remove and reglue all the wedges, and to replace any loose or missing ones. He or she may also decide to glue and screw reinforcing blocks into the angles between each riser and the tread above it to prevent them moving against each other and causing more creaks.

If any damaged treads need to be replaced, freeing them may involve cutting through the tongued-and-grooved joints between the tread and the risers above and below it. Then the tread can be slid out and a matching replacement can be cut to size and fitted in place.

If exposing the underside of the flight is not possible or desirable, the carpenter may be able to carry out some remedial repair work from above, but this will require the stair carpet to be removed. Some of the repairs may involve driving down screws through each tread nosing into the riser beneath and injecting woodworking adhesive into the angles between the treads and risers to bond them together.

When to inspect !

- Check that creaky treads have been silenced before the underside of the staircase is covered or the stair carpet is replaced.

- You should inspect a new balustrade for sturdiness as soon as it is complete.

- When the decoration job is finished, check the paint and other finishes for blemishes and check wallcoverings for dry patches, blisters and lifting seams. Point out any defects as soon as you find them so they can be repaired.

New staircases

You may decide to replace a staircase because it looks old and dated and you want a new look or because its structure has becomed so damaged by woodworm, for example, that it would be dangerous to continue to use it. There are plenty of styles to choose from when it comes to prefabricated staircases. Alternatively, you could have a staircase custom-made, which may be your only choice if you have an old house that doesn't follow standard dimensions.

Before the new staircase is installed the old one will have to be removed, which will mean that you won't have access to any rooms on the floor above. You may want to stay elsewhere while the work takes place.

Replacing a balustrade

Modern replacement balustrade kits make this a relatively straightforward job for a carpenter to carry out. He or she will cut away the existing handrail and balusters, as well as the newel posts if these are being changed too. Then new posts will be mounted on the newel post stubs, new handrails fitted using special brackets, and new balusters slotted into place between a capping on the string and the underside of the handrail to complete the job. Because the new balustrade is not jointed into the strings as the old newel posts and balusters were, you should check carefully for strength.

Decorating the stairwell

The problem of gaining access to the upper walls and the ceiling of a stairwell make decorating it best left to a professional, who will have the appropriate equipment and will be experienced at handling rollers on extension poles or coping with long lengths of wallpaper. He or she will also complete the job more quickly than an amateur decorator, minimizing disruption to the household.

When work starts

Once your decorator has put down dust sheets and set up the access equipment, he or she will begin by stripping old wallcoverings, washing down all painted surfaces and carrying out any preparation work that is needed to plaster or wood surfaces. He or she will paint or paper the ceiling first, then begin painting or staining the woodwork.

The final stage is to paint or paper the walls and to clear up. When it is finished, check the paintwork for blemishes and wallcoverings for blisters, dry patches and lifting seams. Point out any defects, paint splashes or damage to the woodwork as soon as you find them, so that they can be attended to immediately.

Because this graceful, slim balustrade requires less room than a traditional balustrade, it's a good choice for a narrow staircase.

2 Updating the plumbing

Older homes may have plumbing systems that have been modified over the years in a ramshackle way and supply pipes may have become constricted by mineral deposits. The plumbing can be replaced during a bathroom or kitchen renovation.

Household plumbing tends to be a mish-mash of systems laid down over the years. Older systems may contain at least some lead pipework, which will be seriously furred up in hard water areas and which can pose a health hazard if the local water supply is soft. You are especially likely to become aware of your system's shortcomings if you are contemplating changes to your kitchen or bathroom, and this may be a good time to consider having all the old plumbing replaced by a professional plumber. If you want the best service, appoint a services engineer, who can explain which options are best for your home.

Inspecting the system

The first thing your plumber will do is to survey the existing system to see what services are required and to suggest possible improvements. The most fundamental of these is to have plastic hot and cold water pipes instead of the traditional copper. Some plumbers prefer to stick to copper, but plastic has several major advantages: it will not

Extending pipes to the plumbing system was part of creating this stylish shower off a sauna room.

Rules & regulations

All the work your plumber carries out should comply with the requirements of the water bye-laws; make sure that his or her quotation for the work includes a statement that it will. All the fittings that they use should comply with the relevant British Standards.

All work involving the gas pipework should be done by a Corgi registered installer.

develop pinholes, will not burst if a pipe freezes and semi-flexible types such as cross-linked polyethylene can be bent around gentle 90° curves so fewer joints will be needed. It is, however, rather more expensive. Your old taps may then need replacing or at any rate overhauling to cope with the increase in pressure in the new system.

While the pipework is being replaced, the plumber is likely to recommend fitting a new cold water storage cistern and hot-water cylinder if you have a conventional system. Old galvanized cisterns corrode and develop potentially catastrophic leaks and, if you still have one, disaster could be just around the corner. A modern plastic cistern will have a lid and an insect screen to keep dust and bugs out, and can be efficiently insulated against freeze-ups. If access to the loft is restricted, your plumber may suggest the use of two smaller interconnected tanks to give you the storage capacity you need.

If you live in a hard water area, replacing the hot-water cylinder will make the system much more efficient. The old cylinder is likely to be heavily scaled up, so water will take longer to heat and this wastes fuel.

The plumber may also suggest switching from a traditional stored-water system to an unvented one. With this, all the water used is supplied at mains pressure. There is no need for a loft storage tank and its pipework, which can simply be cut off and abandoned. All the cold taps will supply mains water fit for drinking, and hot water is supplied from a special storage cylinder that is fitted with a range of safety devices to prevent overheating. Installing such a system needs Building Regulations approval and must be fitted only by an approved installer – for example, a member of CORGI (the Council for Registered Gas Installers; see pp. 168–171).

When to inspect !

- It is obviously difficult to inspect the work in progress, so you will have to check that everything is water-tight and ship-shape when work finishes for the day.

- At the end of the job, make sure that lifted floorboards are fixed back down securely and floor coverings have been replaced.

- Check all taps to make sure that there are no airlocks in the system.

- Check that lagging has been applied to all pipework exposed to the weather or cold.

- Keep an eye on ceilings for a few days afterwards, just in case any connections are weeping. If you notice any, call the plumber back immediately to fix them.

- Listen for any unusual noises in your plumbing system when you are using newly installed appliances. Notify your plumber if you hear anything odd.

When work starts

There is no disguising the fact that replacing your plumbing pipework, cistern and cylinder will be a massive disruption to everyday life. For a start, you will have no water supply – or probably heating – during the day for the duration of the job, although the plumber should be organized enough to be able to restore supplies at the end of each working day.

Carpets and floorboards will have to be lifted to allow access to underfloor voids so the new pipework can be installed, and your plumber may want to reroute some of the existing pipes. Major plumbing work is best scheduled for the summer months and you should plan on being away from the house for the whole day.

Improving wiring and lighting

Today's homes use more electrical equipment than ever before, and even many new houses lack sufficient wiring and outlets to handle the load. With more activities going on in the house, lighting often also requires updating.

Electricity provision in older houses is especially inadequate to cope with modern demands. Many older houses do not have enough socket outlets for all the array of electrical equipment to be plugged in without a dangerous tangle of adapters and extension leads, and large appliances such as freezers should be installed on their own circuit to avoid overcrowding a circuit (see pp.156–157). The provision of fixed lighting is often below modern standards too – frequently, just a centre light in each room, plus the occasional wall light or two.

Upgrading the power and lighting circuits to modern standards is a job for a professional electrician. He or she will ensure that the work meets the Wiring Regulations requirements and will also be able to advise you on the best way to improve the electrical safety of your house's system.

Inspecting the system

The age of your wiring system will be betrayed by the type of switches and sockets you have and, more impor-tantly, by the state of the circuit cables. Socket outlets taking round-pin plugs are dangerously out-of-date and need replacing with modern 13-amp outlets that take plugs with rectangular pins. However, even if your house does have modern socket outlets, they could be concealing a dark secret – that they were replaced without the old circuit wiring being replaced at the same time.

Another potential problem is light-ing circuits originally wired up with a cable that does not contain an earth core, an old practice that is no longer allowed. These may be unsafe to use with metal-bodied light fittings.

The third area where your wiring may be seriously behind the times is at the fuse box, the nerve centre of the system. If this contains rewirable or cartridge fuses and a simple on-off

Installing new downlighters in this kitchen involved making holes in the ceiling to accept the fittings and running new wiring to a circuit. Downlighters can be planned to provide extra light in work areas.

Rules & regulations

All the work your electrician carries out in your home should comply with the requirements of the Wiring Regulations, although this has the force of law only in Scotland where the Wiring Regulations are part of the Building Regulations. Make sure that you receive a signed certificate on completion so you can be sure that everything is up to standard.

The ever-increasing equipment found in today's home entertainment centres often requires installing extra outlets in the living room or den.

Home computers can be sensitive to electrical surges. You should dedicate an outlet for the sole use of your computer, and equip it with a surge protector.

switch, it definitely needs replacing with a modern consumer unit fitted with protective devices called miniature circuit breakers and with a residual current device (RCD). These can detect minute amounts of electricity

that are not enough to blow a fuse but can still give a fatal shock.

Your electrician will check all these points and advise you on what is needed. This may involve simple extensions to existing circuits if these are safe and in good condition, coupled with the fitting of modern switches and socket outlets. On the other hand, he may recommend a complete rewire from the fuse box, which will give you the opportunity to rethink your wiring needs in detail.

Improving the lighting

Apart from providing extra socket outlets, your electrician will also be able to bring your lighting systems into the 21st century, and it is worth taking some time to plan the effects you want. You no longer have to rely on traditional ceiling and wall lights.

Recessed ceiling lights are usually easy to install (except in a lath and plaster ceilings) and can revolutionize the way a room looks. So can so-called uplighters and downlighters, which can be used to wash wall and ceiling surfaces with light or colour. Low-voltage fittings can create unusual

lighting effects and have the advantage of low running costs. They also produce a lot of heat.

When work starts

Major electrical work is somewhat disruptive, since cables have to be run in floor voids and need concealing beneath wall surfaces. This will mean lifting floor coverings and floorboards, and cutting channels in wall plaster for cables to run to new switches and socket outlets. A professional electrician will do his or her best to reduce the upheaval; for example, by using old cables to draw new lengths into place through floor voids via a board lifted at each side of the room, and by passing cables within partition walls whenever possible. In some rooms you will need some redecoration when work is completed, and also carpet fitters or other flooring specialists to relay floor coverings that were lifted to allow the work to go ahead.

Minor jobs such as upgrading fittings or installing extra lights may take only a day or two, but a full rewire is likely to take at least a week and may put individual rooms out of commission for a day at a time.

Updating the heating system

Central heating systems generally last for decades and are expensive to replace. However, improvements can often be made to increase the efficiency and may be necessary if you have upgraded your plumbing system.

Central heating of one sort or another is now a feature of most homes, but many existing systems are comparatively old and inefficient. The best improvement can usually be gained by replacing the boiler, but there are several other ways of making the most of an existing system. If you have no central heating at present, having a system installed will make your home much more comfortable and also much easier to sell.

Whatever the scale of the work required, you can call in either a plumber or a heating specialist. The latter is likely to have a more extensive knowledge of the latest equipment and is probably a better choice for major installation work,

whereas a plumber will be quite competent to replace individual components such as the boiler, the hot-water cylinder or the radiators.

Inspecting the system

If you want an existing system upgrading, your plumber or heating engineer will look at five key areas. The first is the way the system operates (see pp.158–159). If it relies on gravity circulation between the boiler and hot-water cylinder, he or she will either recommend installing a pump on the circuit between the two, or modifying the pipework so that the pump currently circulating water to the radiators can run both circuits. This involves installing a motorized valve to divert the water flow between the two circuits, a cylinder thermostat to control the hot-water temperature and a new programmer to run everything.

Next is the hot-water cylinder, which will probably have a great deal of scale built upon its heat exchanger over time. Replacing it with a new one will dramatically improve its efficiency. Modern cylinders have shrunk-on foam insulation, and with the addition of a second quilted jacket, they will retain their heat for many hours.

The third potential area for improvement is the controls of your heating system. If it relies on just a clock programmer, a room thermostat and the boiler thermostat to run everything, then an upgrade will bring significant improvements. The fitting of a motorized valve and a cylinder thermostat will bring your hot water heating under much closer

control. A modern electronic programmer will control the heating and hot water supplies independently, ensuring that each part of the system gets heat only when it needs it. Lastly, replacing the existing radiator valves with thermostatic ones will give you better control over the temperatures in individual rooms.

Another option is to replace the radiators. Modern convector radiators deliver more heat from a unit of the same size than their older counterparts, and also fit in better with modern decor. Replacing old single radiators with new double ones means that your rooms will heat up quicker, and they can also free up extra wall space.

Lastly, the most significant improvement to the system will

Some modern fireplaces can be installed without the need of a chimney or the masonry work of an old-fashioned fireplace.

efficient than standard boilers. A combination boiler provides hot water on demand, allowing you to do away with the need for a hot-water cylinder.

Installing a new system

A heating engineer can help you decide what fuel to use, which type of boiler to select, how the system will be controlled and what type of radiators to fit. He or she will calculate how much heat the house requires room by room, how big each radiator needs to be and the required boiler output. He will then plan the circuit layout, size the system pipework and decide on the optimum control arrangement. An unvented system instead of the traditional vented type does away with the need for a feed-and-expansion tank in the loft and makes installation of the system quicker and easier.

Installing a new heating system will involve lifting floorboards to run in the circuit pipework, and this is likely to cause major disruption for the duration of the job. In addition, space has to be found for the boiler and the hot-water cylinder (if one is being used). There will also be some electrical work involved in fitting the system controls. Expect a typical installation to take at least a week or longer. Make sure that your installer gives you the instruction manual about the new system.

A seat around a fireplace is an inviting place to sit when coming inside from cold weather. The glass enclosure provides protection from hot flames.

come from replacing the boiler. You will get more economical heating; you will save space because modern gas and oil-fired boilers are generally more compact than older types; and you may be able to do away with an existing flue by choosing a through-the-wall balanced-flue type. Condensing boilers have a secondary heat exchanger that extracts waste heat from the flue gases, so making them even more

2 Insulation

Insulation performs two important functions in the home: thermal (heat) insulation keeps the house warm in winter and cool in summer; acoustic (sound) insulation stops noise from the outside world getting into your home.

Thermal insulation is regarded as a matter of course in the loft space but it can well be applied elsewhere in the home to improve comfort and increase energy efficiency. Outside noise is very common in today's lightly built housing and can contribute markedly to stress levels. Acoustic insulation is vital if you live in an environment where traffic, aircraft, heavy industry or noisy neighbours are a problem. If your home is deficient in either type of insulation, professional help could go a long way towards putting things right in your home.

The biggest benefits in terms of savings versus expenditure will accrue from having loft and cavity wall insulation installed. Double glazing is expensive, with a long payback period, but may be justified if your windows need replacing anyway. Floor insulation is rarely cost-effective. In all these options, however, it is worth considering the double benefit of the improvement to sound insulation as well as the increased energy efficiency.

Thermal insulation

Your house loses heat to the outside world through the roof, the walls, windows and doors, and perhaps surprisingly, through the floor. In newly built houses, each of these areas is insulated to a standard demanded by the Building Regulations, but many older homes are still seriously under-insulated. The best way of getting your house assessed is to call in a firm of insulation specialists, who will advise on what to insulate and how.

If you have a pitched roof and use the loft merely for storage, the company are likely to advise laying blanket insulation on the loft floor. Even if you have some insulation there already, adding an extra layer can only improve the insulation performance. In awkwardly shaped lofts with uneven joist spacings, they may recommend laying a loose-fill material instead.

Flat roofs are notorious for heat loss, since they are often built with little or no insulation between the ceiling and the roof deck. The professionals will generally opt for insulating from above by laying insulation over the existing roof deck and then covering it with a new waterproof surface. If this is impractical for any reason, and the ceilings in the room below the roof are high enough, the alternative is to put up a false ceiling in the room with insulation above it.

Wall insulation

How wall insulation can be improved depends on how the walls are built. If they are of cavity construction, specialist installers can pump in treated mineral fibres that settle within the cavity to create an insulating layer. This type of work requires Building Regulations approval from your local authority and must be carried out only by approved installers. Ask the local authority for a list of firms operating in your area.

There are no easy answers to the problems of insulating solid walls. If you have solid walls, your installer may recommend externally applied installation finished off with rendering or cladding, but this will

Sound Insulation

The single biggest improvement you can make to improve your home's sound insulation is to have acoustic double glazing installed, because the windows are the chief inlet for noise. Acoustic double glazing differs from thermal double glazing in having a much bigger gap between the panes of glass and in having soundproofing material installed around the sides of the window reveals.

There is little that can be done to insulate external walls against noise. However, noise passing through party walls in semi-detached and terraced properties can be reduced by building isolated timber-framed walls just inside the party wall and fitting insulation behind them.

Floors usually need insulating only in flats and house conversions, but unfortunately the best solution – installing a floating floor over a layer of sound-deadening insulation – involves work in the room from where the noise is coming and access may not be possible. The only alternative is to install a false ceiling beneath the existing one and to fit insulation above it. Sound insulation is always difficult and it may be worth consulting a specialist acoustic engineer.

be an expensive option. The alternative is to have the inside of all the external walls lined with insulating plasterboard – a job that will be extremely disruptive.

Double glazing

The most efficient way of cutting heat losses through windows is by fitting some form of secondary glazing inside the existing frames or by removing them and replacing them with new double-glazed windows. This work is generally carried out by specialist replacement window contractors, who will order and install made-to-measure windows and patio doors. (See pp. 112–113 for more details.)

Floor options

Insulating floors involves lifting floorboards and fitting insulation material between the joists if the floor is suspended, or placing insulation sheets on top of an existing concrete floor and then laying a new "floating" floor on top of it. The first option is disruptive, while laying a new floating floor means raising floor levels throughout the house (see pp. 142–143).

Sound insulation

Noisy neighbours above or below you or noise from the street can greatly increase the stress levels of your household. You should also consider the noise that you or your household produces and whether it is likely to constitute a nuisance for your neighbours. It is possible to insulate separate appliances such as a washing machine or tumble-drier, or separate rooms such as an office. Carpets and curtains absorb noise more than bare floors or window-blinds. Bookcases lining the wall are great sound absorbers.

Make sure that you talk to your neighbours about noise levels as some solutions – such as moving the

DIY jargon !

Double glazing A window comprising two panes of glass separated by an air space that provides insulation. Acoustic double glazing has a wider space between the sheets.

False ceiling A ceiling constructed below the original ceiling with a gap left for insulation material. The ceiling may be suspended on wires from ties to the joists above or rebuilt on extra joists running at 90° to the original ones.

washing machine or the baby's cot – are easier than wholesale insulation. In the last resort, call in an acoustic engineer to pinpoint areas where improvements can be made and suggest the best materials that your contractors can use.

In an uninsulated house, the roof, floors and walls are responsible for 31 percent of air leaks.

Vents and exhaust fans account for four percent of air leaks.

Another 14 percent of air leaks escape through the fireplace.

About 10 percent of air leaks occurs from windows and 11 percent from doors.

Where plumbing enters the house another 13 percent of air can leak; ducts are responsible for 15 percent.

2 Condensation and infestations

Three problems that may affect your house are condensation, woodworm and infestations by insects, mice or other unwelcome visitors. These can cause damage to your house and affect your health.

Condensation can occur due to a variety of causes. Frosty weather will produce condensation on the inside of windows. Some activities in the home such as cooking and bathing will create greater than normal amounts.

Understanding condensation

The warmer air is, the more water vapour it can carry. When warm moist air meets a cold surface, the vapour cools to a liquid and is deposited on the cold surface as droplets of liquid water – condensation. This is found most often on windows in cold weather, but it also forms on other surfaces such as poorly insulated ceilings and external walls, causing mould patches to appear on your decoration. It can form within the structure of the building too, making walls damp and prone to excess heat losses or frost damage, and creating the conditions for rot in structural timbers, especially within the roof space.

Condensation action

Specialist condensation control consultants (whose main specialization will usually be damp-proofing) will visit your home and check whether condensation or damp is the cause of your problems. If it is condensation, they will then have to identify the main causes of the problem and then propose solutions. These generally revolve around three main issues – ventilation, insulation and heating – plus a few common-sense changes to your lifestyle.

Improved ventilation is generally the most important ingredient in the cure. The firm's first step will be to fit extractor fans or hoods in the two main sources of water vapour, the bathroom and the kitchen, to extract steam before it can cause trouble. These can be linked to humidity detectors which will switch the fans on whenever the humidity level rises to the point where condensation will begin to develop.

Better insulation can make a big difference too by ensuring that wall and ceiling surfaces are warmer and less prone to attracting condensation. Loft and cavity wall insulation (see pp. 72–73) can help with severe condensation. In milder cases, the use of warm wall decorations such as cork or blown vinyl wallcoverings may tip the balance. Other materials, such as cold ceramic tiles, should be avoided in condensation-prone rooms.

More controlled heating can also contribute to solving the problem. Unheated rooms are obviously more prone to condensation, so maintaining a constant level of background warmth will be better than heating the room up and the letting it get cold. If you do not have central heating, the firm may recommend the installation of electric panel radiators with thermostatic control to provide the necessary background heating at an economical rate.

Once these improvements have been carried out, you can help to make condensation less of a problem with a few simple steps – close bathroom or kitchen doors when running a bath or boiling saucepans, open a window in steamy rooms, avoid drying clothes on radiators and never use paraffin heaters to warm cold rooms. Every litre (1¼ pt) of paraffin burnt produces a litre (1¼ pt) of water vapour to condense on your walls.

Tackling woodworm

You can tell if you have an attack of woodworm by looking for the small round exit holes left in woodwork by the emerging beetles. The beetles lay

---

Alternative choices !

Double glazing can be a mixed blessing when it comes to condensation. It will increase the warmth of a room and possibly therefore decrease the likelihood of moisture forming on the windows, but double glazing reduces ventilation. Loft insulation also reduces ventilation and, in increasing the warmth in the house, increases the cold in the loft space. Mould can form due to condensation in the loft space without you noticing.

Alternative steps to reduce condensation include:
- Closing bathroom doors when bathing or showering.
- Keeping pans covered when boiling large quantities of water.
- Opening a window in steamy rooms.
- Avoiding drying clothes on radiators.
- Keeping few indoor houseplants if you have restricted living space.

To help reduce condensation in the kitchen, you can have a hood with an extractor fitted above the cooker. If there is one there already, it may need updating to a model that is a larger size or offers proper venting.

Building Regulations will specify ventilation requirements for houses but these vary between local codes. As a general rule of thumb, bathroom air should be ventilated at a rate of at least 54 cu m per hour; kitchens at a rate of at least 216 cu m per hour.

Bear in mind that if a survey done for a building society reveals woodworm or dry rot in your structural timber, you will have to get the timbers treated by a professional firm who can give you guarantee afterwards. Check this before employing them.

eggs on unprotected wood surfaces, and once these hatch the grubs bore into the wood and tunnel around, creating winding galleries beneath the wood surface that can eventually weaken it seriously if the outbreak persists. You may be able to treat an isolated attack in a piece of furniture using proprietary woodworm treatments, but an attack in the house woodwork should be dealt with by a wood treatment specialist.

Once they have assessed the extent of the outbreak, they will arrange to treat all the affected areas by spraying on woodworm fluid. The work will be disruptive and time-consuming, especially if the loft needs treating and has to be cleared of stored goods and insulation materials first. It is wise to get at least three opinions on whether treatment is necessary before going ahead. You must distinguish between holes that are an indication of an old infestation and holes that indicate current activity. In the latter case, you will find minute pockets of wood dust near the holes, perhaps on the carpet below or simply round the mouth of the hole. If the outbreak occurred years ago and there is no sign of fresh infestation, treatment may be a waste of time and money.

Dealing with infestations

There are many pests and vermin that could infest your home, from obvious contenders such as bees and wasps, ants and fleas, cockroaches, mice and rats, even birds or squirrels in the loft or moles in the garden. If you have a problem with any of these, first contact your local authority's Health Department. They will normally assist with infestations that are judged to be a health hazard, such as wasps, cockroaches, mice and rats, but they may charge for their services.

In the case of a bee swarm forming in the house or garden, a call to your local authority, the police or a Citizens' Advice Bureau will put you in touch with a local beekeeper who may agree to come and remove it.

For other infestations you will have to call in a pest and vermin control specialist. Many offer a 24-hour-a-day service. When telephoning them, ask about their charges as well as their response time. Their charges are likely to be higher than the local authority's pest control officer. Bats are a protected species and must not be killed by law. If a colony starts nesting in your loft, contact your local authority Health Department for advice.

In all cases of infestation, it is worth asking yourself (or an expert) why it occurred. The answer can range from loose pointing or fascia boards (wasp nests) to improper food storage (mice, cockroaches) or inadequate rubbish storage (rats, foxes) – it will certainly be worth your while to fix the cause of the problem.

2 Modifying existing rooms

The day you moved into your house, the functions of its various rooms probably seemed predetermined – living room, dining room, kitchen, bathroom and bedrooms. However, there is no reason why you should not put rooms to different uses.

Generally speaking, the rooms of a house are laid out to be most convenient for a normal lifestyle – bedrooms upstairs where it is quieter and the bathroom above kitchen to rationalize the plumbing – but they are not irreversible if a different layout suits your family or your lifestyle. Some of the changes may be simple and within your own abilities to organize. Others may need professional help to plan the best layout for your needs and carry out the alterations.

Options for change

Altering the way you use your living space is the first place to start. For example, if you have separate living and dining rooms, you could simply swap their functions. The shapes of the two rooms may suit certain pieces of furniture better than the existing arrangement. Perhaps one has a long uninterrupted wall against which your three-seater sofa could be placed, while the other has a bay window that would take the dining table. Trying this out will involve moving a lot of furniture about, so make sure you have

Rules & regulations

You do not need any permission from your local authority unless you are altering underground drainage, perhaps for a relocated bathroom or kitchen. The new drainage work must comply with the Building Regulations requirements, so make sure that your installer gives the necessary notice to the local Building Control office.

enough help for the job. This change-over is also worth experimenting with if you have a large through room where one end has been the established sitting area and the other the dining zone. Changing ends may simply work better for you.

Another way of changing the living space is to turn the existing main room into a combined kitchen and dining area, and to reclaim the existing dining room and kitchen for other uses. One could be the home entertainment centre, for example, with television and hi-fi equipment for family use. The other could then become a quiet zone for reading, homework and the like. Whether this change is possible will depend on how easy it is to provide services to the new kitchen site, especially getting rid of waste water from the sink, washing machine and dishwasher. This, and the planning of the new kitchen, is a job you may prefer to leave to professional kitchen installers (see pp. 44–49 for more details).

If you are fortunate enough to have a conservatory, improving its heating and ventilation could allow you to use it as the dining room or as a second living room to enable parents and children to have their own spaces for leisure activities.

One further possibility is to redesign the existing kitchen to provide space for family meals, perhaps by removing some of the kitchen units you do not really need and making better use of the storage that remains. Because dining rooms are often used for less than an hour a day for meals, it may make sense to reclaim them for use as alternative

living space. One could even provide an extra bedroom, especially for a teenager to use as a bedsit if there is pressure on bedroom space upstairs.

Underused spaces

You should also think about the way you use the existing bedrooms. Parents usually have the biggest bedroom but use it only for sleeping, while children often spend far more time in theirs during the day, so it may make sense to change places. The larger room could then become a study bedroom and a retreat for entertaining friends.

A spare bedroom that is rarely if ever used for overnight guests can be put to better use. Get rid of the beds and turn the room into a children's playroom, a space for hobbies such as sewing or painting, or even a home office (see pp. 60–61).

If the smallest bedroom is all but redundant, you could use it to provide a second bathroom or shower room (see pp. 50–53) and relieve the pressure on the existing family bathroom. Once again, the feasibility of this will depend on getting rid of waste water, but pumped waste systems can get around the problem of taking waste water to a distant soil stack. Calling in a plumber or a firm of bathroom installers will give you the opportunity to get some professional advice and solve any problems of this nature.

Turning a large living room into a combination kitchen and dining room allows the homeowner to prepare food while entertaining his or her guests.

2 Connecting rooms

In examining the way your home works and trying to make the best use of the space, you may come to the conclusion that its layout needs redesigning. One way to do this is to create fewer but larger rooms by removing one or more internal walls.

If you knock rooms together you will not gain any additional floor space, but you may end up with rooms that work better for you. Factors to think about are the number of people in your household, whether this may change in the near future, and the kind of different activities that may be going on at the same time. It is tempting to create a feeling of spaciousness, but you may find you have reduced your privacy or made the house noisier.

If you decide to go ahead, it is well worth enlisting professional help, both in the planning and the execution of the work. This will ensure that the alterations not only provide workable solutions from the practical point of view, but also that the structure of the building is not compromised in any way or rendered unsafe.

DIY jargon !

Joist A horizontal length of 200 x 50 mm (8 x 2 in) timber that helps to support the floor above it and/or the ceiling below. A number of joists are laid running in the same direction across the room.

Load-bearing wall An internal wall that helps support the weight of the framing of the house above it.

Transverse brace In the context of load-bearing walls, a wall that is linking two other walls together and holding them apart.

Options for change

In theory you can create a through room anywhere in the house by removing the wall between adjacent rooms. The most popular conversion is to amalgamate the living and dining rooms. If the dining room and kitchen are next to each other, the two could be combined to create a spacious kitchen with an eating area. This can become a focus for social living in a way that many dining rooms are not. You could also remove the wall between the hall and the front living room, but this is not a good idea unless you have a front porch with an external door, or the front door will open directly into the living room.

If you have a spare bedroom upstairs, the most beneficial conversion will involve knocking two adjacent rooms into one large master bedroom to create space for a dressing area and even an en-suite bathroom. You could also consider amalgamating a separate bathroom and an adjoining cloakroom as part of a radical bathroom refit (see pp. 50–53); however, if this is the only toilet in the house, remember that it will then be unavailable for others to use when someone is bathing.

There are a few points to bear in mind when thinking about having a through room. The first is the resulting loss of wall space for furniture to stand against. This may be offset by the fact that a doorway will become redundant and blocking this off may give some wall space back. The second is the need to redecorate the two rooms as one, and possibly to lay a new floor covering right through the conversion as well.

Where rooms are knocked together, in most cases, you will find that the light has changed entirely and the lighting will need rethinking to create an effect of continuity. A lighting designer or electrician can help.

What type of wall?

By far the most important factor in creating a through room is whether the wall you want to remove is load-bearing or not (see pp.136–137). The likelihood is that downstairs walls will be load-bearing, however, upstairs walls are more likely to be simple timber-framed partitions, especially in recently built houses.

Correctly identifying the type of wall involved is crucial, and this should always be left to a structural engineer. If the wall is load-bearing, the correct type and size of supporting beam must be specified. Consideration must also be given to the effect on other walls in the house – removing a wall amounts to removing a transverse brace between other walls. Transferring the load of the floor or roof above via a beam to the side walls may also transmit extra loads down to the foundations, and it takes an expert to assess this correctly and recommend any necessary strengthening work. He or she will also be responsible for drawing up plans and getting the necessary Building Regulations approval for the proposed work.

When work starts

The first job in removing a load-bearing wall is to provide support for the floor above using props. Once that has been done, any services such as electricity cables or heating pipes that

If the dividing wall was load-bearing, a structural beam or RSJ will be necessary here. Painting the walls the same colour will help join the rooms together.

Furniture and decorative elements from the two smaller rooms can be redistributed in the larger room to provide a balance in the style.

If the original flooring in the two rooms was different, consider replacing it with a continuous flooring material to help link the two rooms visually.

Ask yourself ❓

- Are there never enough seats in your living room? If not, this is an indication that you could benefit from a larger living area.

- Do you like to talk to your guests at the same time as you prepare the meal? An adjacent dining room and kitchen would be ideal for you.

- Are you tired of battling with your children to get into the bathroom first thing in the morning? Consider changing the function of two bedrooms to create a master bedroom with an en-suite bathroom.

cross the wall are isolated and cut back. Next, the masonry at the top of the wall is chopped out to create a slot for the support beam – usually an I-section rolled steel joist (RSJ). Thicker side piers may have to be constructed to support the ends of the RSJ, or slots may have to be cut in the flanking walls to take short bearer beams on which the main RSJ will rest. Then the RSJ is lifted into place in its slot and is jacked up tightly against the underside of the wall above so that mortared support pads can be positioned beneath its ends.

Once the RSJ is in place and the support pads have hardened enough to take the load, the props are removed and the beam is encased in plasterboard to give it the necessary resist-

ance to fire specified by the Building Regulations. Any other damage to the rooms' plasterwork is repaired, ready for redecoration and finally, the skirting boards are replaced and the floor recovered (see pp.40–43).

Partition walls

Removing a non-load-bearing timber-framed partition wall is a simpler job. Once services in the vicinity have been isolated and cut back, the plasterboard cladding is prised off to reveal the wall framework. This is then cut away section by section, and the head and sole plates are freed from the ceiling and floor. Once the framework has been removed, the wall, ceiling and floor surfaces are prepared and the room is ready for redecoration.

The opposite of enlarging rooms is to create more but smaller rooms by installing new partition walls within existing large rooms. This is a relatively straightfoward job, but dividing the room may mean changes to the electricity, heating or plumbing.

The creation of extra rooms with partition walls can be the answer to the requirements of a growing family or the need for an extra room for an office but it does need to be thought out carefully. Existing services will probably need to be repositioned and extra services supplied, and you may also need to provide an additional window.

If you are planning anything more elaborate than a simple partition wall, it is worth enlisting the help of an architect or surveyor to help you. Otherwise a good builder should be able to plan and carry out the work for you. Remember that stud walls do not provide the sound insulation of a solid wall. If necessary, you can ask to have sound insulation added in.

Options for change

The main reason for dividing rooms is to gain an extra bedroom. You may be able to partition one existing large room, but you may get a more satisfactory result by removing an existing partition wall between two rooms and then dividing the total floor space up to create three rooms. A variation on this involves removing an existing partition and re-erecting it to form one larger and one smaller room – for example, to create a master bedroom suite with an adjacent dressing room or en-suite bathroom.

Another possible conversion is the partitioning of a bathroom to create a separate cloakroom – this could be a worthwhile project if the house contains just one toilet and more than one inhabitant.

Ask yourself ?

- Is the room that you are thinking about dividing large enough to accommodate two rooms comfortably?

- Are both rooms to be used as bedrooms? If so, you may have to add windows.

- If you are creating another bathroom, have you planned to provide adequate ventilation (see pp. 150–151)?

- Have you thought about how to provide access to the room?

Downstairs, the most likely partitioning you may consider is the creation of a separate utility room using part of the existing kitchen (see pp. 62–63 for more details). You may want to reverse an earlier through-room conversion by putting back the dividing wall that was removed to create it. This conversion not only recreates two separate living spaces but also gives back wall space in the two rooms, with more options in positioning furniture such as bookshelves, dressers and large settees.

This high-tech bathroom – with a shower, basin and toilet – was designed to make the best use of available space without detracting from the style. A space for it was carved out of the main bedroom.

Planning access

If you are planning to partition up a large bedroom, remember that each room needs its own door opening. One room leading off another is not a satisfactory solution as it means that the outer of the two will get

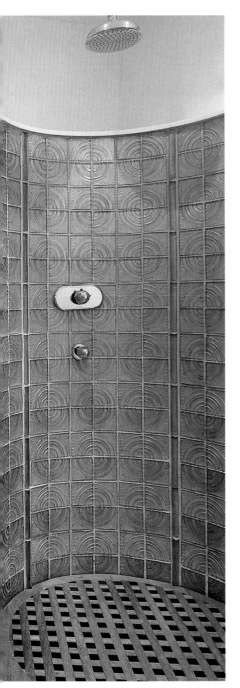

through traffic. Part of the available floor space will have to be taken up by a lobby or passageway giving access to the door of the new room from the existing door position.

When work starts

Once the planning is complete and the precise positions of the new walls have been agreed, your builder can start work. After clearing furniture and lifting floor coverings, he or she will begin by checking which way the joists run beneath a suspended timber floor. They will be able to support a wall running at right angles to them, but the builder will have to insert transverse noggings between adjacent joists to give extra support to any section of wall running parallel to them.

The next job is to screw the wall's top section, called the head plate, to the ceiling joists. The builder will have to insert noggings between these joists too if the wall runs parallel to them instead of across them. He or she will then fit a matching bottom section, called the sole plate, to the floor vertically beneath the head plate. On a concrete floor this will be secured with screws driven into wallplugs.

He or she will start to build up the wall framework with vertical members called studs, screwed to the existing room walls at each end

of the structure and nailed between the head and sole plates at 400 mm (16 in) centres in between. The builder will form door openings where necessary, cutting away the sole plate and framing the sides and head of the doorway. He or she will complete the framework with horizontal noggings fixed between the studs; these give the plasterboard cladding extra support and also provide fixing points for wall-hung fittings such as shelves and radiators.

Then any wiring or pipework can be run in before the wall is clad on one side with plasterboard and insulation fitted between the studs. The other side will then be clad and all the joints taped and filled. The finishing touches include connecting up switches and socket outlets on the wall, fitting any radiators, hanging the new door and adding decorative trims such as skirting boards, architraves and coving.

Light and ventilation

Each new room must have adequate natural light and ventilation. This means providing an openable window plus background trickle ventilation in each room. Since you are not allowed to share an existing window between two rooms, a new window will have to be installed in one unless the existing room already has two in suitable positions. Another possibility is a rooflight. If the newly created room will be used as a kitchen, utility room or bathroom, it need not have an openable window, but it must have adequate mechanical ventilation provided by an extractor fan that complies with the Building Regulations. If the room will contain a fuel-burning furnace, gas water-heater or gas clothes dryer, check with an installer to be sure the appliance will have adequate ventilation to run safely.

2 Conversions and extensions

By adapting and extending our homes to cater for our changing needs, we are reducing the burden on green land for new home developments, as well as choosing how we want to live. The floor space of our existing homes can not only be increased to match those of new houses but usually to exceed it. The opportunity to add on extra rooms, altering the layout of your living space and controlling the quality of the building is an opportunity that cannot be had from buying an existing house. You can decide on the energy-efficiency of the extension, the levels of daylight, the sound insulation and the robustness of construction that you want. In doing so and by taking a careful interest in how the work is planned and done, you will undoubtedly add value to your biggest asset – your home.

With the help of an imaginative architect, you can convert just about any room in your house; this individualistic bathroom (far left) was once an underused bedroom. An architect can also design an extension, such as this appealing kitchen (left).

Converting a loft

Converting a loft can enhance your home by creating attractive and interesting living space. The extra room you gain may also add to your home's value if you plan to sell it at a later date.

Loft conversions can enhance your home by creating attractive and interesting living space. You may not require planning permission if you are not extending your home by less than a certain amount.

Building regulations

The work will always have to comply with the Building Regulations to ensure that the converted roof area is safe. The two main issues and, therefore, Building Reg-ulations that control the design of loft conversions relate to structural stability and to fire safety. Even if you only intend to add a floor to your loft for storage or use it as an occasional hobby room for the train set, you should consider the implications on the structure. What were previously ceiling joists are now effectively floor joists and as such the load may be up to four times greater. Ceiling joists are invariably only 100 mm (4 in) deep and will

Rules & regulations

Planning permission is needed for loft conversions if you are increasing the size of your house by a certain percentage (i.e., by adding large dormer windows) or by adding to the roof slope that faces the highway.

Building Regulations are more complex and lay down rules about fire doors, ceiling height, ventilation and access.

need to be strengthened before starting any other part of the con-version. The most common way to do this is to install new deeper joists alongside them.

In conventional designs a short timber stub wall, also known as "ashlaring", is built a metre (yard) in from the wall plate to help sup-port the rafters. This stub wall can replace any purlins and struts in the loft (see pp.128–129), which can then be safely removed. It is worth asking your structural engineer to design the floor joists so that they will also support the stub wall, the most cost-effective option. The alter-native is to install beams of steel or timber to support it, but builders often dislike using steel beams in attics where access is difficult and working space tight. If RSJs are to be used it may be necessary to deliver them in manageable sections with end plates that will allow them to be joined together when they are in position. As a compromise between timber and steel beams, flitch beams are ideal because they

A curved window was artfully fitted into a gable wall for this renovation. Allowing for natural light is an important factor in any loft conversion.

In this loft conversion, the rafters were left exposed as a design feature and the space in the "peak" of the roof was left accessible to store belongings.

to the window face – however, be aware that you might need to obtain planning permission. If correctly proportioned dormer windows can make attractive features externally, as well as increase space inside.

Rooflights do not usually require planning permission because they do not alter the shape of the roof. However, a rooflight on the south-facing slope of your roof will probably need a blind as loft rooms can get very hot. For rooflights that are out of reach, a range of accessories is available such as electrically operated blinds.

It is also worth ensuring that your window has a "crack vent" position or "trickle vent" fitted that allows some air to enter even when the window is locked and secure. Special designs that can be used for fire escape exits and others for conservation areas are available from manufacturers.

are made up of two sections of timber bolted together with a steel plate sandwiched in between.

If the loft conversion changes your house from a two-storey to a three-storey dwelling, then a host of fire regulations will come into play – for example, you will probably have to have automatic closers on doors and other fire precautions.

Possible problems

If your home was built before the mid 1960s then your roof will be of a traditional construction, perhaps of 100-mm (4-in) deep rafters and joists with a purlin supported by a few diagonal struts. Measure the vertical height from the ridge at the apex down to the joists. If you have 2.3 m (7 ft 6 in) or more available you should be able to make a habitable room, perhaps with the addition of a dormer window.

Properties built after this time may have used roof trusses and,

although it is still possible to convert the loft, the process is then more complicated.

The proper sequence of construction must be followed. The web of diagonal struts must never be cut out until the new floor and roof supports are in place to take the load, and you must definitely use a specialist's advice. As trussed rafter members are invariably smaller in size than traditional roof timbers it is common that more support beams will be needed.

Floor layout plans of loft conversions always look deceptively large because the ashlar walls shown edging the rooms may only be 60 cm (24 in) or 90 cm (36 in) high. Find out where the full headroom stops and mark this line on the plan.

Because of this problem dormer windows are often favoured over rooflights, which lie flat to the roof slope. Dormers allow the full ceiling height available to be extended out

2

DIY jargon !

Collar ties A part of the roof frame near the "peak" of the roof, these lengths of timber tie rafters together to prevent them from spreading outward.

Stub wall or ashlaring A low wall that supports the rafters about 1 m (3 ft) in from the wallplate, replacing purlins and diagonal struts.

Purlin Horizontal timbers running under long rafters.

Rafter The sloping parts of the roof frame that support the roof covering.

Ridge piece The central horizontal support at the peak of the roof.

Trusses Prefabricated roof frames replacing rafter and purlin construction.

Positioning the stairs

Probably the most important element of a loft design is siting the staircase. Fire safety is an important issue when you're creating a third floor to your house and especially when the loft room is used as a bedroom. Your new staircase should ideally come up from the landing or lobby area below and not from within another room as someone could be trapped in the loft should a fire break out in the room below. It is much better to have your stairs enclosed throughout the house so that you can pass straight down to the hall and front door, even if it means walling off part of an existing room with partitioning to accommodate the new stair. Space-

saving stairs, with a steep almost ladder-like pitch and paddle-shaped treads can be used if space is too limited for a normal staircase.

Fire Safety

Fitting self-closing devices to the existing doors on the landings and hall will help to contain a fire by keeping doors shut. These, together with a new fire-rated door to the loft storey, are basic requirements of the Building Regulations. Fire doors are available in a variety of styles so they can fit the look of your house.

For increased safety at very little expense, you can have a mains-wired smoke alarm fitted to the ceiling of your loft. This should be wired in to either the lighting circuit (if the alarm has a battery back-up) or a separate fused circuit.

The existing ceiling directly below the new loft room now protects the floor above it and needs to have a measure of fire-resistance. If it is plasterboard, the thickness of the board and any finish to it should be checked to see if it is sufficient. If it is not, a PVA adhesive can be applied to create a bond, then the ceiling can have a skim finish of plaster to upgrade it.

Plumbing

You will probably need to find a new home for the water tanks in the loft, and the space behind the stub wall where the tanks can be supported by the new floor joists will be ideal. (In any event, access should be provided to this space, both for future checks on your house and so that it can be used for storage.)

If your loft is to contain a bathroom, the cold water tank must be positioned high enough to provide adequate water pressure, and this

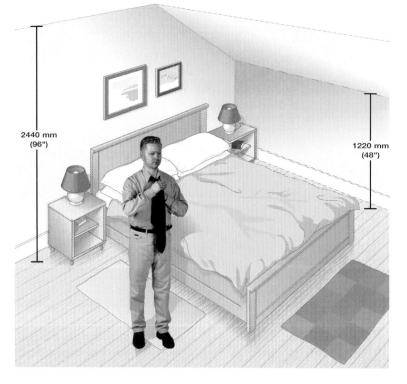

2440 mm (96")

1220 mm (48")

The ceiling of a gabled roof should be high enough for you to walk around without hitting your head; stub walls define the floor space.

may mean locating it beneath the apex of the roof. Long thin tanks, known as "coffin tanks", are available for this situation. You should make sure that your designer has allowed for its weight in the structural design.

Insulation

Insulating should be done before boarding out begins, but an air space must be left above the glass fibre insulation in between the rafters or condensation will build up within the construction. Check that a gap of at least 50 mm (2 in) is left for airflow on the cold (outside) face of the insulation. If your rafters are only 100 mm (4 in) deep, you must make them deeper to accommodate the necessary thickness of glass fibre or use a high performance insulation board such as polyurethane foam, which can achieve the same results in a much reduced thickness. Rafters can easily be made deeper by nailing timber battens to their underside. Vents should also be fitted at the eave and ridge positions to allow the air in and out.

An attic staircase with open treads (without risers) and a simple balustrade allows more light into a constricted hallway.

When work begins

Nearly always, the first tradesperson needed in a loft conversion is the plumber. Once the old insulation material has been bagged up and removed, the plumber can relocate the water tanks and demolish their support stands. Until the plumbing services are sorted out, the new floor can not be fully constructed so the plumber and carpenter must agree on where the tanks are to be temporarily positioned.

Where long steel beams are to be used in the conversion, it may be easiest to allow the builders to make a hole in an external gable end wall to feed the beams in. This is often preferable to jointing the beam from shorter lengths inside the loft or manhandling it through the house.

The plasterboard ceiling will be cut where the new staircase is to be positioned. It will probably not be possible to trim the joists themselves at such an early stage, but once the new floor joists are installed the old ones can be cut out, making access easier. If you are having a large dormer or rooflight opening, once it has been cut the materials and workers could come in through the opening from an external scaffold, at least until the windows are fitted. This will reduce the mess and disruption inside your home.

2 Converting a basement

Basements are often overlooked but can provide ideal space for many activities. Home offices, play or recreation rooms, bathrooms and workshops are all suitable candidates for a basement conversion.

Basements have many advantages: they are soundproofed from outside noise and free from dramatic changes in temperature. Providing you can introduce sufficient daylight and ventilation, cellar space that has long since been abandoned or used only for storing wine can become part of your home. They make for ideal kitchens and playrooms or can be opened up to extend living room space.

As with loft conversions, one problem with a basement conversion may be restricted headroom – however, you do have the added possibility of lowering the floor a little. Basements must also comply with stringent Building Regulations if they are to be used as living space, and you should use an architect or surveyor to oversee the project.

The basement space

Before embarking on a basement conversion it is important to understand how the space relates to the structure of your home and the ground outside it. Victorian houses were built with cellars beneath the timber ground floors to store coal for the fires, but often these cellars did not extend to the full width of the property and hence do not have the benefit of an external wall, let alone a window. An interior room basement like this is best converted by opening it up to another room, in

Part of this basement has been converted into a bathroom. It offers more space and quiet than the conventional above-stairs room.

Rules & regulations

There are stringent Building Regulations on the use and conversion of basements. These can vary from authority to authority but they generally define the requirements for fire safety arrangements, ventilation, lighting and access and egress.

If you are changing the use of the space – for example, to a home office – you will also require planning permission and will need a professional to guide you in this.

effect creating a split-level open-plan arrangement. By doing so, the below-ground space can benefit from the daylight and ventilation of the ground level room above. The stairwell opening will have to be enlarged and this will depend on the layout of your house and the position of the existing windows.

Obviously it will be a matter of balancing the loss of some ground floor space against the need for light and air below, but this type of layout can add interest and value to your home. It will also avoid the creation of an "inner room", where you could become trapped in the event of a fire above.

The larger basement

Of course, some basements may already have windows and light wells in the garden outside and you can convert them into enclosed rooms in their own right. What you have to consider is access and emergency exits. First, look at the opening size of the windows and see whether they can be used or replaced to form a minimum of a 500 mm (20 in) wide by 850 mm (34 in) high opening casement. If you can do this, then this window will double as an emergency exit if you have to position the basement stair within an existing room above, so that the basement space is an inner room. A suitable window such as this can be locked securely with a quick-release catch rather than a key-locked fastening to make it possible to use the basement as a bedroom.

If you are unable to provide a large enough window, then you should try to position the stairs in the hallway of the ground floor. As with loft conversions, an essential safety precaution is the installation of a mains-wired smoke alarm inter-linked with one on the floor above. Mains-wired smoke alarms should always be used in preference to the battery-operated type.

For daylight provision, the window area should add up to at least 10 percent of the floor area. With basements relying on light wells outside, the decor you choose can be used to help reflect the light around the room. White painted walls are ideal, and you can always add warm colours in furnishings if you wish.

For adequate ventilation, window openings should be equal to at least five percent of the floor area and fitted with background or trickle vents. If you're planning on using the space for a kitchen, utility room or bathroom then you will need to have an extractor fan installed to sufficiently remove steam – and, therefore, potential condensation – rapidly. It should be mounted on the ceiling, and the duct will be run between the joists and through the wall to the outside air.

As the natural light is never likely to be as good as in rooms upstairs, remember to pay especial attention to your lighting design. You will need plenty of light, but you will probably need to use warm colours in the furnishings to counteract the starkness of the basement space.

Ask yourself

- Are there enough windows to provide adequate ventilation? If not, is it possible to add windows or ventilation?

- Once the floors and ceilings are installed, would there be enough headroom?

- Is there a door to the outside? If not, the basement may not be suitable for a conversion. Remember, you need two exit doors for sleeping quarters.

- What is the condition of the staircase? It will have to take more strain than the occasional use many basements get.

Floors

It is unlikely that the existing basement floor is resistant to damp or insulated against heat loss, and it may not even be particularly level. Most of the conversion work will probably include the construction of a new solid floor.

If you are short of headroom, there is the possibility that you can break up the existing floor, dig down a little and reform it lower. However, great care should be taken not to extend the digging below the wall foundations unless you are prepared to pay the extra cost of underpinning. Small trial holes can be dug to check the depth of the foundations before starting. At this stage, it is a good idea to go around the outside of the house with your builder and check that your garden or even the rainwater drainage system is not contributing to the damp in the basement.

Floating floors

It is often not possible to include a suspended timber floor in a basement conversion since they need to be served by good ventilation from the outside air and installing air bricks wouldn't be possible. If you would really like the warm feel of a timber floor rather than a solid one,

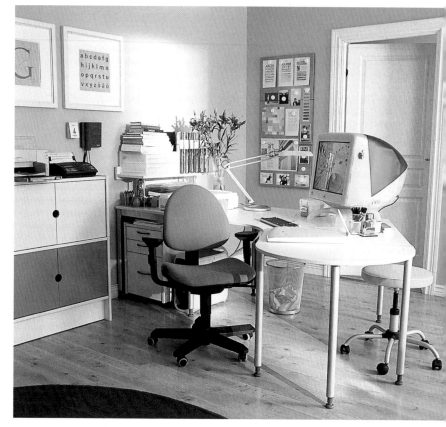

In a basement with little or no natural lighting, choose light colours to help the room appear brighter and provide plenty of electrical lighting.

you could choose a floating floor finish where tongued-and-grooved floorboards or chipboard sheets are laid over the insulation instead of screed. It is vital that the screed and concrete is completely dry before the floor is laid. This can take from three months to a year. (For more details on floors, see pp. 98–99 and pp. 142–143.) If you opt for a floating floor, make the following checks:

Ensure that the insulation is laid perfectly flat and level on the concrete slab. To achieve this the slab will need a trowelled finish or levelling compound.

Check that a polyethylene vapour barrier is laid over the insulation before the boarding is laid.

Check that the joints between boards are all glued and that the skirting pins down the floorboards all around the edges.

Is the floor level? Check it in several places with a 1.2-m- (4-ft-) long spirit level or straight edge.

Other types of flooring

A brick cellar floor could be left rustic and uneven if you aren't planning on fitted units such as floor cupboards. The surface could be cleaned and painted with a clear silicone water sealant to finish it, but remember that the adjustable feet on some kitchen units will only allow a limited adjustment.

Assuming you are lucky enough to have a sound existing floor but you are hoping to achieve a level finish, a product known as levelling compound is ideal for overcoming small discrepancies in level and is floated on as a slurrylike mix. If the levels are too far out, it will need to be screeded with a mixture of cement and sand in a ratio of 1 to 3 parts. Before this can be done, however, the concrete floor should be cleaned and treated with three coats of liquid-bitumen-based damp-proof membrane. This will ensure that the floor finish remains free from damp.

Take this opportunity to install a layer of floor-grade insulation before screeding, but check to make sure that the thickness of the screed is at least 65 mm (2½ in). If it is any less, the screed will crack later.

Tanking

Of course it is not only the floor that will need damp proofing: the basement walls will also need it. Because you are below the main damp-proof course of the house and below ground level, you don't have the option of choosing a chemical

injection damp treatment being applied to the walls. In a conversion such as this you will have to accept the fact that the walls themselves may always be damp and concentrate on ensuring that the damp doesn't get through to the inside surfaces. Damp proofing a whole wall such as this is called "tanking", and it is possibly the most important element of the conversion.

Tanking choices

There is a variety of methods and materials for tanking and specialist advice should be sought to establish which one is best for you. The choice will depend a great deal on the condition of the walls and the extent of the dampness. Tanking used to be done with asphalt but this is seldom used today. Bitumen-based products that can be applied in self-adhesive sheets or painted on (with a broom) to set as a rubber latex seal are more popular. The drawback with them is that they usually require the wall to be dry and primed before they are applied, otherwise they simply won't stick.

If you have a wet wall subject to active ground-water pressure, you will have to use one of the dimpled semi-rigid sheet membranes (known as Newtonite) that allow the water to flow behind them safely, or you can address the problem from the outside with land drainage. Whichever method you select, the wall treatment should be compatible with that used in the floor to achieve a continuous seal if your new room is to remain dry. Most damp proofing products come with guarantees if they are applied in accordance with the manufacturer's instructions, so obtain a copy of the instructions from the supplier.

Finishings

An ideal internal finish for tanked walls is plasterboard secured on dabs of a specialized adhesive to

When to inspect !

- If you are laying a new floor structure, check the sub-base (oversite) before they concrete over it. (For details on hardcore fill beneath floors, see pp. 98–99.) Your Building Control Surveyor should also be invited to inspect the work at this stage.

- Check the tanking of the walls and look to see that every inch is thoroughly covered. Damp is quick to take advantage of poor workmanship.

- Check that each stage of the floor and wall rendering is completely dry before your workpeople move on to the following stage.

- Check that all ceiling timbers have been inspected and treated if necessary.

avoid fittings that can puncture the tanking. Any out-of-plumb in the walls can be rectified with this type of finish. If you want to insulate the walls against heat loss, specially laminated plasterboard is available with the insulation already stuck to its back. A waterproofing additive can be mixed with ordinary plaster as an added precaution.

Before the ceiling can be lined with plasterboard the builder should inspect the timber joists. If there hasn't been much ventilation in the basement in the past, the joists may have suffered from dry rot, which will mean they will need replacing; otherwise, a thorough treatment of preservative will be sufficient. Remember that ventilation will be needed during this process.

If all the processes for damp treatments are carried out properly, there is no reason why your basement should not be a pleasant environment to relax or work in.

Lighting

Overhead lighting – in particular, fluorescent fixtures – can be easily installed above acoustic ceilings and covered by translucent panels designed for the purpose. However, some people find fluorescent lighting impossible to live with.

Track lighting with surface wiring is easier to install, but the fittings must be located so that they are out of the way of people's heads.

2 Converting a garage

If you need extra room and don't use your garage, you may consider converting it into living space. Integral garages can provide sizeable, well-lit spaces suitable for a study or a lounge.

Rules & regulations

You will need planning permission to convert a garage to a habitable space, because you will be changing its original use and probably adding services such as new electrical circuits, plumbing and heating.

You will probably need planning permission to convert a garage not only because of the change of use, but also because in modern housing the garage space is seen as part of the off-street parking. You may have to create additional space in your garden to extend the parking area, and you should also bear in mind the resale value of your house if you do away with the garage.

Doors and windows

The garage door will provide the ready-made opening for your new room's window. If you want to match the appearance of the house frontage, then you can have the lower part of the opening bricked up. Windows less than 800 mm (32 in) from the floor should be of laminated or toughened glass for security. Background ventilation can be provided by installing trickle vents to the frames.

Your new external wall must be built on a suitable foundation. This should be of a similar width and depth to the existing foundation if possible to avoid the risk of differ-

The floor was relaid and new windows and doors were installed, making this garage conversion a delightful, airy family room.

ential settlement between the two. Instead, you could choose a purpose-made glazed screen, perhaps one that incorporates French doors to the full size of the existing opening. Low-e (low-emissivity) double glazing has the same thermal insulation capacity as triple glazing and will reduce the heat loss in winter. Large areas of plain glass can be dangerous, so break up the area with framing or decorate the glass to make it more noticeable.

Walls and roof

Garage walls are often built of only half-brick thickness, 100 mm (4 in), and these will need to be upgraded. If the roof is adequately supported, the best option is to build an inner skin wall to improve its weather-resistance and thermal insulation. This can be of lightweight insulation blocks bonded to the old wall with remedial wall ties. Cavity wall insulation can be included or a clear cavity retained, which may be best if the walls are exposed to wind-driven rain. Alternatively, the inside may be timber studwork with the cavity insulated between the timbers with glass fibre quilt. As a moisture barrier against possible condensation, a polyethylene sheet is pinned over the frame and quilt before the plasterboard is nailed on.

When to inspect !

2

- Check that the new damp-proof course is in position and overlaps the existing one.

- Make sure insulation is fully installed to walls and ceilings.

- Make sure that the roof is well ventilated.

- Check that specialized remedial wall ties have been used for bonding the wall.

Check that any clear cavity in the wall is closed at the edges of window openings with a vertical damp-proof course (dpc) incorporated. Proprietary cavity closures can be used, which are insulated to avoid cold spots. The cavity should also be closed at the top of the wall with the roof, and a strip of cement-fibre board is ideal for this purpose.

The garage roof may either be flat or pitched. If it is in good condition, it will only need insulating and ventilating over the insulation. In the case of a flat roof this can sometimes cause problems because if the joists run from side to side, with one end supported on the house wall, ventilating this end can be tricky without cutting back the roof deck and fitting a specialized abutment vent. Do not allow your builders to simply install vents at one end of the joists – you need to have a flow of air through the void above the insulation if you are to avoid condensation. The void should be at least 50 mm (2 in) deep and glass fibre insulation at least 150 mm thick (6 in) – so if the flat roof joists are less than 200 mm (8 in) deep, they will need battens before the plasterboard is nailed in place. A pitched roof garage will not be so difficult to insulate and ventilate, as a variety of vents are available to be located in the tiles or at the eaves.

Garage floors

If your garage has a door to the house, the floor level of the garage is probably considerably lower that in the house – Building Regulations have required for some years that the garage should be at least 100 mm (4 in) lower. The new floor insulation and screed (a minimum of 65 mm/2⅝ in thick) should bring it up to level. The concrete surface may need repairing, then damp proofing, and any floor drains need plugging to prevent the release of sewer gas and odours.

The floor will also need careful levelling. Garage floors also usually slope towards the door opening to drain off water dripping from vehicles. Sleepers or other framing on which the subfloor will rest must be tapered or else set on strategically placed shims to compensate. The door to the house will probably be a fire door and you can now, if you like, remove the closer.

Adding a conservatory

Conservatories are a popular way of extending living space and providing a quiet retreat for reading or sunbathing. Larger conservatories can even be furnished with dining tables for summer evenings.

As most conservatories weigh very little, they are built on a simple slab of concrete, about 100 mm (4 in) thick. On clay soil, which is liable to shrinkage, the concrete slab can be thickened and strengthened with a fabric steel reinforcement to give a more robust foundation.

If your conservatory is quite large, the wall and roof panels may need to be strengthened with a steel or timber frame to break up their span. The manufacturer should provide you with a structural guarantee for the superstructure even if they are not providing the base foundation. The manufacturer's design calculations for the structure need to be approved by a building inspector before the work starts.

If you are planning on a normal roof over your conservatory, you should remember that the metal strengthening included within uPVC window frames will not be adequate in itself to support it. An independent frame of metal or timber will have to be formed, within which the windows can later be installed. Hardwood can be used instead of uPVC for the frames, but check to ensure that the timber comes from a truly sustainable source. The Forest Stewardship Council's "FSC" label endorses this.

Retaining an external door between the conservatory and the house will prevent heat from escaping in the winter and allow heat to enter in the summer. Patio or French doors are ideal since they benefit from larger openings and can be opened up to extend the space when needed.

Heating and insulation

However high a grade double-glazing panels you have, there will be enormous heat-loss from your conservatory if you have artificial heating. When the sun is on it, however, it can produce enough heat to warm adjoining rooms for free.

If you do decide to extend your heating system to the conservatory, check that a thermostatic radiator valve (TRV) is fitted to the radiator. It will allow you to isolate the conservatory from the rest of the house.

Ventilation and shade

The conservatory has a tremendous ability to absorb solar heat and can very quickly become unusable. Not only that, but the roof sheets may buckle and furnishings degrade. It is vital that you consider the provision of plenty of shade and good ventilation. These are several important considerations at the design stage – you need to select the position and size of window and roof openings and be aware of the options and cost for blinds. Tinted glass and polycarbonate is available and will help to some extent.

A roof vent is a good idea and will allow warm air to be exhausted out, as well as relieve wind-pressure inside the room. Light-weight structures can be damaged by wind uplift created inside from a single open window, so a vent allows the air to flow through your conservatory and not just in.

Weather resistance

The most common problem arises at the intersection of the conservatory roof and the house walls where rain can penetrate if the joint isn't properly sealed. Lead flashing is not suitable as it cannot be easily hammered down onto a plastic roof. Invariably silicone mastic is used in large quantities to seal joints such as these, often with a self-adhesive "flashing" material. Although it will cost more, you could consider safety glass for the roof material and incorporate it with as steep a pitch as the house will allow. This will help to make it self-cleaning, as well as reduce the risk of leaks.

A conservatory can give a view of the outdoors while offering a comfortable warm place to relax. This conservatory provides an inviting and peaceful sitting area.

Rules & regulations

Conservatories with floor area of over 30 sq m (323 sq ft) are subject to Building Regulations. You must ensure that your builder invites the building inspector over for inspections at the required stages.

You must also consider both whether your proposed conservatory is near enough to the boundary between your and your neighbour's property to need planning permission and also whether it will interfere with their visual amenities. In either case, you should inform your neighbour about your plans before starting work.

Adding a porch

The porch is an underestimated and underused space that can provide more than merely a storage for outdoor clothes. With a little planning it can offer shelter in wintry weather and a warm place to sit or to keep some plants in summer.

The front porch tends to be the smallest addition it is possible to make to the home, but it serves as a valuable space to hang coats and hats, kick off one's shoes and stop the wind from whistling around the front door. When developers of new houses include porches in their designs they are seldom larger than 2 or 3 sq m (2 or 3 sq yd), and if you are aiming to avoid the planning application process, you will also be limited to this size. However, if you can obtain planning permission, a larger porch can be a delightful place to relax in warm wheather.

Design choices

The front porch is much underestimated. It will dramatically alter the design of the front of your house and hopefully it will either enhance it or improve it. Sketch your options for pitching the roof, including windows or glazed doors and other features. A small circular or arched window can make an interesting feature for a porch and, as this may be the only room in the house where single-glazing will suffice, the cost can be modest. Stained windows or door sidelights are also effective on the inside, adding light and colour to a small room that can be difficult to decorate creatively.

Structure

Since small porches, like conservatories, are generally exempted from the Building Regulations, the quality of the design and construction rests solely with the builder and homeowner. As a valuable extension to the house, you should aim for the style of the porch to be similar to the house as far as possible.

It is hardly worth extending the central heating system to provide a porch radiator unless the layout lends itself to the job easily; instead a slimline electric radiator with a thermostatic control will be more than sufficient in most cases. You may decide not to heat the area at all, but to simply use it as a draught-lobby that allows the front door to be opened without exposing the living area to the elements. The

Screening in a porch

If you have a porch big enough to sit in, a screen to keep out insects helps to make the porch habitable during the summer months in some areas of the country. Insect protection can range from simple curtains to mesh screens that can be bolted to a framework and removed when they are not needed.

In the parts of the country where winters are fierce, double-glazing will decrease draughts, add a measure of heat through solar gain and increase the potential of the space for light utility use without having to go outdoors. If your porch is to be mostly built of glazed panels, then double glazing is a must. However, you should also consider fitting some sort of vent, especially if the porch will face south, because the heat can build up to be stifling in the summer.

extent to which you insulate a porch is a matter of personal choice and it makes more sense to concentrate on ensuring its weather-resistance.

Roofs

For such a small addition, the design of the roof is all-important. Flat roofs are to be avoided unless the part of the house it is adjacent to also has a flat roof. A steep pitch of at least 40 degrees is to be favoured with a covering of plain tiles or

Rules & regulations

Because a porch alters the appearance of a house, especially on the front elevation, you may need planning permission in some areas. Also make sure that your design does not interfere with your neighbours' visual amenities. Porches are exempt from Building Regulations unless they are very large.

Few outward aspects of a house spell charm, domestic tranquillity and comfort more than an inviting porch. This pleasant feature provides an area for sitting and protection from summer sun, winter winds and rain.

Many uPVC doors present a formidable trip hazard as a threshold but, to counteract this, the floor can be laid level with the bottom of the door. You should locate the door on the sheltered side of the porch, especially if the porch is on the side of the house that faces the prevailing wind and rain.

For the inner opening think about providing a door wider than the standard 762 mm (30 in) internal door. Over the years you will be bringing furniture in through here, as well as prams or pushchairs and shopping, and you'll be giving yourself room to manoeuvre. If the old front door opening is to become the new inner door, the width should, in any case, make it suitable for replacement.

When changing doors or adding new ones, remember to make sure that the locks are adequate (see p. 101). If your builder is unsure about security, you can always get advice from your local police station or home insurance company. Lastly, your outside light may need to be relocated and your doorbell will need to be extended.

Back porches

If you have a garden or workshop at the back, with people coming and going with muddy feet, or if your children are at the age of playing outside, it is worthwhile considering the benefits of a back porch. It can provide an invaluable space to change muddy boots, to store a few gardening tools or to wipe the dog's paws. It is also a good place to locate an outside tap.

It may be that the back of the house catches the most sunlight, so you could make the porch double as a small conservatory. As with the front porch, you could have a small window in one wall, but here it may be worth installing narrow fitted shelving or racks on one wall for the family's boots and other gear.

small slates – large interlocking tiles or slates will be out of scale. Even if the roof area is small, aim to collect the rainwater run-off and discharge it with the existing surface water drains. Do not be persuaded to save money here by doing without guttering, as you don't want drips falling exactly where you and visitors will enter the house.

Make sure that the join between the new roof and the house wall is sealed properly with flashing.

Front door

In Britain new homes have to be built with a degree of accessibility for people with disabilities, and a key part of this consideration is the front entrance. The doorstep is a thing of the past and it makes sense to include in your porch design a more accessible entrance to your home. Even if you aren't disabled it will prove an asset to children and elderly relatives, or indeed yourself in your old age.

Adding an extension

Adding a room to your house provides extra space for living arrangements, activities, guests and storage. A skilfully budgeted extension can also increase the resale value of your home and bring a healthy return on investment when you sell.

If you are thinking of having an extension to your house, you need to decide what type of space you'll need, where to add the space and in what shape or form. You should also consider how it will fit with your existing house, both internally and externally. Once you have formulated your ideas, you should discuss them with a professional such as an architect, or perhaps several builders.

Foundations

For most extensions foundations of one of two types are appropriate. Strip foundations are usually about 600 mm (24 in) wide, with a concrete thickness from 225 mm (9 in) to 300 mm (12 in); trench-fill foundations are somewhat narrower (450 mm/18 in wide), but filled to near ground level with concrete. The latter are more popular with builders in clay soil areas where foundations have to be at least 1 m (3 ft) deep, because they reduce the need for bricklaying within the trench. This should be weighed against the cost of extra concrete.

Before the concrete is poured into the foundation:

Check that the base of the excavated trenches are level (on a sloping site vertical steps can be cut in the bottom to ensure this).

Check that the subsoil appears to be reasonably consistent (reinforcement may be needed in the concrete where there are dramatic changes in the nature of the soil).

Check that the foundations have been inspected and passed by your Building Control officer.

Your house's potential

Before making a final decision on the type of extension you have in mind, make an inspection of your house to see how it may influence your choice.

- If there is enough extra ground, you can build out; otherwise, you'll have to build up. (If up is your choice, you'll have to determine whether the foundation and walls of your house are strong enough to support a second storey.)

- Any angles in the existing house might be convenient locations for an extension to nestle into or spring from.

- Think about access to the extension from inside the house. For example, you may need further conversion work to create a hallway to it.

- If you think the siting of the extension will block natural lighting in another room, consider having additional windows or a skylight installed as a new source of natural lighting in the affected room.

Solid ground floors

After the foundations have been concreted and the external walls built up to damp-proof course (dpc) level – which is at least 150 mm (6 in) above the finished ground level – the ground floor construction can begin (see pp. 142–143). The key element for a good solid concrete floor is the preparation of what is known as the oversite, on which the concrete slab will sit.

It is essential that the oversite is laid using the correct materials and with good workmanship if the floor isn't to subside or crack later. Stone aggregates or hardcore rubble can be used but a hardcore mixture of broken brick and concrete must be clean and free from plaster, wood, wire or any other debris, and it must be broken into small pieces not larger than 100 mm (4 in) or a half-brick size. It should also be compacted, preferably with a mechani-

cal plate compactor, to form a solid and level base. Before the oversite is concreted, inspect the following:

The oversite fill material is between 150 mm (6 in) and 600 mm (24 in) thick.

It is blinded with a layer of sand or ballast before the polyethylene damp-proof membrane is laid over it.

It is reasonably level, particularly if you are using rigid floor insulation such as polystyrene sheets below the concrete slab.

Timber ground floors

For suspended timber floors (see pp. 142–143) it is important to ensure that the joists can span between the walls without bending and that good ventilation and damp proofing is provided beneath them. You should check that:

The earth beneath the joists is covered with at least 75 mm (3 in) of concrete on a polyethylene layer.

A well-equipped kitchen with extra room for a breakfast table occupies this extension. The architect planned a change of ceiling height to help separate the preparation and dining areas.

- What do you need from an extension? More living space? A larger kitchen? Additional sleeping space for guests or a growing family? A home office? The use of the space may affect the demands on the services, especially plumbing.

- What about the outward appearance of the house? Is there an architectural style you must incorporate in order for the addition to blend in with the existing house unobtrusively? Will landscaping or a new driveway be required?

There is at least 125 mm (5 in) of air space free beneath the joists.

There are plenty of airbricks built into the walls on both sides to allow air to flow freely across this gap.

The damp-proof course (dpc) is in place beneath the joists on all walls.

For insulation, it is easiest to suspend a mineral fibre quilt between the joists on chicken wire pinned to the timber. Precast concrete joists (or "T" beams) can be used instead of timber, and these are infilled with concrete blocks laid flat. This is only economical for a large extension over a sloping or problematical site. The damp-proof course shouldn't simply be aligned with the existing dpc but should allow for the finished level of any proposed paths or patios. They need to be at least 150 mm (6 in), or two brick courses, down. You may also need to relocate or bridge drains.

Cavity walls

By including an air gap between the two brickwork leaves (or skins, which are held together by ties), cavity walls can keep dampness out. In recent years with the demand for greater energy efficiency, the cavity has become insulated and the air gap lost. If the cavity wall is to be built with a total fill insulation, it must be built very well if damp is to be kept at bay, particularly where the outer skin is facing bricks and the extension walls are exposed to wind-driven rain. In these situations you may prefer to retain some cavity by using a high-performance insulation board designed for partial instead of total filling of the gap.

Once the external walls have reached windowsill height:

Check that the cavity is clear and not bridged by accidental mortar droppings on the wall ties.

Check that the insulation boards fit neatly together without mortar droppings between them.

Check that if fibre insulation boards have been cut to fit, they are

Once the foundation was laid for this living room, the framing structure for the walls – and windows – were next to be installed.

still installed with the outer face facing out.

Check the damp-proof course (dpc) in the cavity around windows. It should fit in a groove in the window frame and extend into the cavity.

Solid walls

If you want to finish your external walls with tile hanging, rendering or timber boarding, then you may build the walls out of solid insulating blocks instead of cavity wall or timber frame construction. It is the quickest way to build a masonry wall but there are drawbacks. The blocks themselves have a low

strength and can be difficult to fix things to internally. If you anticipate that you will always have to use special fixings to put up shelves, for example, this need not be a problem but, even with special fixings, heavy items like kitchen wall cabinets and bedroom bridging units may present you with an undesirable challenge. You won't gain much room space from using this method of construction, because the blocks themselves are about 230 mm (9 in) or 255 mm (10 in) thick in order to meet insulation requirements.

Check that fresh mortar is always being used (less than 2 hours old)

Make sure that mortar that is going off is not recycled by the addition of more water.

In cold or very wet weather, brickwork should be covered when work is finished for the day.

In very cold weather, an anti-freeze agent should be added to the mortar or work suspended.

Timber frame walls

Cavity wall construction with an inner leaf timber frame and an outside leaf of masonry provides an excellent construction for a damp climate. The studs are usually 100 x 50 mm (4 x 2 in) timber and are insulated to the full 100 mm (4 in) depth with mineral or glass fibre quilt, creating a very warm house. However, 150 x 50 mm (6 x 2 in) studs would improve the structural stability of the wall and the insulation. The latter size is usually best where a cladding such as shiplap boarding is fixed to the frame without a masonry skin.

Whichever method is chosen there are some basic rules that should be observed:

Baseplates need to be level and bedded on a dpc. They should be anchored down with special angle brackets to the floor slab and not fixed through the dpc.

The walls should be made up in panels with either diagonal braces between the vertical studs or plywood (or oriented strand board/ OSB) sheets fixed to the outer face.

The wall panels should be fitted together without gaps between them and should be vertical. They must not lean to accommodate incorrectly made roof trusses or beams.

Once the timber-frame is up, make sure that the roof is pitched and the windows and doors are installed to weather it in. It should not be left for too long exposed to the elements.

There is a tremendous difference in cost and quality of windows and doors at the top and bottom ends of the market. Apart from needing more maintenance, the security of your home could be compromised by the wrong choice.

Look for internally glazed units and locks that comply with BS:3621. Your home insurance policy may be invalidated if you extend your home and use a lower standard than stipulated. For external doors, at least a five-point dead lock mechanism should be used and sliding patio doors should be fitted with extra locks that prevent intruders lifting them off their runners.

Tying-in

If your house was built before the mid 1970s, the foundations may be shallower than those required on your extension. This may cause a problem because in drought weather some soils, especially clay, shrink dramatically near the surface. If your extension differs greatly from the existing house in this respect or indeed in the design of its walls, it would be a good idea to allow for some differential movement between the two. Instead of bonding in the masonry at the joint, a proprietary brickwork profile bolted to the wall can tie the two together and still allow for some movement without cracking.

You can turn your extension into a luxurious modern bathroom. If you want windows similar to those in the bathroom shown here, make sure the bathroom is situated where you will have plenty of privacy.

Pitched roofs

If the roof of your extension is pitched, it may be formed on-site by carpenters or it may be a prefabricated trussed rafter roof manufactured off-site (see pp. 128–129). Trussed rafters are particularly suited to large spans but they still need bracing timbers and even the tiling battens contribute to the stiffness. Special fixings such as truss shoes are used to secure them to the wall plates instead of skew nailing.

The builder must take accurate measurements on site before the trusses can be fabricated. Key dimensions are the span including the wall plates (not the clear span between the walls); the roof pitch (angle of the truss) or the height; and the size of any overhangs at the eaves.

A roof built on site has the advantage of providing more space in the loft and allowing the carpenter the chance to align it with the existing roof as he or she builds. Check that the design of the construction has been approved by the Building Control officer.

Flat roofs

Regardless of their span, flat roofs today tend to need quite large joists because of fitting in the insulation material and allowing plenty of airflow above the insulation. The insulation is usually glass-fibre quilt as lagging fitted between the joists, but it means that the depth of the joists need to be 200 mm (8 in) or more. Your only other choice is to use a modern high performance insulation, to have warm roof deck construction or to batten out the ceiling before applying the plasterboard to increase the depth.

If the warm deck roof is covered by glass-fibre or elastomeric roofing felt, you should be able to expect a 20-year guarantee. However, the life expectancy of the traditional flat roof built up with three layers of bitumen-based roofing felt can be less than 10 years.

You should check the following:

Flat roofs should not be flat; a fall of 1:60 is ideal.

Plywood or oriented strand board (OSB), 18 mm (¾ in) thick, should be used for the decking.

Some traditional felts require solar reflective chippings or paint finish to stop ultraviolet light breaking down the membrane.

If the extension roof abuts the house wall and your existing house has brick-faced cavity walls, a remedial cavity tray damp-proof course (dpc) must be installed in the wall, just above the extension roof abutment. Purpose-made remedial trays are now available preformed, and only two courses of bricks need to be removed before they are inserted.

The tray is essential to stop rain that has penetrated the outer skin of a cavity wall from tracking down the inner face of the brick skin, which will become the inside face for your new room below. The tray collects the water in the cavity and returns it via weepholes in the mortar joints to the outside.

Materials

The bricks and the roof tiles will determine the appearance of the completed extension. There is a vast choice of colours and style of bricks and some merchants have brick

---

Careful planning is necessary to ensure that the floor levels align and the wall surfaces match. Matching or complementary materials, such as wood flooring and bricks, help tie in the new room with the existing house.

When to inspect ❗

- Inspect the progress at the end of each day, especially work that will be concealed such as wiring and plumbing.

- Inspect the walls, floors and ceilings of the new extension to see if they tie in with the existing house. For example, any steps needed should be at a comfortable height.

- With the room (or rooms) completed, inspect the decoration to ensure that there are no problems with the work.

- Inspect the garden around the extension to ensure that it has been properly landscaped.

libraries that you can visit. But what you really need to do is check them against the existing house. Make sure that the colour and type of pointing is appropriate.

If it is necessary for you to use second-hand tiles, they will need to be inspected to make sure cracked and broken ones are discarded. Welsh slate is still produced and easily obtained but your roofers may have to drill the holes for the fixings themselves. Again, subtle colour changes in slate from different mines occur, so obtain a sample before ordering.

When work begins

Extensions may not require planning permission if they are within permitted development rules, but they will require Building Regulations approval and inspection at various stages by Building Control officers. You should decide whether you or your builder will notify them.

The first step will be to clear the site area. Any patios or paths will have to be broken up before the foundations can be excavated. There will obviously be some disruption during groundwork, with spoil being removed from the site by a skip or lorry. It is not unreasonable to insist that scaffold boards be laid on your lawn to reduce the damage. It may also sometimes be necessary for the builders to rig up a temporary drain while work is underway, but it is seldom necessary to disconnect services or drains totally for more than a few hours.

As the homeowner, you are responsible for the health and safety of people visiting your home, so make sure that excavations left open are covered adequately or fenced off.

When the superstructure is complete, secure and weathered in, the extension will need to be opened through into the existing house. This is a job that can be done carefully and considerately, or it can be quickly with a lot of mess, using a masonry disc cutter. This may be acceptable in the unfinished extension side but in the house you'll be cleaning up brick dust for months afterwards. It can be finished inside with a hammer and bolster and a few dust sheets with the minimum of disruption. It's worth staying at home that day.

Creating a self-contained space

Finding self-contained space for elderly or disabled relatives or grown-up children living at home can be difficult under any circumstances, but in modern houses it is likely to be impossible without planning a purpose-built extension.

A single-storey extension that includes all the essential amenities of a separate dwelling on a smaller scale is the perfect answer for a "granny flat". Most of the structural building problems are similar to those of other extensions.

Where to build

You will probably have to build the annexe as an extension with access to it through your house rather than it having its own front door (see pp. 98–103). It may be possible to construct the annexe as a detached building, but you may have difficulty in obtaining consent if it is too large or it appears to have its own separate parking, access or garden.

In most annexes the intended occupants will be looking for some level of independence and to this end, a kitchen, bathroom, bedroom and lounge area, albeit on a miniature scale, need to be included.

The drainage system

One of the primary considerations for positioning the extension will be the drains (see pp. 154–155). It is essential that the existing drainage runs and levels allow new connections to be made. If they are especially shallow or just simply in the wrong place, you may end up incurring additional expense or at worst aborting the project. Check

A self-contained apartment for a member of the family may have unusual arrangements but they should be both practical and comfortable for the occupant.

your drainage first by lifting manhole covers, flushing toilets and running water. New uPVC drain pipes can be laid at very shallow falls, but you should aim to get them at a 1:40 gradient if possible. You can establish the gradient by measuring the

Rules & regulations

Most planning authorities are reluctant to give permission for the creation of self-contained living accommodation that could be later sold off separately. This means that you may have to have access to the annexe via the main house.

Building Regulations will also have to be followed with regular inspections, and services should be installed by registered contractors. Alterations to drainage also need approval from your local authority.

depth of the manhole from the cover level to the entry of the pipe and the distance from the manhole that your new drains will travel.

The below-ground drainage can be installed at any stage but is best tackled once the work has reached damp-proof course level, before the builder starts on the superstructure. Pipes should be laid straight without bends, and inspection chambers or rodding points should be installed wherever the pipe changes direction or gradient so that blockages can be easily cleaned out. The plastic pipes are also accompanied by plastic

manholes; the small ones are known as "shallow access drains" and have a limit on their depth of 900 mm (3 ft). If you need manholes deeper than this, they will have to be either solid brick or sectional concrete with step irons in the sides and to a size of at least 1200 x 750 mm (48 x 30 in); they will obviously cost more. Deep access plastic chambers are now available but they are usually more expensive.

When checking the drains:
• Look for straight pipe "runs"; use a spirit level to check the gradient – it should have a half-bubble fall.
• Look for a bed and pea gravel surrounding the pipes before they are covered.
• Make sure that plastic manholes have not been "stretched" beyond 900 mm (36 in) by adding bits on.

Rainwater disposal can be handled in a number of ways. Soakaways can be dug in the ground as pits filled with hardcore rubble: these should be at least 5 m (16.5 ft) from any building. Their size will depend on the porosity of your soil and the amount of roof area that they serve. You may be able to collect the rainwater for use in the garden, but any tank or water butt should be fitted with an overflow.

Services

If your house boiler can cope with the central heating in the annexe as well, separate thermostatic controls will be needed on the radiators or roomstats. Two zones should be created if possible: one for the sitting area, one for the bedroom. You should check with a heating engineer that the rated output of your boiler is sufficient to cover the new rooms. It is much easier to upgrade it rather than install a separate system in the annexe.

Electrical layouts for power circuits and lighting circuits are usually separate, with their own fuse on the consumer unit. Posi-

Architects and designers are increasingly specializing in so-called accessible home design; that is, making living areas accessible to occupants with physical infirmities such as those caused by ageing. Hiring such a professional is recommended if you need planning help of this kind. You will need not only the normal planning permission, but also the expert knowledge of many unfamiliar specifications and details in designing spaces for disabled or elderly occupants. For example, you will get advice on the amount of room necessary to turn a wheelchair and the most convenient height for wall outlets and light switches.

Even if you don't need an architect or full-scale building designer, hiring a qualified kitchen or bathroom designer for either of those areas will pay dividends. Their knowledge of how to arrange and furnish kitchens and bathrooms for occupants with special needs is invaluable, and you will be glad to have their expert opinions when it comes to choosing from among the growing array of fixtures, appliances, furnishings and decorations for the disabled and infirm.

tioning socket outlets higher up the walls is something simple that can make life much easier for an elderly person. The electrician should also install a mains-operated smoke detector close to the bedroom. It can be wired to either the lighting circuit if it has a battery back-up or to a separate fused circuit.

Carbon monoxide alarms are also available for kitchens and areas where heat-producing appliances can leak this invisible and odourless gas. Select an alarm that complies with British Standard BS:7860.

Creating an outbuilding

There are many reasons to add an outbuilding or two on your property – if space allows for them. An outbuilding can be a place for storage, a workshop or studio space, or a place to relax or play.

Garden buildings can be put up that will enhance the garden as well as serve a basic function. They can be used as garden sheds, workshops, studios or just summerhouses.

Garages and workshops

Detached garages will probably be exempt from planning consent below a certain size. Most single detached garages are also exempt from Building Regulations, as they are less than 30 sq m (323 sq ft) in floor area. Larger double garages and those with loft areas in the roof are controlled under the Building Regulations, as are those constructed with combustible materials that are near the property boundary (within 1 m/36 in). The standard garage is 2400 mm (94 in) wide. Make sure

Shed kits

For a simple shed, many attractive models for a variety of uses are available in kit form from manufacturers, timberyards, home and garden centres, and landscape design firms. These sources may supply or recommend trained carpenters to erect the building as part of the purchase price, or you can hire your own carpenter.

Kits may cost almost the same as having a similar building made on site and, although they are made in a controlled factory environment and may be better built in some ways, most won't match the quality of a good custom-made shed.

you measure your vehicle (with the doors sufficiently open and room at the back to get the shopping out) before the plans are finalized.

Unless you are proposing to heat the garage, there is little point in constructing it with cavity walls. It is usually sufficient to use a half-brick (112 mm/4⅜ in) construction with solid (215 mm/½ in) brick piers internally to strengthen it. The wall on either side of the garage doors – as short as it may be – should be constructed with piers because the action of the doors may put a strain on it. The corners of the walls should also be formed by solid piers and the walls themselves split by a central pier or have at least one every 3 m (10 ft). Gable end walls can be built in the same way but lateral restraint straps should be used at the ceiling and rafter levels so that the roof is helping support the wall against wind. Pitched roofs are more attractive but a flat roof covered with a sheeting material, adequately secured and with well-lapped joins, will last for years.

Sectional garages are available as either timber frame or precast concrete panel kits. The latter come in a variety of finishes from pebble-dash to a brick look. The timber kits can be either a standard timber frame construction or a "barn-style" building formed with oak beams traditionally jointed. These make for very striking buildings, weatherboarded on the outside and with roofs covered in traditional clay peg tiles.

It may be possible to construct the garage with a loft that could

Ask yourself

- How do you plan to use the outbuilding? Is it intended for storage, as a place to work or to relax in?

- Will you need electricity or heating in the outbuilding? If you intend to use it for work, both of these are considerations. A building used for relaxing may be restricted to warm weather use if you don't want to include heating.

provide workshop space or even living space. Workshops may need a stronger floor if they are to house heavy benches or timber but you will be able to access them by an open stair from within the garage. If you want to use the loft as living space, the stair should be either external or enclosed with fire-resistant construction, and the garage will also need a ceiling.

Garage doors range from the simple double timber doors to metal or fibreglass up and over and even roller shutter doors that disappear into a neat barrel above the door opening. Electronic devices are also available so that you won't need to step out of the car to open the doors when you arrive home.

Gazebos and summerhouses

Garden buildings do not normally require permission of any kind, providing they are not more than 4 m

An outbuilding can be as useful yet attractive as this work studio.
The interior provides a place to work away from the main house, but
the attached deck allows you to take a break in the sunshine.

(13 ft) high for a pitched roof or 3 m (10 ft) high for a flat roofed building – however, if there is a public highway within 20 m (65 ft), this may also affect the exemption.

As with the garage, you can buy kits or whole sheds or build to your own specifications. The suppliers often provide the labour to erect their products on site as an optional extra. Ready-made sheds are usually fairly flimsy and for a little more you can have something solidly built in timber that will last forever.

Choosing materials

The quality of the timber is the prime consideration, together with its treatment. For increased life expectancy, any timber that has been pressure-treated will outlive the paint on surface-treated wood by many years. This is because the preservative has been applied under vacuum and has impregnated the timber throughout, rather than just soaked in a little below the surface.

The quality of the timber itself will also determine its appearance and durability. The weight of dry timber is an indication of its density and strength. Scandinavian redwood and spruce are popular choices because of their rich warm colour and tight grain, but as with red cedar, it may look and smell wonderful when it is new but you need to be aware that it doesn't stay

that way. As it ages it dries and splits and takes on a shiny grey patina. You can help delay the ageing process by applying an oil-based preservative every year, but you will never stop it.

You should apply preservative every year, in any case. Some are coloured and will produce a rather uniform dull appearance. The most efficient timber preservatives are highly toxic and require some protective clothing when being applied, but with increasing environmental awareness, new water-based products are available that are free of solvents and will not harm pets, plants or people. Look for the low VOC (volatile organic compounds; see p. 37) content on the tin.

Timber that has been labelled with the FSC mark will be from sustainable forests where logging is not causing environmental damage.

The outside of your house needs more regular care and attention than the interior. If its condition is allowed to deteriorate, the whole property can be affected and damge is often not immediately visible. This section explains what professionals can offer when it comes to exterior maintenance, replacing windows and doors, maintaining or replacing roof coverings and coping with the ultimate property disaster – subsidence. It also tells you how they can help create patios, garden paths and steps, build boundary walls and fences and add unusual features such as timber decks. Knowing what each project involves will make it easy for you to deal with specifications, make informed product choices and keep an eye on the installation. That way, you will get the results you want and avoid many of the pitfalls.

A patio (far left) partially surrounded by walls provides an intimate setting for entertaining guests. Keeping the exterior of your house in good shape (left) will be a welcomng sight whenever you return home.

Maintaining the house's exterior

The outside skin of your house is the building's defence against the elements. It must be kept in good condition, otherwise wind, rain, sun and frost will eventually attack the various materials that make up its structure.

The paint on your house is responsible for protecting the structural materials. If it is not maintained, rot may attack wood, damp may penetrate masonry and rust may attack metal. To begin with, the house will simply look rundown, but as time goes by a range of serious defects will begin to appear. To prevent this from happening, your house needs an annual service in much the same way as your car does. This is a job that a firm of general builders or decorators should be able to carry out for you, guaranteeing you peace of mind and your house a longer life.

Before your professionals arrive to look at the property and assess what needs to be done, it is a wise precaution to carry out your own survey first. Although there are plenty of honest firms around, there are some people who will invent extra work and charge for either a shoddy repair or not carrying it out at all. This is especially true of hidden parts of the structure such as roofs and drains, which are usually difficult for most homeowners to inspect closely.

A well-maintained house will not only be more attractive, it will also be a less expensive house to maintain. Repairs to run-down houses are often more expensive than the cost of maintenance.

Roofs and gutters

Start by checking the condition of the roof, either by climbing to the eaves of each roof slope with a ladder so you can inspect it at close quarters or by using binoculars from ground level. Look for tiles or slates that are cracked or missing, and for ridge and hip tiles with faulty pointing between or beneath them. Check lead flashings for signs of lifting and tearing, especially around chimney stacks, skylights and soil pipes. Check the condition of the chimney stack itself, looking for frost-damaged brickwork, failed pointing or cracked rendering, and for any signs that the mortar bedding the pots on top of the stack is cracked or missing.

Finally, if you are up a ladder, take the opportunity to examine the state of the gutters, which should have an even fall towards each outlet and no signs of rust, cracks, leaks or blockages. Some checks can be made from inside the house, which is better if you don't like heights. You may be able to check the inside of any skylights for leaks or tell-tale patches of corrosion and you can also see stretches of the guttering from the windows. Again, leaks, if not actually wet, can be detected by discoloured patches under the guttering. (For details on roof maintenance or replacement, see pp. 116–117.)

Walls and paintwork

Give the house walls a close inspection, looking for failed pointing or cracked rendering, patches of mould or other discolouration, and for gaps opening around window and door frames that could let in water. Finally, look closely at the paintwork on windows, doors, timber cladding and the eaves woodwork – fascias, soffits and bargeboards. Make sure that putty around window panes is intact and not lifting away from the glass, and that there are no signs of rot anywhere beneath lifting or peeling paintwork. You can press a screwdriver or bradawl into soft wood to assess decay. If the wood is no longer fibrous and does not resist the bradawl, it needs either treating for rot or replacing.

You should check especially on the side of the house that is the most exposed to the prevailing wind and rain. However, the paintwork is often also in a poor state on the sunny side of the house as wood and other materials (such as steel and aluminium) shrink and expand with changes in temperature, thus pushing off the paint cover. Make a note of all the faults you discover, so that you can compare them with your builder's or decorator's assessment.

When work starts

You and the professional should first agree on what work needs to be carried out in detail and what it will cost. It is important to specify the types of paint to be used from the primer right through to the top coats. Microporous or breathable paints are good for exterior work but they are more expensive.

Redecorating exterior woodwork will involve sanding and washing down all sound paintwork, and stripping any defective paint back to bare wood ready for priming and recoating. This can be a messy job if the paint is burnt off, and the painters should use every effort to stop scrapings being blown all over the garden. As with any decorating job, but especially on the exterior, the finished job will only be as good as the preparation. Most decorators will carry out the work from a ladder, although some may prefer to use a slot-together platform tower if there are paths and other solid paved areas around the house on which to set it up.

Painting rendered walls is also usually carried out from ladders. If you are offered the option of having the walls sprayed rather than brushed or rollered, all windows, doors and downpipes will need masking off first, and the work should be carried out on a still day to minimize the risk of paint mist drifting. This is certainly far quicker than painting by hand, and the time gained more than offsets that taken up in masking off surfaces.

Gaps around frames and defective putty around window panes can be tackled at the same time as the paintwork. Old mortar filling around frames should be raked out and deep gaps filled with inert material such as glass fibre insulation or filler

foam before the gap is sealed with a bead of nonsetting mastic. Defective putty should be chopped out and replaced with acrylic putty or, better still, with hardwood glazing beads bedded in putty.

Repairs to masonry may require the use of scaffolding, although localized repairs can be carried out from steps or ladders. Make sure that dust sheets are used to catch the inevitable mortar droppings beneath the work area.

Replacing windows and doors

Owing to rising energy costs, replacing draughty single-pane windows and ill-fitting doors is one of the fastest growing sectors of the home improvement business – and replacing windows and the front door is one way to make a house more attractive.

If you decide to replace your windows or doors, one route is to choose a windows specialist. Pick one with a good local trading record who can put you in touch with satisfied customers in your area, rather than simply taking the cheapest quotation. The alternative, if you want to replace your existing windows with new ones of the same style and material, is to call in a firm of local builders to carry out the work for you. This may be less expensive than a package deal, and you can organize the timescale to suit your finances.

Window options

Most window replacement companies offer a choice of two types of replacement window, with frames of

timber or steel-framed plastic (unplasticized polyvinyl chloride, or uPVC for short). The best timber-framed windows are made from rot-resistant hardwood (this does not mean that they will not rot – any wood will rot if neglected), although cheaper preservative-treated softwood windows are also available. They are made in a wide range of standard sizes and styles, or can be made to measure to fit nonstandard window openings. High-performance types have double glazing and integral weatherstripping.

Windows made from uPVC are maintenance-free if installed correctly. They do not need painting, and the use of glazing gaskets means that there is no putty to deteriorate. They also feature double glazing and integral draughtproofing and are available in a wide range of designs. Most firms offer a choice of white or dark wood-grain finishes, but a few can supply other colours on request. It is difficult to fit additional security devices to plastic windows after installation, so it is important to check that any windows you choose offer adequate built-in security.

Whether you choose timber or plastic windows, picking a frame style that suits your house is of paramount importance.

Glazing style

Most replacement windows are fitted with clear glass as standard, but windows can be made to special order using obscured, patterned or even coloured glass. You can also have sealed units with the appear-

When to inspect !

- As soon as the work is completed, check that all opening casements, sashes and top lights can be opened, closed, locked and unlocked easily. Inspect the external seals and any internal filling work to make sure there are no gaps or cracks. Finally, make sure the frames and glazing are clean and free from mastic or finger marks.

- Check that all doors open and close properly and lie flush to the frame at the top and bottom. Check the clearance over the floor covering. Make sure that some form of finish has been applied so that the door will not warp in the warmth from central heating.

ance of leaded light or small-paned Georgian-style windows if that suits your house style.

If you have large areas of glazing, it may be worth considering having solar control or low-emissivity glass, which will help reduce heat gain in summer and also keep rooms warmer in winter. Low-level glazing in doors and full-height windows must now be fitted with safety glass (it does not disperse shards of glass if it is shattered) to comply with the Building Regulations.

Replacing doors

A window replacement company will also be able to supply front and back doors, plus any French win-

Low-e glass

Insulated windows are available with invisible metal coatings that make the glass more energy efficient. Low-e glass (the term stands for low-emissivity) stops heat escaping from a room. It allows the sun's rays through and then stops the heat seeping back into the ambient air. It also reflects heat from fires and radiators back into the house, helping to reduce heating costs. On a double-glazed unit the special metal-coated surface should be used on the inner pane and should be within the cavity of the unit. Consult with a supplier or window contractor to determine your optimum use of these panels.

When choosing a new door and windows, make sure the style is in character with the rest of the house. Installing small windows around a door enhances the entrance and provides natural light indoors.

patio doors. You should also consider having security glazing with laminated glass in vulnerable doors.

When work starts

Once the firm's surveyor has measured up all the windows you want replaced and you have decided on which material, style and glazing you want, your order will be placed and manufactured. You will normally have to pay a deposit at this stage, but you should never pay the full amount in advance.

You will be notified when work is scheduled to begin. You will be expected to take down curtains and blinds, and it is a good idea to move any furniture away from the window area and to cover it and other belongings (such as books on shelves) with dust sheets. The window installers should put down dust sheets inside and outside the windows, and some will fix polyethylene sheeting to the window reveal on the inside to minimize the dust.

The old windows will then be stripped of moving parts. Timber frames will be cut into sections and prised free, while metal-framed ones will usually have their side fixings cut so they can be lifted out whole. There should be minimal damage to internal plaster as this is carried out.

The installers will check at this stage that vertical and horizontal damp-proof courses are present and intact, and will fit them if they are absent in older properties. Make sure that this stage is not skimped as it is vital. They will then slot the replacement window into position and secure it to the masonry at each side of the opening, and seal around the exterior with nonsetting mastic. Finally, they will repair any damage to the internal plasterwork and fit a new internal window sill.

When employing firms of this sort to replace windows and doors, you should stipulate that your house should be left secure every night.

dows or patio doors you require, in a style and material that matches the new windows.

If you just want a replacement timber front or back door, a builder or carpenter will probably be able to offer you a quicker and cheaper service, and you will also have a larger range of door styles to choose from. Make sure that your new doors feature top-level security – locks that meet British Standard BS:3621, plus additional devices such as mortise and hinge bolts for back doors and integral three-point locking for French windows and

Improving home security

Most burglars are amateurs and opportunists. They look for a property that is easy to break into, easy to get out of and not visible to neighbours. By eliminating these characteristics from your house, any burglars will probably try elsewhere.

Home security can be expensive but it is vital to the safety of your property and your own peace of mind. You can get detailed advice on how to improve your home's security from the Crime Prevention Officer at your local police station. Call on a security specialist to install locks, burglar alarms and other security equipment.

Security weak spots

Windows, especially those at the back of the house, are the entry point for around 60 percent of burglaries. Small-paned windows are often broken almost silently to allow the burglar access to interior handles, but few will risk smashing large panes because the noise may attract attention. If the burglar cannot break the glass, he or she may use a crowbar to force the casement or sash open. Since these are usually held closed by fittings with short screws, it takes little force to tear them out of the wood.

Doors, especially back doors, account for the other 40 percent of forced entries. Glass or flimsy plywood panels may be broken to allow the locks or bolts to be reached from outside, or the door may simply be kicked in. Outward-opening French doors and old-style patio doors with few security devices are particularly at risk.

Porches, conservatories and atached garages with internal access to the house are also weak spots. If they are not themselves secure, they give a burglar the perfect cover to work on the enclosed entry door to the house out of sight.

Lastly, check your property perimeter – easily climbed walls and fences or unlocked side gates can all give access to the often poorly secured rear of the house. High fences or hedges hide the burglar from passers-by or neighbours. Remember, too, that your house becomes more vulnerable when you are having building work done.

Security survey

When you call in a firm of security specialists, they will survey the property and recommend what action is needed to make it secure, beginning with the front door. Since this is your final exit door you must rely on good locks to secure it, reinforced with some additional security features. If you have only a surface-mounted cylinder rim latch, they will recommend the fitting of a mortise lock made to the requirements of British Standard BS:3621, ideally with up to seven levers for maximum security. They will want small glass panes replaced with laminated glass or polycarbonate sheeting. For extra security they may also suggest hinge bolts to strengthen the hinged edge against forcing, as well as the addition of steel plates to reinforce the frame and the lock area. Lastly they may offer to fit a door viewer and a door chain or limiter so you can vet callers before opening the door.

For back doors, they will recommend a mortise sashlock and the addition of extra internal bolts to improve security. Again, they will want to replace glass panes with unbreakable materials, or will

recommend the fitting of a security grille on the inside of the door. For patio doors, they are likely to suggest adding surface-mounted locking bolts, and they will recommend mortise rack bolts and hinge bolts for French doors.

For windows, key-operated locks with long fixing screws will make both casement and sash windows secure, including those accessible from flat roofs or external soil pipes.

Electronic systems

Modern alarm systems can also detect emergencies and monitor household systems. They incorporate smoke detectors and sensors for gas leaks and flooding. In case of fire, some systems turn on lights to enable exit in the dark and turn off air circulation equipment to prevent smoke spreading through the house.

These systems may also function as a speaker phone, allowing you to listen for noises in your house or to broadcast your voice through a speaker. Some systems can also operate lights and thermostats, not only to give an empty home a lived-in look but to save energy by regulating temperatures. The most basic of these is the external light with its own movement sensor.

Vulnerable ground-floor windows, especially in basements, may need external or internal grilles.

Alarm systems

Your security specialists may recommend the installation of a burglar alarm. These can either set off a bell or siren on the house wall when an intruder is detected or alert a remote monitoring station, which then notifies the police. The former may well be ignored by neighbours, but the visible external alarm box and the noise will act as a deterrent to many burglars. The latter is a better choice if you live remote from other properties. Whichever type you choose, make sure the firm installing it is a member of NACOSS (the National Approval Council for Security Systems) and that the installation meets the requirements of British Standard BS:6707.

When to inspect

When all the security equipment has been installed, check that door and window locks operate smoothly and that window locks can be released in an emergency. It is especially important that upstairs windows can be unlocked quickly for use as escape routes, and keys should be located close to the windows (but out of sight of a burglar).

Make sure you (and others living in the house) know how to arm and disarm the system while going in and out of the house. Have it serviced annually to ensure that it remains in perfect working order.

A low roof can be climbed onto from a nearby tree or fence. If either is near your house, make sure you keep upstairs windows secured. Always keep ground floor windows secured, especially those at the back of the house.

Windows near a front door may be smashed to reach the lock. Consider replacing ordinary glass with a stronger version, such as one of polycarbonate plastic glazing or a laminated type, for greater security.

A garage door may be forced open to gain entry through an internal door to the house. When upgrading your home's security, make sure you include any garage doors.

The roof is the most important part of the house structure when it comes to keeping the building weatherproof. Any roof should give decades of good service with little maintenance. However, most roofs do wear out over time and require replacement.

It is vital that you give your roof regular checks. Remember that rainwater can accumulate in a loft space for some time before it becomes apparent. It takes little effort to glance up at your roof to check for loose tiles or slates or broken ridge tiles. In older houses, you should also look for the line of the ridge sagging or the development of concave areas in the slates or tiles.

Damage can be dramatic – after a hurricane, for example – or it can develop gradually over time, allowing water to penetrate and wind to lift and loosen tiles, slates and the metal flashings (see pp. 146–147) that waterproof junctions between the roof and the chimney stack. If these faults are not remedied, the roof will eventually deteriorate to the point where its covering, and possibly parts of its supporting framework too (see pp. 128–129), will need complete replacement.

Roofing specialists
Work on the roof is one area of home maintenance that is best left to the professionals. They are experienced in working at heights, have the proper access equipment and possess the necessary technical knowledge to ensure that the roof is restored to peak performance.

Roofing is an area to beware of cowboy operators, who may recommend treatment that is not needed or will fail to carry out properly what should be done, often for exorbitant charges. For your own peace of mind, you should use either personally recommended contractors or firms that are members of the National Federation of Roofing Contractors (see pp. 168–171).

Localized repairs
Your roofing contractor will be able to carry out a range of localized repairs to your roof. These may include replacing cracked or missing tiles with matching replacements, rebedding loose ridge and hip tiles on a fresh mortar bed and repointing the junction between tiles and gable ends. If you have a slate roof, he or she may have to secure slipped slates with lead or zinc support tongues or replace cracked or broken slates. Any lead flashings that have been lifted by the wind should be dressed down, and any that are torn or missing should be repaired or replaced. Check that old lead flashings are replaced with new

A wood or slate shingle roof may be an appropriate choice for a traditional house in some areas.

lead. Mortar flashings are cheap, but they are no substitute for lead in the provision of long-term weatherproofing for your roof.

The roofer will also tackle any repairs needed to flat roofs, whether these are felted or coated with hot asphalt. Localized areas of damage may be patched, or the roof may need resurfacing with a fabric reinforcing membrane bedded in a fresh layer of waterproofer.

Replacing the roof covering
Stripping an existing tiled or slated roof and replacing the covering with new materials is a major project that needs careful planning and dry weather. Unless the existing roof is

When to inspect !

There are several points you can check as work progresses.

- Sarking felt should be pulled taut across the roof slope, with a generous overlap between the sheets. There should be no holes or tears in it.

- Tiling battens should be intact, nailed to every rafter and neatly butt-jointed, with the same spacing on adjacent roof slopes.

- Eaves tiles should project over the gutter to ensure that rainwater drains off into the guttering – however, they should not be drooping into the gutter.

fully boarded, it will also make a considerable mess in the loft space, so you will be well advised to clear everything that has been stored in the loft – including the existing loft insulation – and to ask your contractors to vacuum the loft when the work is finished so that new insulation can be laid before all the stored items are replaced.

Before work starts, discuss with your contractors what new covering is to be used to ensure that the roof structure is up to the job. If you are replacing plain clay tiles or slates with their modern counterparts, there should be no problems, but replacing slates with heavy concrete tiles could overburden the structure and some strengthening work may be needed first.

The roof timbers should also be inspected for signs of rot and woodworm. If present, the roof may need to be retimbered (see p. 102). If the whole structure needs replacing, you may be advised to use an architect or surveyor to oversee the job.

This new asphalt shingle roof uses shingles of different shades in the same colour range; the irregular pattern helps break up the large area of roof.

When work starts

The work will involve removing existing flashings, stripping the roof from the top down and inspecting the state of the transverse battens over which tiles are hooked and to which slates are nailed. These will generally be replaced; there is little point laying a new roof covering over old battens that may be split or damaged by rot. Similarly, if the roof has underfelt beneath the battens, this will also be replaced with new rot-proof tear-resistant sarking felt to ensure that the roof is completely wind and waterproof. Then new preservative-treated battens will be fixed at spacings to suit the gauge of the new tiles or artificial slates, using rustproof fixings for long life.

The new roof covering will then be placed course by course, working from the eaves upwards. With traditional roofing, slates will be nailed at every course and tiles at every fourth or fifth course. With modern dry roofing systems, individual elements are held to the battens with clips and ridge and hip tiles are bedded on dry gaskets.

Ventilation is an important aspect of reroofing to ensure air circulation in the loft. This can be either at the eaves with special ventilation strips, or special ventilation tiles can be fitted at the ridge or on the main slope.

Finishing

The finishing details are very important for your roof's integrity. The tiles or slates at the gable should be neatly pointed where they meet the top of the wall, or driving rain could penetrate underneath. Ridge tiles should be pointed or securely clipped in place to the ridge board. Hip and valley tiles should be neatly cut with an angle grinder.

Finally, ask your contractors to make sure that the gutters are clear of mortar droppings and tile fragments before they take down their access equipment.

DIY jargon !

Sarking The layer of material laid over the rafters, under the tiles or slates. It is laid horizontally in overlapping strips from the bottom upwards.

Battens These are thin strips of timber nailed horizontally across the rafters and over the roofing felt to support the tiles or slates. They must be treated with preservative to prevent rot or decay.

Coping with subsidence

Settling of the foundation, or subsidence, is one of the most serious problems that can affect a house. Settling in older houses is common; however, provided the condition has stabilized, corrective action is usually not warranted.

Subsidence can eventually lead to severe structural damage to your house. Evidence of subsidence can be seen in zig-zag cracks in exterior brickwork or internal partitions appearing to pull away from load-bearing walls. If you find such symptoms, you need to call in a building surveyor at once to track down the cause of the problem and recommend a solution.

Causes of subsidence

House foundations are designed to support the weight of the house and to transmit the load evenly to the subsoil beneath it. If the foundations fail to do this properly, the house will begin to move and, being a rigid structure, something will have to give. There are several possible causes of such movement.

If the original foundations were inadequate – they may have been too narrow or too shallow – they

---

When to inspect !

• The quality of subsidence repairs to foundation work will be beyond your ability to judge. You should leave this for the building inspector to handle. Once the work is finished, make sure you obtain a certificate of guarantee – this will be important if you sale the house at a later date.

• Your specialists should leave the site clean and the ground level; it will be up to you to deal with the garden.

---

will gradually subside as time goes by. Certain types of soil, notably clay, can also cause what is known as sulphate attack, weakening concrete foundations and leading to their gradual collapse. This type of subsidence is often a problem in older properties, but will generally have occurred long ago and should by now have been corrected.

If the house has been extended and a different type of foundation used for the later work, differential settlement can occur and cause cracks to appear between the old and new sections of the building.

Ground movement is the most common cause of subsidence, especially on clay soils. These soils can dry out and shrink in long periods of dry weather, causing foundations to collapse. They then swell and heave upwards again when they become saturated with water, and thus cause further movement and damage to the building. Similar effects can be caused by large trees growing near the house. The roots extract a lot of water from the subsoil, leading to soil shrinkage and subsidence. Felling them can then cause ground heave as the soil regains its natural moisture.

Other causes of ground movement include leaky drains causing soil erosion beneath the building, a high water table resulting in frost heave in cold weather, and general subsidence due to poor subsoil conditions. This happens in houses that have been built on land-fill sites or where old underground workings have collapsed, in coal-mining areas, for example.

Testing methods

The two most common tests for analyzing subsidence include gluing thin strips of glass or other material across foundation cracks, or simply marking across cracks with an indelible pen. Any substantial movement will affect the materials. It is often necessary to monitor a building for months or even years to learn whether a problem warrants repair.

Assessing the problem

The first thing your surveyor will do is to check all parts of the house structure to find out whether the movement is due to small-scale settlement of the whole structure – something that occurs to a greater or lesser extent with most houses – or to serious subsidence. Settlement usually takes place with a year or two of the house being built, and most often results in nothing more serious than small gaps opening up at floor and ceiling joints. Subsidence, on the other hand, has more serious tell-tale signs.

The most obvious are cracks in the outside walls, usually near the corners of the building and starting at weak points such as door and window openings. The cracks often widen as they travel upwards – a clear indication that parts of the building are moving independently. Irregular gaps may also open up around window and door frames. Internally, subsidence beneath a

---

Any large trees growing within 15 m (5 ft) of a house can potentially contribute towards subsidence. Before having the tree removed, consult a specialist to determine the best way to handle the situation.

solid floor slab may result in the slab dropping, taking internal partitions with it and opening up wedge-shaped gaps between floor, ceilings and the walls. Doors may become difficult to open, and the floor slab may even crack.

Your surveyor will measure and record details of all such movement, using devices called tell-tales – strips of glass stuck across the cracks – to reveal whether movement is still taking place. He or she may also want to expose suspect areas of the foundations to assess their condition. This assessment may take up to a year befor the surveyor will be able to recommend the appropriate remedial treatment.

What the work involves

A process called underpinning is the only effective long-term cure for subsidence caused by inadequate foundations or ground movement. This involves excavating the subsoil beneath the existing foundations, propping up the structure temporarily and placing new stronger foundations to support the building. It is a job for specialists who will be recommended and overseen by your building surveyor.

Where floor slabs have subsided it may be possible to pump in consolidating material from outside the building, but in severe cases the slab will have to be removed and

Rules & regulations

Most if not all of the cost should be covered by your buildings insurance, so you should notify your insurance company who will appoint an experienced surveyor to handle the work and design the solution. Your certificate of guarantee is essential in obtaining further insurance cover.

reconstructed. The work will be time-consuming (therefore expensive), noisy and disruptive.

After the underpinning there may be a lot of further work to repair the damage caused by the subsidence – cracks in brick and plasterwork, loose fixtures and damaged decoration – and this process can be as lengthy and disruptive as the underpinning work itself.

Garden landscaping

Structural landscaping, such as terracing, paths or patios, can make your garden both more practical for all ages to use and more attractive. Garden designers and landscapers can increase the possibilities of any space, however small.

Home improvements do not have to be confined solely to the house. Increasingly, homeowners are planning structural alterations and improvements to the garden as a natural extension of the house. Small-scale works are often within the scope of the average do-it-yourselfer, but larger projects involving major building work may need professional help, and the advice of a landscape designer can be sought at the outset for major garden makeovers.

Options for change

The improvements you can carry out in your garden will depend on its size, its orientation to the sun and its basic geography – whether it is flat or sloping, wide or narrow, long or shallow. One feature that many homeowners want is a patio – a paved area where they can sit and relax or have meals. This is usually sited at the back of the house for easy access, but could also be built at the side or the end of the garden if this gets more sun or enjoys a better view.

The patio needs to be large enough to accommodate chairs, tables, barbecue equipment and other outdoor comforts without overcrowding. Its shape also needs to be considered – patios do not have to be square or rectangular, and curves or other irregular shapes often suit a garden setting very well.

Paths link different areas of the garden together, providing access to washing lines, compost bins and outbuildings such as sheds and greenhouses, or simply allowing

One feature many homeowners want is a patio where they can sit and relax, eat meals in the open air and entertain friends. A garden that has had time to mature around a patio is a particularly relaxing place to sit.

people to walk in the garden without treading on the grass. They can run straight, follow flower borders or meander down the lawn in a haphazard and natural way.

Changing levels brings in a third dimension to garden design. If the garden slopes, you can create different levels and planting areas with retaining walls, and you can use steps to link the separate parts of the garden.

The interest in a garden is greatly enhanced if the whole garden is not open to view at once. Long narrow gardens can be divided by a free-standing trellis with a climbing rose or a vine trailing over it. Square gardens are more difficult but an area could be separated off to make a secluded corner, perhaps with a gazebo or pergola.

Another possibility might be a garden pond with or without an electric pump to provide circulation of the water. Once planted up and with resident fish or frogs, even a small pond provides an especially attractive feature.

You may have an idea of what you want and be able to draw up detailed plans that you can show to a builder. If not, then calling in a firm of garden landscape specialists will sort out both the planning and the construction of your garden.

Planning the work

Your landscapers' first step will be to visit the site, take measurements of the area, produce basic scale plans and discuss with you what you want to achieve. Once the basic plan has been agreed, they will then move on to choosing materials and finalizing the job in more detail.

Paving materials for paths and patios will probably be the first consideration, and your choice is likely to lie with paving slabs, block pavers or crazy paving – all much more sympathetic than concrete or tarmac. Slabs and pavers can be laid on a sand bed – indeed, pavers are designed solely for such installation, but you may prefer the more permanent bed of concrete for slabs and, of course, for crazy paving. A brick base for a patio can be built in different patterns such as herringbone or cane-weave, and second-hand bricks can be used to give a pleasing aged look. As for walls, these can be of brick, man-made walling blocks or natural stone, but all need building up on suitable concrete foundations if they are to remain strong and stable.

Once all these details have been agreed, your landscapers will produce three-dimensional drawings and final plans, possibly with the aid of a computer program.

When work begins

The contractors will start by removing plants and turf from the work area. They will mark out the positions of the walls, paths, steps and the patio with string lines, and then start work on digging and placing concrete foundation strips for retaining walls and free-standing steps. As these are built up, they should incorporate weep holes between the bricks or blocks to prevent water building up behind them, and the inner face of the walls should be damp-proofed to prevent mineral salts leaching through and perhaps staining the outer surface of the masonry work.

To create a patio or path, they will excavate down to firm subsoil, saving any topsoil for use elsewhere in the garden. They will consolidate the ground with a layer of crushed rock, called hoggin, before laying concrete or a sand bed according to the agreed specification.

At this stage, they may need to add new drainage for this area. They will install edge restraints for block paving before bedding the blocks into place with a powered tool called a plate vibrator. Slabs and crazy paving will be laid on a mortar bed, and the joints will be pointed. All paved surfaces, including step treads, should incorporate a slope to encourage rainwater to drain off them.

Once all the masonry work is complete, the landscapers will replace topsoil in planting areas and replant shrubs that had to be moved for the building work to be carried out. If your designer has given you a full planting plan for your new garden, the new plants, shrubs or hedges will be planted out, pots sited and turf laid.

Building decks

Wooden outdoor decks for seating and entertaining are becoming popular alternatives to traditional paved patios. Unlike masonry, decks can be framed to rest at any height on posts or piers set into the ground, so a level site is not essential.

A deck is an outdoor seating area built from timber as an alternative to a traditional paved patio. On a level site it is raised slightly above ground level to protect it from rising damp, and it can be built on the same level as the indoor rooms to which it provides a natural outdoor extension. However, it is on sloping sites that decks really come into their own, since the supporting posts can cope with changing levels and avoid the need for the retaining walls and backfilling that are essential with masonry structures. Specialist firms offer a complete design and construction package that will ensure you make the most of your site's potential.

Deck options

The simplest deck is just a level planked platform with a frame of joists resting on short in-ground posts – in effect, a timber patio. It can be open to the elements, enclosed at the sides with trellis-work for shelter, or roofed with an open pergola, over which plants can be trained for shade and colour. Shallow steps can allow easy access to the rest of the garden, and railings can be added around the edge – indeed, they should be for safety reasons if the deck level is somewhat higher than the garden underneath.

Raised decks on sloping sites allow for more variation, especially in the creation of different levels.

The design can also incorporate raised walkways leading to the house or to other areas of the deck.

Because timber is such a versatile construction material, it lends itself to the building of decks in almost any shape or size. Apart from this basic design flexibility, the way the deck is planked can also add to its visual appeal. For example, the planks can be given neat mitred joins at corners, or they can be laid diagonally or in parquet patterns. They can be finished naturally or treated with coloured wood stains. The only requirement is that they are placed with slight gaps between adjacent boards so that rainwater can drain off freely.

Remember, however, that any outdoor timber structure will need regular checking and maintenance, especially in a damp climate. At the least, it will need regular treating with preservative.

Planking patterns

The way a deck is planked adds to its visual appeal and creates deliberate effects. Planks laid parallel to the house can make a wide deck seem narrower. Angling planks away from the house can make the deck seem larger and can lead the eye to attractive views or areas of intended focus such as gardens or trees.

Planking can be arranged in herringbone or parquet patterns. Varying patterns can make a single-level deck more interesting; but overusing this technique can spoil the effect.

Decks can be built in almost any shape or size. Decks that are built on sloping ground allow for more variation in design.

- Check the overall finish. It is essential that the boards have a smooth surface finish with no splintered edges or ends, and that all fixing nails are punched in below the board surface.

- Check that all cut ends are treated with wood preservative as extra back-up to the preinstallation preservative treatment the wood will have already received.

- Check that provision has been made to prevent vegetation from growing beneath the deck area, especially with low-level decks. Laying a weedproof plastic membrane below the deck and topping it with coarse gravel is one of the most effective methods, but this will need regular maintenance.

This deck was built on several levels, with the top platform leading directly to the first floor. The different areas offer a number of options for relaxing.

Planning the deck

After discussing your requirements and surveying the site, your installers will produce plans and three-dimensional drawings of how your deck will be built and how it will look when completed. At this stage you need to make all your requirements clear, including the choice of wood type and finish. Most decks are built from preservative-treated softwood and are finished with a water-repellent wood stain, but you can choose hardwood or a naturally rot-resistant timber such as cedar if appearance is more important than price. You also need to ensure that the deck specification includes any necessary steps, railings and other decorative or practical features.

Remember that if the deck is on very sloping ground, the space underneath should be included in your plans. It may serve for storage or even make a shady place to sit when the deck is in full sun.

When work starts

Building a basic deck will begin with the clearance of the site such as removing turf and any plants from within the deck area. If the deck adjoins the house, the installers will attach the main wall plate to the house wall to act as a reference level for setting the outer support posts in place. They will then set the main support posts in the ground in concrete, bracing them upright while the concrete sets.

The next stage is to link the support posts with the outer support beam, which is fixed to them so it is parallel with the wall plate but at a level that will give a slight fall away from the house across the deck surface. Then the deck area is defined by nailing on the outer side joists and the outer header joist parallel to the outer support beam. Intermediate joists can be skew-nailed into place (with the nails set at an angle) between the wall plate and the header joist, but it is quicker and easier to use steel joist hangers.

Once the deck structure is complete, the bracing is removed from the support posts. The planks are nailed on, working from the house towards the deck's outer edge, and they are cut flush with the outer side joists with a circular saw. The board ends can then be covered with nailed-on facing boards for a neat finish. If the deck is raised, the installers will add steps to link it with the lower garden level, then they will finish the structure by adding railings and handrails around the deck perimeter. Finally, they should ensure that the garden and lawn are back to their original state.

Fences and walls

Fences or walls can be erected along the boundary of your property or internally to divide up the space. They can be attractive features in themselves and serve as a framework for climbing plants but also offer a degree of privacy in your garden.

Installing new boundary fences or walls, or replacing existing ones, is a relatively large-scale job that involves plenty of manual labour. It is well worth calling in professional contractors to carry out the work, especially if you need to get the job completed quickly.

Fence options

All fences need secure posts to hold them up, but there are various materials that can be used in between. The cheapest and quickest method is to fit prefabricated fence panels, which are available in a variety of styles and heights and in standard 1.8 m (6 ft) lengths. Individual panels can easily be cut down in width to complete a fence run

that is less than a whole number of complete panels in length. Panel fences offer good privacy, but are not very strong and can easily be damaged by high winds.

The close-boarded fence consists of tapered overlapping vertical boards nailed to horizontal rails called arris rails, which are fixed between the posts. The rails are put on the inside of the fence, so it is difficult to climb and offers good security as well as strength and privacy. It is also more expensive.

Post-and-rail (ranch) or picket fencing do not offer security, but they make attractive boundary markers. The former consists of low posts linked with two or three widely spaced horizontal rails, while

the latter has two horizontal rails to which closely spaced uprights (pickets, often with decoratively shaped tops) are nailed.

Wall options

Brick is the most widely used material for high walls and is cheaper than man-made walling blocks or natural stone. High boundary walls need both solid foundations and the correct construction to ensure that they are safe and not likely to collapse. Recommended wall thicknesses and heights vary according to the degree of exposure. In relatively sheltered areas a wall one-and-a-half bricks (340 mm/13.5 in) thick can be built to a height of 2.4 m (8 ft), whereas in a severely exposed area the maximum safe height is reduced to 1.8 m (6 ft). Walls that are one brick (225 mm/9 in) thick should not be built higher than 1.45 m (4 ft 9 in). Make sure that

A traditional picket fence or rustic rail fence is an inviting, friendly way to establish the boundaries of the property and suits an older style house.

Rules & regulations

Boundary fences and walls that are more than 1 m (about 3 ft) high and erected along road frontages may need planning permission. Check with your local authority before proceeding, even if you are replacing an existing boundary that exceeds that height.

Planning regulations also apply to building works along boundaries between properties or within 3 to 6 m (10 to 20 ft) of a neighbouring building, depending on the depth of the foundations used.

the base to discourage rot. In a close-boarded fence, the rails should be housed in mortises cut in the posts or should be secured to the posts with stout galvanized brackets. The boards should rest on a horizontal gravel board at the foot of the fence posts to stop rot. The posts should be fitted with timber caps to protect the vulnerable end grain from water penetration.

High boundary walls will take several days to build, not only because of the amount of bricklaying involved, but also because the mortar will be squeezed out of the joints if too many courses are laid in a day. Long straight walls should incorporate an open vertical movement joint filled with mastic every 6 m (20 ft) to prevent any slight movement in the wall structure from causing cracks.

A close-boarded fence provides privacy in a residential area in an urban setting. The top edges of the boards are enhanced by being cut in a pattern.

When to inspect !

- Before construction begins, confirm the route of the fence or wall after it has been marked out by the builder.

- For a wood fence, make sure the concrete surrounding the posts is properly sloped at the surface. Check that all wooden parts are aligned and evenly spaced. The posts should be plumb – vertical from all sides. Any fastenings should be galvanized to avoid rust stains. Make sure they are sunk flush with or below surfaces so they don't snag clothes or skin. Also check that the posts have been fitted with timber caps.

- Footings for walls must be the correct size; confirm their dimensions before they are poured and inspect them immediately afterwards. Walls should not have excess mortar squeezed out of the joints.

your builders are aware of these recommendations and use the appropriate construction.

When work starts

Old fencing will have to be broken up section by section and the posts removed, plus any concrete used to secure them. The old foundations of a wall may be suitable, but your builder should expose their full width and depth first to make sure they are large enough to support the new wall. If the new wall will be thicker or higher than what it is replacing, the old foundations will need strengthening or replacing.

New fence posts should be set in concrete for complete security; metal fence spikes can work loose and are, in any case, difficult to drive precisely vertically unless the ground is soft. They should have one-quarter of their length below ground. If panels are being used, they should be secured to the posts with C-shaped mounting brackets, and they should be clear of the ground at

How your house works

3

One of the most important things you can do before working with professionals is to learn how your house works. Your new knowledge may help you avoid potential problems during the planning stage – for example, you will understand why a load-bearing wall cannot simply be knocked down or why an electrician cannot add a new socket outlet to an already overcrowded circuit. It may also provide you with ideas for improving your home, or confirm your own ideas that you have already been considering.

There are many components to a house, from its gutters, downpipes and roof on the outside to its floors, plumbing and electricity inside.

3 Roofs

House roofs look relatively simple from the outside, but the shingles conceal complex framing that supports the roof's weight and the extra loads that wind or snow can impose on it.

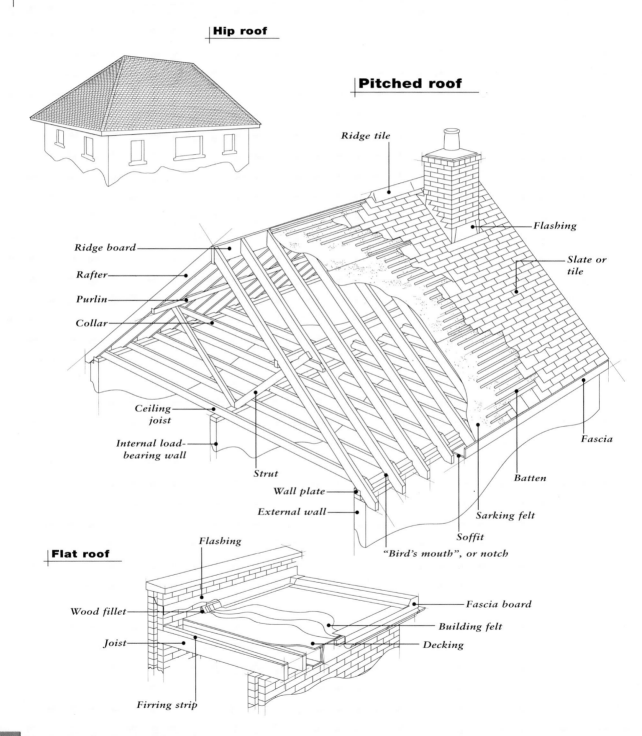

Hip roof

Pitched roof

Ridge tile

Flashing

Slate or tile

Ridge board

Rafter

Purlin

Collar

Fascia

Ceiling joist

Internal load-bearing wall

Strut

Batten

Wall plate

External wall

Sarking felt

Soffit

"Bird's mouth", or notch

Flat roof

Flashing

Wood fillet

Fascia board

Building felt

Joist

Decking

Firring strip

Water-tight covering

A well-constructed roof will last for decades as long as attention is paid to the condition of the individual components that keep it weather-proof – the tiles, slates, shingles or sheet materials that cover it, and the flashings (see pp. 146–147) that waterproof the junctions with chimney stacks and adjoining walls.

Traditional pitched roofs

In its simplest form a pitched roof consists of two roof slopes meeting at a central ridge. The sloping rafters, which support the roof covering, rest on timber wall plates at the eaves and are nailed to the ridge board. The ends of the building fill in the triangular sections beneath the roof slopes to form gable walls.

In relatively small houses the rafters may be linked at eaves level by horizontal ceiling joists to form a single or close-coupled roof. However, this type is impractical on larger houses because of the large size of timber needed to span the full width of the building.

The double or purlin roof is more common on houses. The rafters are

Trussed-rafter roof

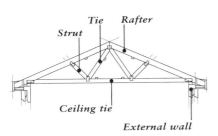

Strut
Tie *Rafter*
Ceiling tie
External wall

supported by horizontal members called purlins, which lie parallel to the ridge and eaves, roughly midway between the two. A central load-bearing wall inside the house provides a bearing for angled struts

to be fitted between the purlins and the wall, transferring the roof load down to that wall. Shorter, slimmer joists span the spaces between the external walls and the internal one.

A hipped roof has one or two sloping ends, which run down to the building's end walls, intersecting with the main roof slopes at an angle called a hip. If the house has a floor plan in an L or T shape, two or more roof slopes will intersect at right angles, with a sloping valley formed between the two.

Trussed rafter roofs

Traditional timber roofs were built on site by a team of carpenters, but today prefabricated timber roof trusses are installed. Quickly erected and covered, these span the width of a building without need for internal load-bearing walls. The main triangle of the truss is divided up into a series of smaller triangles, which give the frame great strength, despite the use of slim components.

Trusses for the main part of the roof structure are symmetrical A-shapes, and they are secured to wall plates on top of the external walls. Smaller trusses are added to form hips and are also used to create monopitch roofs on lean-to structures such as attached garages. There is no ridge board. Instead the trusses are kept in position by horizontal braces nailed to both the rafters and joists, and by diagonal braces fixed to the rafters' undersides. Overhanging roof edges at gable ends (verges) are created by fixing a prefabricated gable ladder to the truss next to the gable wall.

Eaves details

The rafters of both traditional and trussed-rafter roofs may project beyond the face of the external wall or may finish flush with it. In either case the cut rafter ends are covered with a vertical fascia board, and if the eaves project, a horizontal soffit

board bridges the gap between the wall and the fascia's lower edge. At gable walls, the verge tiles may be bedded directly onto the masonry. Alternatively, barge boards may finish off the roof edge, with soffits beneath them if the verge projects.

Tiles and slates

Both tiles and slates are fixed on horizontal battens, which are nailed across the rafters on top of a layer of sarking felt (this may be absent in older buildings with their original roofs). On high-quality older roofs there may also be a layer of soft-wood boards beneath the felt.

Slates overlap each other by about two-thirds of their length, and every slate is nailed to a batten. Tiles generally overlap by less, and have moulded nibs on the back, which hook over the battens. They are usually nailed at every fourth or fifth course.

Ridges and hips are finished with ridge tiles. These are bedded in mortar on traditional roofs but on modern ones they are often fitted dry with clips and sealing gaskets.

Flat roofs

Flat roofs are usually only used for extensions. Despite the name, they have a slight slope (about 1 in 60) running towards the eaves. The roof is supported on parallel horizontal joists spanning the width of the building and resting on a wall plate at each side. Tapered wooden firring strips are nailed to the tops of the joists. The roof decking – usually pretreated board, or planking on older houses – is nailed to the strips.

Domestic roofs are waterproofed with either hot-laid asphalt or a three-layer covering of roofing felt. The edges are finished with fascia boards. Junctions with walls are waterproofed with a flashing strip. Angle fillets at each side of the roof guide the water down the slope to the gutters.

3 | Gutters and downpipes

Rainwater running off roofs is collected in gutters that run along the eaves of the building. The water drains along them into a vertical downpipe, which carries it to ground level for discharge into the drainage system.

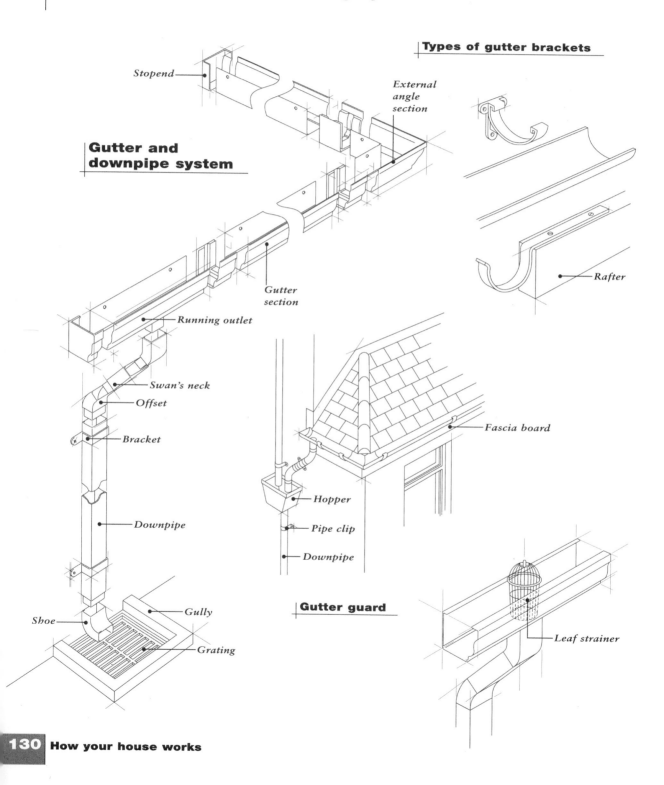

Stopend

Types of gutter brackets

External angle section

Gutter and downpipe system

Rafter

Gutter section

Running outlet

Swan's neck

Offset

Bracket

Fascia board

Downpipe

Hopper

Pipe clip

Downpipe

Gutter guard

Shoe

Gully

Grating

Leaf strainer

Cast iron components

Most older properties were built with gutters of cast iron or, sometimes, of asbestos cement or lead. Cast iron gutters are usually either half-round or ogee. The half-round type are supported by brackets, which are either screwed to the fascia board or to the top surface of the rafter ends. The ogee type has a moulded front and a flat back, and is generally screwed directly to the fascia. The gutter lengths, approximately 1.8 m (6 ft) long, has a socket at one end to take the plain end of the next length. The joints are sealed with putty and secured with a nut and bolt. Corners are turned with angle sections.

Unless they are well maintained, both types suffer from rust damage and eventual structural failure, especially along the back of ogee types, and have to be replaced.

Downpipes on older properties are almost always of cast iron, each having two shaped fixing lugs cast on the socket that forms the upper end of each length, which accepts the lower end of the length above. The joints between lengths are not sealed. Holes in these lugs allow the pipe sections to be fixed to the wall. Where there are overhanging eaves, angled connectors and a short section of pipe, called a swan's neck, link the gutter outlet to the top of the downpipe.

Plastic systems

The most widespread material used for gutters and downpipes today is PVC (polyvinyl chloride). It has many advantages over cast iron. Being light in weight it can be made in longer lengths, which requires fewer joints, and it can be supported on unobtrusive brackets. It is easy to cut to length and to install using connectors with integral flexible seals. Its smooth surface helps water flow through the system efficiently. Most important of all, it needs no painting and little maintenance, apart from the annual removal of any debris that has collected inside.

PVC gutters come in half-round, square and ogee patterns, and they are made in white, green, grey, black and brown to match the house's colour scheme. Separate mouldings form corners and downpipe outlets. The downpipes interlock, but they are fixed to the wall with separate brackets. They are also available in round and square cross-sections.

Aluminium gutters

On older properties aluminium is used mainly as a replacement for cast iron guttering. It is formed into cross-sections that match traditional cast iron shapes, but since it is much lighter it is easier to handle and install. It can be left unpainted or can be decorated on the outside.

Aluminium gutters can also be cold-formed by a special machine on site from flat strip. The resulting continuous runs avoid the need for joints except at corners and outlets. However, this system is little used in the house-building sector.

Sizing and siting

Gutters must be able to carry away all the rain running off the roof without overflowing, so the cross-sectional size and the number of downpipes must be matched to the roof area. In general it is better to have a downpipe in the centre of each run of gutter, rather than at the end, because this halves the volume of water each section has to carry. If this is not possible, the gutter should slope down from its mid-point, and there should be a downpipe at each end of the run.

There is another reason for keeping gutter runs short. There is an optimum gap between the edge of the roof slope and the lip of the gutter to ensure that water runs cleanly from one into the other without overflowing or trickling back between the two and down the house wall. Because each run of gutter must have a slope, this gap will be too great towards the lower end of a long run and water will spill out as a result.

For an average house, 100 mm (4 in) gutters and 65 mm (2½ in) downpipes are generally adequate. If your house has an unusually large roof area, fit the next available size.

Water discharge

Where rainwater disposal is via the drainage system (see pp. 154–155), downpipes discharge into a gully. This contains a trap to prevent drain smells rising up the downpipes. In older systems the downpipe discharged over a grating in the gully; if this became blocked, water would flow onto the surrounding surfaces. On newer homes the pipe discharges into the gully below the grating, avoiding the problem.

If disposal is via separate storm drains or a local soakaway, there is no need for a trapped gully. The pipe runs straight into the ground, turns through 90° below ground level, then runs underground to its destination. The only requirement in this situation is an access point (rodding eye) close to where the pipe enters the ground.

Routine checks !

- Remove leaves and debris from gutters, downpipes and leaf strainers in the autumn.

- Annually flush cast iron and aluminium gutters and downpipes with a hose to check for leaks. Have a leaking joint resealed or a length of gutter or downpipe that has rusted through replaced.

- Paint cast iron parts on a regular basis to prevent rust.

Warmth was once provided by the fireplace, but central heating systems have replaced this inefficient method of heating. However, the fireplace is still used as a cheerful way to supplement heat in a room – and modern styles are more efficient.

Masonry fireplace

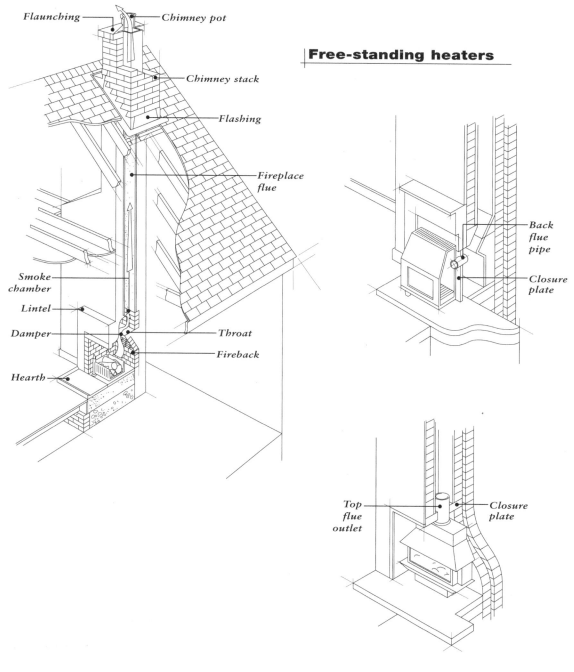

Flaunching — Chimney pot

Chimney stack

Flashing

Fireplace flue

Smoke chamber

Lintel

Damper

Throat

Fireback

Hearth

Free-standing heaters

Back flue pipe

Closure plate

Top flue outlet

Closure plate

Chimneys and flues

Many older homes had a fireplace in every room, a flue for every fireplace and often two or more chimney stacks as a result. By the 1970s, however, open fires and stoves had gone out of fashion as central heating systems became commonplace, and many houses built at that time had no fireplaces and chimneys at all. But by the end of the following decade, a fireplace in the main living room was back in fashion, and demand from house buyers meant that houses were once again being built with chimneys.

A typical masonry chimney is basically a tower of brickwork or blockwork, enclosing one or more flues. The flue rises vertically from the fireplace recess, then turns at an angle for a short distance before reverting to the vertical and rising through the roof to the top of the chimney, where a flue terminal (usually a terracotta chimney pot) discharges smoke to the atmosphere. The turn in the flue prevents rainwater from falling directly into the fireplace and also helps to improve the flue's draw – the efficiency with which smoke is drawn up the flue instead of being blown back into the room.

In a modern home built to meet current Building Regulations, the flue serving an open fireplace must have a minimum diameter of 200 mm (8 in) or a square section of about 180 x 180 mm (7 x 7 in). Smaller flues are allowed for closed appliances and room heaters. In older homes flues were not standardized, and a range of flue sizes will be found, depending on the size of the fireplaces being served.

Chimneys often contain several flues. For example, four flues in a square chimney built in the centre of the house will serve back-to-back fireplaces in adjoining ground-floor and first-floor rooms, while side-by-side flues in rectangular chimneys will be found on party walls between adjacent properties. Where the chimney is built within the house, the projecting masonry structure in a room is known as the chimney breast. Where the chimney is external, the fireplace recess indoors is flush with the face of the internal wall.

Modern chimneys are lined with interlocking clay or masonry lining blocks, with the joints pointed with fire cement and any gaps between the lining and the surrounding masonry filled with weak mortar or insulating concrete. Older chimneys are generally unlined, with the result that condensation can carry tar and soot through the brickwork to the face of the chimney breast. Flues suffering from this problem, or from failed pointing allowing smoke to escape from within the flue, can be cured by lining the flue. For open fires this is done by lowering a flexible liner down the flue and then pumping lightweight insulating concrete into the space between the liner and the flue. When this has set, the liner is withdrawn to leave a smoothly lined flue. For oil and gas-burning heating appliances and boilers, a flexible stainless steel liner is fitted instead and left in place to serve as the new flue.

At the top of the chimney the terminal (pot) fits over the top of the flue and is held in place by a bed of mortar called flaunching, which is sloped to shed rainwater. The masonry incorporates a damp-proof course close to the level at which it passes through the roof slope, and this may be linked to the lead flashings that waterproof the junction between chimney and roof slope.

The top of the stack should be a minimum of 1 m (3 ft) above the highest point of contact between chimney and roof. Where the stack is within 600 mm (24 in) of the roof ridge it should project above the ridge by at least 600 mm (24 in).

Fireplaces

At the base of the stack the flue opens out into the fireplace recess – a square or rectangular opening in which a free-standing heater fits or where an enclosed fireback is installed. Beneath the recess is a concrete slab, the constructional hearth. This rests on hardcore where the ground floors are solid, or it is supported on low brick fender walls where they are of suspended timber construction. In a modern house the hearth must project at least 500 mm (20 in) beyond the face of the fireplace recess, but in older buildings it may be smaller (or larger). The projection into a room is superimposed by a decorative hearth, often of tiles or natural stone laid on a mortar bed.

The masonry above the fireplace opening is usually supported on an iron bar in older properties, and on a precast concrete lintel in modern ones. If the recess has been built for use with an open fire, the shaped clay fireback stands on the back of the hearth, and the space between it and the back and sides of the fireplace recess will have been filled with a mix of lime, sand and broken brick or, in a modern house, with insulating concrete. A smooth throat is formed at the head of the fireplace opening to connect it to the flue above, with mortar in older properties and with preformed concrete units in modern ones.

Routine checks !

- Have the flue checked for tar build-up and the chimney inspected and cleaned annually.

- Ensure chimney pots are sound and flaunching and flashings are in good order.

- Check that a mortar throat in a fireplace is sound.

Fireplaces and chimneys 133

3 External walls

In older houses the external walls were built of solid brick. Newer homes have external walls consisting of two skins of brickwork, with a cavity between the two. Some new homes have adopted a timber-framed construction.

Cavity-wall construction

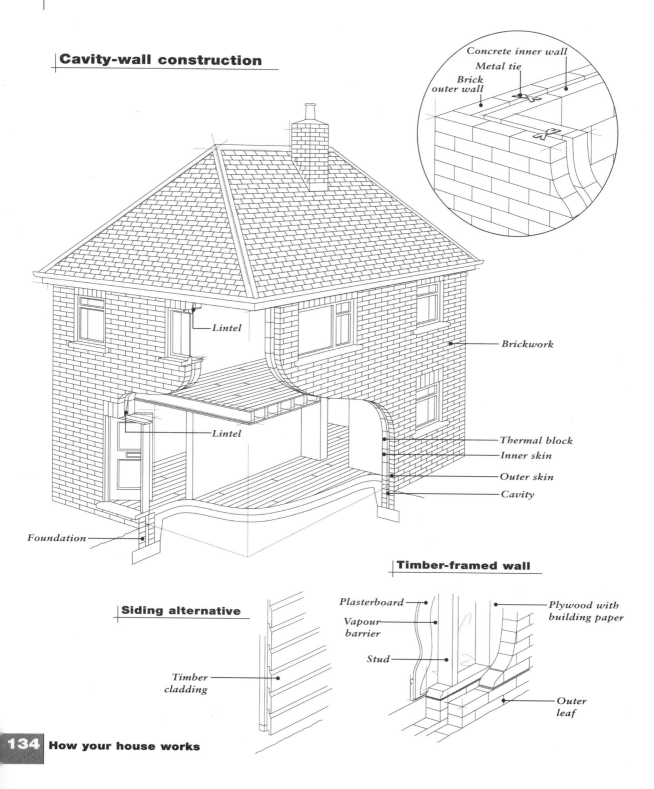

Concrete inner wall
Metal tie
Brick outer wall

Lintel

Brickwork

Lintel

Thermal block
Inner skin
Outer skin
Cavity

Foundation

Timber-framed wall

Plasterboard
Vapour barrier
Stud

Plywood with building paper

Outer leaf

Siding alternative

Timber cladding

Solid walls

Until around 1920, most houses were built with solid walls of brick, stone or a combination of the two (brick inside, stone facing outside). Two-storey buildings usually had walls 230 mm (9 in) thick – the length of a standard brick. Taller town houses had thicker walls up to first or second floor level. Where the brickwork is visible, you can identify this construction by the presence of headers (brick ends) alternating with stretchers (brick faces) in each course of brickwork, or by alternate complete courses of headers and stretchers. If the brickwork is concealed by rendering or other cladding, or the house is built of stone, you can measure the wall thickness at windows or doors.

Walls with cavities

Solid walls have always been at risk of damp penetration, especially in exposed locations. They are also relatively poor insulators. To help eliminate these problems, the cavity wall was developed late in the 19th century. It consisted of two skins, or leaves, of brickwork 102 mm (4 in) thick – the width of a brick – built with a gap in between.

The purpose of the cavity is to prevent any water penetrating the outer skin from reaching the inner one; instead it should run down the inner face of the outer skin to ground level, where weep holes will allow it to escape to the outside. The relatively still air in the cavity will also help to improve the wall's insulation performance.

Because high walls as thin as this are relatively unstable, metal links called wall ties were placed in the mortar bedding at regular intervals to span the cavity, effectively tying the two skins securely together.

Various cavity widths were tried out initially, but eventually the gap became standardized at 50 mm (2 in). This gives an overall wall thickness, including the interior plaster, of about 280 mm (11 in). Where insulation has been built into the wall, a wider cavity may be found.

More insulation

While the cavity wall helped eliminate damp penetration, it was still not a very good insulator. The next improvement was to use lightweight thermal blocks instead of bricks for the wall's inner skin, and high-performance types are still used today. Both skins may be of blockwork if the building is finished with rendering or other cladding.

By the 1970s, better insulation was being achieved by inserting insulating material in the cavity. In new homes, slabs of mineral fibre are placed in the cavity as the wall was built up. In existing buildings, various materials can be injected into the cavity through holes drilled from outside. These included urea-formaldehyde foam, special fibres and coated pellets of insulation.

Timber-framed walls

Timber-framed construction is an alternative to traditional masonry walls, developed from American and Scandinavian building methods, which began to be used from the 1960s. The most common form uses storey-height prefabricated timber wall panels to build up the internal skin of the wall. These are clad on the outside with plywood and a layer of waterproof building paper. The spaces between the vertical supports (studs) are filled with insulation material, and are covered on the inside with a polyethylene vapour barrier to stop moist air from within the house penetrating and condensing in the insulation. This is covered with plasterboard to form the internal wall surfaces.

The outside of the wall panels can be protected with cladding, tiling or, most commonly in this country, an outer leaf of brickwork.

The brickwork is tied to the wall panels with special wall ties, maintaining a narrow cavity.

The overall thickness of a timber-framed wall is roughly the same as for a traditional cavity wall. Tapping the inner surface of the outside walls will identify a timber-framed house. These will sound hollow because the wall panels are clad with plasterboard. This has obvious implications for making fixings, as only the frame members can carry any substantial load. In addition, care must be taken not to penetrate the vapour barrier.

External wall finishes

Fair-faced brickwork with mortar pointing is the most common external wall finish. Where this is not used, the external wall surface may be covered with smooth or textured mortar rendering, with pebbledashing (rendering with fine aggregate), with clay tiles hung on horizontal timber battens, or with timber or plastic cladding fixed to vertical battens. Pebbledashing and rendering are often painted for decorative effect, while cladding may be painted or stained.

Routine checks !

- Periodically, check the rendering for cracks or the brickwork for cracks or crumbling mortar in the joints. Also look for a loose or cracked brick or stone.

- Scrape off any fungal growth with a wire brush and apply a propriety fungicide to prevent it from recurring. Have the source of dampness that caused it, such as a leaking gutter, fixed.

- Every 3 to 5 years, reseal or restain timber cladding; or repaint it every 7 years.

3 Internal walls and ceilings

Traditionally, the solid walls inside a home are built of bricks or blockwork and coated with layers of plaster. Ceilings are also coated with plaster. Modern homes or upper stories may have timber-framed walls and ceilings covered with plasterboard.

Stick-built walls

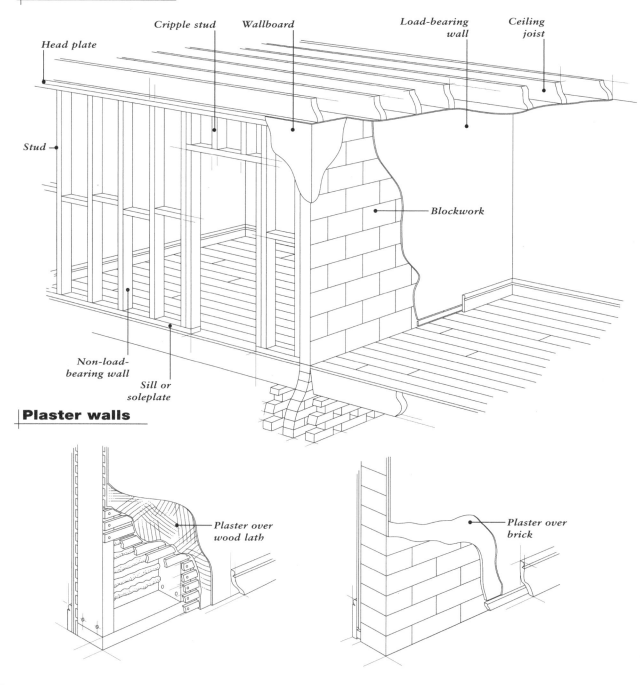

Head plate

Cripple stud

Wallboard

Load-bearing wall

Ceiling joist

Stud

Blockwork

Non-load-bearing wall

Sill or soleplate

Plaster walls

Plaster over wood lath

Plaster over brick

Older houses

Until the 1930s, most internal partition walls were built of brickwork one brick (102 mm/4 in) thick, with the surface covered with a three-coat lime plaster finish. The plaster was traditionally made with lime and hair and called course stuff. In some older houses, a framework of vertical timber battens was fixed to the wall surface, and a lath-and-plaster finish applied. Thin rough-sawn wood strips called laths were nailed across the battens and a thick two-coat plaster surface was applied over the laths. Where this system was employed, it was also used on the inner face of external walls. The void between plaster and masonry is a common place for dry rot to attack – it can thrive on the hidden woodwork and travel the entire height and width of the wall surface.

Where upstairs walls were not supported by those in the floor below, a lightweight timber-framed construction was used instead. This was again finished with a lath-and-plaster surface, with the laths nailed across the faces of the vertical frame members (studs). Apart from their location in the house dictating their construction, tapping the surface will reveal that a wall is hollow.

Lightweight blockwork

By the 1930s, lightweight blocks began to be used instead of bricks for internal walls, as well as for the inner skin of external cavity walls. These are the same thickness as a single brick, but test drilling will reveal the difference; blockwork produces grey drill dust, whereas brickwork produces red or yellow dust. The wall surfaces are finished with a two-coat plaster surface that is thinner than the traditional three-coat lime plaster system.

As in older houses, some upstairs walls will be solid where they are built directly over a partition in the floor below. Where they are not so supported, timber-framed walls will be found. These will still be finished with lath-and-plaster; its modern replacement, plasterboard, was not used for housing until the 1950s.

Modern homes

Modern traditionally built houses still have lightweight blockwork partition walls on the ground-floor. However, upstairs walls are now commonly timber-framed partitions, whether they are located over a ground-floor wall or not. This allows far greater flexibility in room layout. Blockwork walls will have a thin two-coat plaster finish, while timber-framed partitions will be clad in plasterboard and finished with a skim coat of plaster.

Timber-framed houses

Internal walls in houses built using the timber-framed system will often be timber-framed partitions. The inner leaf of the external walls will also be timber-framed, clad with plasterboard, behind which is a polyethylene vapour barrier and a layer of insulation. All wall surfaces will sound hollow when tapped.

Load-bearing walls

Apart from construction type, the other important factor you need to be aware of if you are planning alterations inside the house is the wall's purpose – in other words, whether it is load-bearing or not. A load-bearing wall supports part of the house structure – a wall in the storey above, for example, or the floor and ceiling joists spanning the rooms. This means that it cannot be removed, or have an opening made or enlarged in it, without steps being taken to carry the load it bears.

One way of identifying whether a wall is load-bearing or not is to examine which way the floor or ceiling joists run. If the joists are parallel to the wall (and therefore the floorboards run at right angles to it), the wall is not load-bearing and can be removed or altered. If joists are at right angles to the wall, alterations to it must satisfy the requirements of the Building Regulations (see pp. 16–17). Always get advice from a builder or surveyor as to what is involved.

Ceilings

The majority of houses have timber upstairs floors and a timber roof structure. This means that rooms are spanned by timber joists, which are set at 400 mm (16 in) centres in modern homes and at 300 to 450 mm (12 to 18 in) in older ones.

In houses built before the early 1950s, the ceilings will be finished with lath-and-plaster. This may have been replaced in some rooms with plasterboard if the property has been restored, since the plaster key can fail over time.

In modern homes the ceilings will be surfaced with plasterboard and finished with a thin skim coat of plaster, applied over taped joints to ensure that cracks do not open up across the ceiling. Ceilings beneath a loft space often have plasterboard backed by a plastic vapour barrier to prevent moist air from the house rising and causing condensation.

Routine checks !

- In the spring inspect walls and ceilings for dark stains, bulges, and peeling paint; if any exist, you should seek advice from a qualified builder.

- Periodically, look for cracks in the walls and ceilings.

- If you have a wallcovering, occasionally inspect its seams to see if they are lifting at the edges. If so, adhesive should be applied to reseal them.

The majority of 20th-century homes have wooden windows with hinged panes (casements), although plastic-covered steel frames are becoming more widespread. Plain steel-framed windows were in vogue from the 1930s to the early 1950s. Older properties generally have vertically sliding wooden box sash windows.

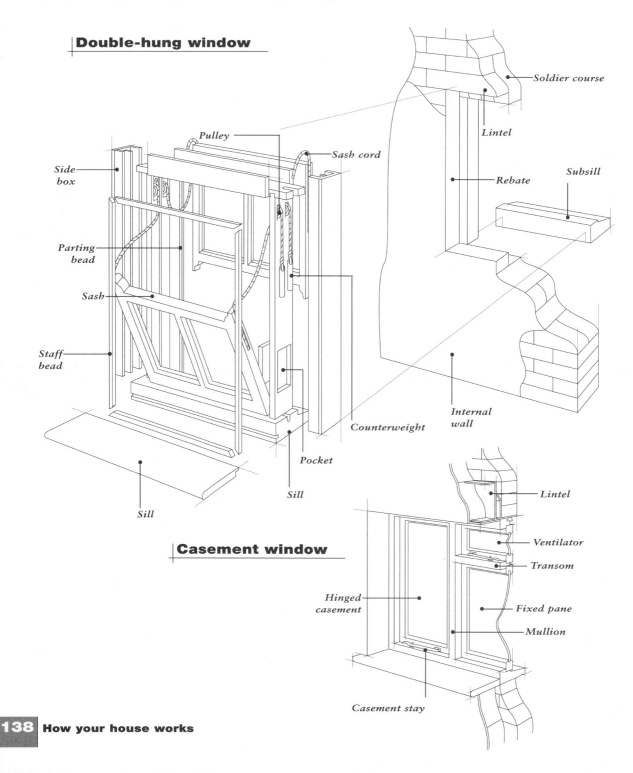

Double-hung window

Pulley

Sash cord

Side box

Parting bead

Sash

Staff bead

Counterweight

Pocket

Sill

Sill

Soldier course

Lintel

Rebate

Subsill

Internal wall

Casement window

Lintel

Ventilator

Transom

Hinged casement

Fixed pane

Mullion

Casement stay

Window openings

The opening in the external walls in which a window fits is bridged in one way or another to carry the load of the wall structure above it. In houses built before the First World War, this will usually be a brick or stone arch (or a one-piece stone lintel). Galvanized steel and reinforced concrete strip lintels came into use in the 1920s, and today steel and concrete lintels are virtually universal. They come in a range of lengths and are designed to carry the external brickwork over the opening, sometimes in the form of a soldier course of upright bricks. Some structures also carry lightweight blockwork above the opening on the inside, while others have an integral metal mesh inner face ready for plastering over.

In older houses built with solid walls, the window frame is usually set back within the opening by 100 mm (4 in) or more to give it better protection against the weather. The timber sill of the frame often rests on a stone or tiled subsill. The sides of the frame are nailed in place to timber plugs set in the surrounding masonry.

If the window is a sliding box sash type, the masonry will have been built with vertical rebates on the inside to accommodate the sash mechanism at each side of the frame. If the wall is of cavity construction, the opening in the inner skin will be slightly wider than in the outer one for the same reason, with the sides of the window frame completely closing the wall cavity at each side.

In houses built with cavity walls, the window frame is inset only slightly from the face of the outer skin so its timber sill projects beyond it. It is secured to the masonry by metal ties, which are attached to the sides of the frame and then built into the masonry as the wall rises. The open cavity is closed at each side with blockwork or, in recently built houses, with a plastic cavity closer; this is then plastered over.

Sash windows

The sashes in a traditional sliding sash window are raised and lowered using ropes called sash cords, which run over pulleys fixed at the top of the frame sides. The sash cords have counterweights attached, which fit within concealed compartments at each side of the frame. Once the frame has been installed, the only access to the weight compartments is through small openings called pockets near the bottom of each compartment. These enable the weights to be removed and put back when a worn sash cord breaks and needs replacing.

Modern timber sash windows, which are commonly used in replacement work, are much simpler in construction than the earlier design, using springs or spiral balances at each side of the frame to raise and lower the sashes. This means that the frame is far less bulky. These windows also often incorporate draughtproofing strips, which makes them much more effective in combating heat loss.

Casement windows

Casement windows consist of a head, a sill and two vertical side members (jambs). The outer frame may be subdivided by one or more vertical members called mullions to create openings that can contain a fixed pane of glass or a hinged opening casement. The casements are usually hinged at the side, but top-hung and centre-pivot types are also found. There may also be a single horizontal member called a transom, which subdivides the window opening so that a small top-hung ventilator can be fitted above the fixed pane or opening casement beneath it.

There are semi-circular drip grooves machined into the edges of the opening casements and ventilators to help prevent rainwater from being driven in around them. There is also a similar groove along the underside of the projecting sill. This encourages rainwater to run off instead of finding its way back to the wall beneath the sill, where it could cause penetrating damp.

Glass and glazing

Most older windows have a single thickness of glass, held in a rebate in the frame with a fillet of putty, which sets hard after it has been applied, or by a wooden strip known as a glazing bead, which is pinned into place over a thin bedding layer of putty.

Modern timber and plastic windows often have double-glazed units instead of plain glass. These retain heat better and also offer a degree of noise insulation. The units may be fixed in the same way as plain glass in wooden windows, but in plastic ones they are usually held in place by flexible sealing strips called gaskets. Double-glazed units need to be installed carefully as a breakdown of the edge seal leads to condensation between the panes.

Routine checks

- Have new sealant applied around windows, if necessary, in spring and autumn.

- Lubricate movable hardware, such as hinges and catches, in spring and autumn.

- Have any cracked window glass replaced and loose windows reputtied as needed.

- For wood window components, have peeling paint repainted before wet rot sets in.

3 Doors

Most houses have a number of doors – manufactured of solid wood, plywood, or a composite material – both for the front door (and any other external doors) and for internal doors to rooms.

Internal door

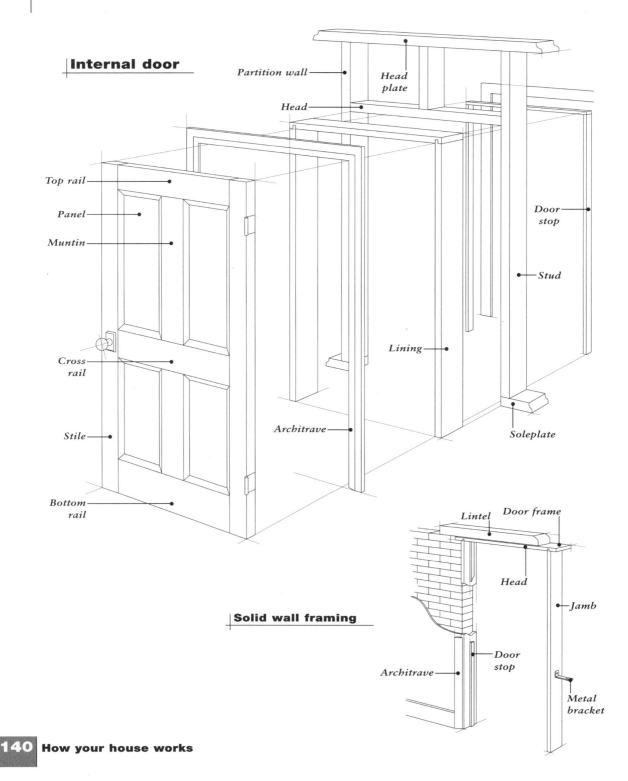

Partition wall
Head plate
Head
Top rail
Panel
Muntin
Door stop
Stud
Cross rail
Lining
Stile
Architrave
Soleplate
Bottom rail

Solid wall framing

Lintel
Door frame
Head
Jamb
Door stop
Architrave
Metal bracket

External door openings

Openings for external doors are bridged in the same ways as window openings – brick or stone arches in older homers, concrete or steel lintels in newer ones (see pp. 138–139).

External door

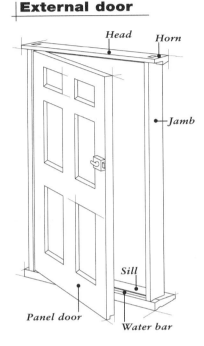

Head *Horn*

Jamb

Sill

Panel door

Water bar

The door frame that is set inside the opening consists of a head, two sides (called jambs) and a sill. The sill projects outwards beyond the face of the frame to throw off water running down the door, and a raised metal strip called a water bar is fixed across its width to stop rainwater from being blown in beneath the door in high winds. A rebate across the bottom edge of the door closes against this bar to form a watertight seal. The sides and head of the frame also have a rebate on the inside, into which the door closes.

As with windows, the door frame in older houses is generally nailed to wooden plugs let into the masonry at either side of the door opening. In more modern construction, metal ties are fixed to the outside of the

frame and are built into the brickwork as the walls rise. In addition, there will be a vertical dampproof course at each side of the door opening to prevent water penetration between frame and masonry. This is bedded into the cavity as it is closed during construction.

Internal door openings

Door openings in internal load-bearing walls are bridged by a timber beam in older houses and by a short concrete or steel lintel in more modern buildings. The door lining – a head and two jambs – is nailed or tied to the masonry at each side. Unlike an external door the lining is not rebated, allowing it to take a door hinged in either direction. Instead, slim lengths of wood called stop beads are nailed to the lining in the appropriate position when the door is being hung.

In a timber-framed partition wall, vertical studs are spaced to create the door opening, and a horizontal member called a nogging is nailed between them to form the head of the opening. Then a door lining like that used in a load-bearing wall is nailed in place, ready for the door.

The door lining projects beyond the face of the masonry or timber frame, creating an edge up to which the plaster or plasterboard cladding can run. This join is then concealed beside and above the door opening with a pinned-on cover strip known as an architrave.

External doors

To be secure external doors need strength, and the most common type is a panel door. It has a sturdy timber (usually hardwood) frame consisting of two side members called stiles linked by top and bottom rails. This is further subdivided by one or two intermediate cross rails and a central vertical member called a muntin. All these compon-

ents are assembled with mortise-and-tenon joints.

The spaces between the frame members are filled in with solid timber or plywood panels held in grooves machined into their edges. If the door includes glazed panels, these are generally set into rebates and secured on the inside with pinned-on glazing beads. The glass used should ideally be toughened or laminated for extra security, since ordinary glass could be easily broken by an intruder.

Flush doors are also used as external doors, especially for secondary doors at the side or rear of the property. These have a strong softwood frame and are clad on both faces with plywood. Glazed areas may be included in the design.

Internal doors

These doors do not have to be strong, so they can be lighter (and cheaper) than external doors; they are 35 mm ($1^3/8$ in) thick compared with 45 mm ($1^1/4$ in) for external doors. In certain situations, internal doors must offer fire resistance, in which case they are of heavier construction and 45 mm ($1^1/4$ in) thick.

Internal doors may be flush or panelled. Flush types have a lightweight timber frame clad on either side with plain plywood or hardboard for painting, or with a veneered plywood for staining and varnishing. The interior of the door is reinforced with a stiff cardboard honeycomb, and there are solid wood blocks fitted next to each side edge to allow door handles, latches and locks to be fitted.

Panelled doors may be made in the same way as external types, in softwood or hardwood, or may be a flush door with facings that have been machined out of medium-density fibreboard or other man-made sheet material. Where privacy is not important, some of the panels may have glass to let light through.

3 Floors

The most common type of floor in houses is the suspended timber floor, consisting of timber joists covered with floorboards or flooring-grade chipboard. Solid concrete ground floors are the norm in most houses built since the Second World War.

Joist supports

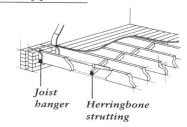

Joist hanger *Herringbone strutting*

Timber ground floor

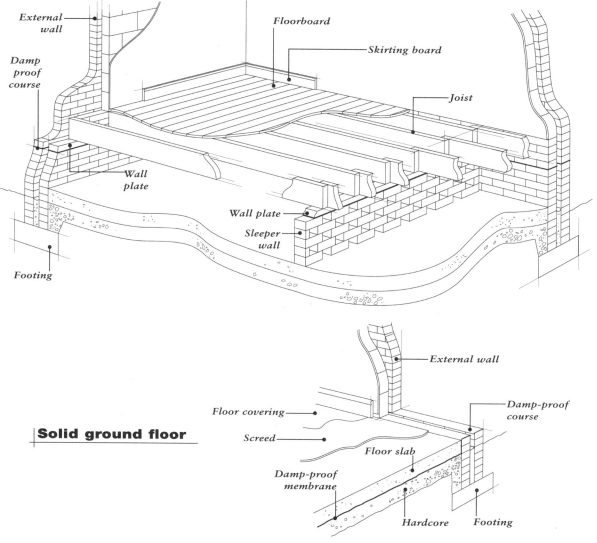

External wall

Floorboard

Skirting board

Damp proof course

Joist

Wall plate

Wall plate

Sleeper wall

Footing

External wall

Floor covering

Damp-proof course

Solid ground floor

Screed

Floor slab

Damp-proof membrane

Hardcore *Footing*

Timber ground floors

Suspended timber ground floors in older homes are supported on dwarf brick walls called sleeper walls, built up off the over-site concrete. These support the joists at each end and at intervals across the room, allowing shallower joists to be used than upstairs, where they have to span the room unsupported. The sleeper walls are of honeycomb construction to allow air to circulate through the underfloor void, and air bricks were inserted in the outside walls to encourage this air flow so that the timbers remain dry and free from rot. Each wall is topped by a horizontal timber wall plate, which rests on a strip of slates or other damp-proof material. Then the joists are nailed to the wall plates, ready for the floorboards to be nailed to them. Their ends are usually cut back so they do not touch the walls—another precaution to prevent damp from getting into the wood and encouraging rot. The floorboards usually have tongued-and-grooved edges to cut down draughts rising from the underfloor void, but many older homes have square-edged boards. You can tell which is which by trying to insert a knife blade between adjacent boards.

Where a suspended timber floor is found in a more recently built house, the joist ends will be supported in metal sockets called joist hangers, which are set into the walls. The floorboards will be tongued-and-grooved and generally narrower and thinner than those found in older houses.

Solid ground floors

As the name implies, solid ground floors are laid between the perimeter walls as a solid concrete slab. They were introduced initially because of post-war timber shortages, and they persevered because they are not affected by rot. The rough ground inside the building is covered with a layer of well-rammed hardcore, topped off with a "blinding" layer of sand or stone dust to prevent sharp stones piercing the damp-proof membrane that is laid next. This is a sheet of heavy-duty polyethylene, which is lapped up the perimeter walls and into the same mortar bed occupied by the wall's damp-proof course (see pp. 146–147). Then the concrete floor is poured, levelled to a thickness of between 100 mm (4 in) and 125 mm (5 in) and left to harden. Just before the building is completed, a mortar screed about 50 mm (2 in) thick is laid over the concrete to provide a dense and smooth finish suitable for carpeting or another floorcovering.

In a variation on the above method, which is used to speed up the drying-out process, the damp-proof membrane is sometimes laid between the concrete slab and the mortar screed. Since this prevents the screed from bonding to the slab, a thicker screed up to about 65 mm (2¹/₂ in) thick has to be laid to ensure that it does not crack. In both instances, a layer of high-density insulation is laid on top of the damp-proof course.

Suspended block floors

Some modern houses have suspended block ground floors rather than solid concrete ones. These are used where the subsoil may shrink and cause cracking, where the house is on a sloping site or where the soil is itself unstable and a lot of expensive excavation and backfilling would be needed.

The floor consists of parallel T-shaped concrete beams, which are supported by the external and internal load-bearing walls. Then insulating blocks are placed between them, resting on the projecting flanges at each side. Once the floor deck is complete, a moist mortar mix is brushed over the blocks to fill the gaps between them. A fine mortar screed is then laid over the surface as the building nears completion, as for a conventional concrete slab floor. So long as the void beneath this type of floor is well vented and the ground is well drained, there is no need for a damp-proof membrane.

Upper floors

Other floors in the house are invariably constructed by spanning each room with timber joists and nailing floorboards or chipboard sheets to them. The joist ends are built into the masonry in older houses, while metal joist hangers will be found in more modern ones.

Because these joists have to span relatively long distances, they are often up to 230 mm (5 in) deep. Such wide beams can warp, and to prevent this happening solid or herringbone wooden strutting is sometimes fitted between the joists to stiffen the structure.

Openings are needed in the floor structure around the stairwell. Thick trimming joists flank two sides of the opening, parallel with the other joists in the floor. Short trimmer joists are then fitted at right angles between the trimming joists to form a square or rectangular opening.

Routine checks !

- Periodically, check wooden floors for loose or split floorboards and for wear.

- If windows or doors stick, check the floor for sagging; if there is a sag, you should call in a builder or surveyor to inspect it.

- Periodically, inspect floor tiles and vinyl flooring for cracks and other damage.

One of the most complex components in a house is the staircase. It provides access between floors and consists of two main parts – the stairs themselves and handrails or balustrades to guard against users falling while climbing or descending them.

L-shaped staircase

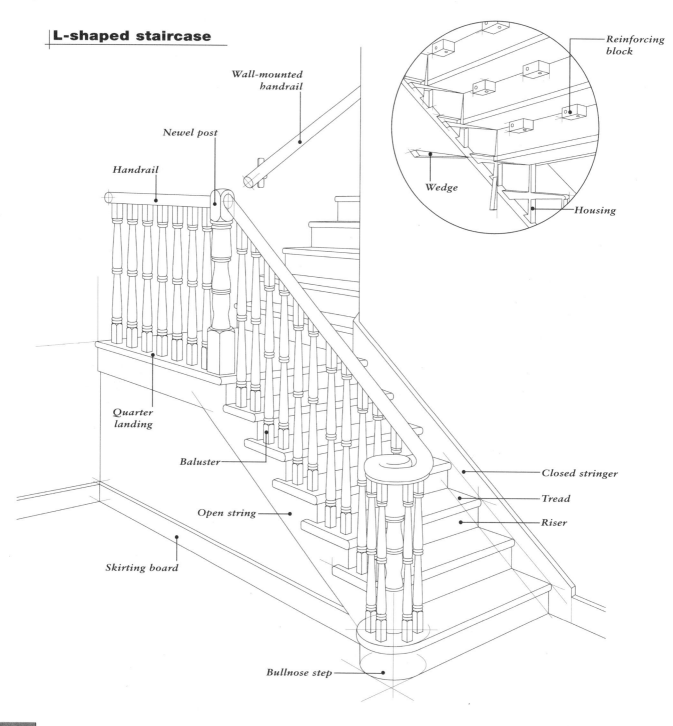

Reinforcing block

Wall-mounted handrail

Newel post

Handrail

Wedge

Housing

Quarter landing

Baluster

Open string

Skirting board

Closed stringer

Tread

Riser

Bullnose step

Staircase configuration

The basic ingredients of a staircase are horizontal treads, vertical risers and side members called strings, which support the ends of the treads and risers. The simplest staircase is a straight flight that rises directly from one floor to the next.

Other staircase arrangements where the flight changes direction as it rises are common, because they make more economical use of the floor space available. The flight may turn a 90 degree angle, reaching a square quarter landing the same width as the flight. Or it may turn 180 degrees, using a half landing twice as wide as the flight; this is known as a dog-leg staircase. A dog-leg staircase with a wider half-landing and clear space between the two flights is known as an open-well staircase. The staircase may also turn through the use of a number of triangular steps called winders, or there may be a continuous spiral with wedge-shaped steps, which requires the least amount of space.

Staircase construction

Where one or both strings are fixed to side walls, the treads and risers fit into slots (housings) cut into their inner faces, and are retained in their slots by long thin wooden wedges. This is a closed string. Where the staircase abuts just one wall, the inner string will be closed while the outer string may be closed or open. In the latter case, the top edge of the string is cut into steps on which the treads rest.

On a traditionally built staircase, the back of each tread will fit in a slot cut across the face of the riser above it, while the top edge of the riser below will engage in a slot cut across the underside of the tread. On a modern prefabricated staircase, these joints are often simply glued and nailed together. Triang-ular reinforcing blocks may be added underneath the staircase, fitting in the right angle between tread and riser. Some wide staircases have a stout timber support called a carriage fitted beneath the treads midway between the two strings.

A staircase built against one wall has a balustrade along the open side. This runs between stout vertical timbers called newel posts, which are bolted to the floor joists at the top and bottom of the flight. Extra newel posts are also fitted wherever the flight changes direction. The handrail is then fixed between the newel posts, and the space between the handrail and the outer string is filled in with a series of closely spaced balusters or other open or solid infilling. Where the staircase is fitted between two walls, a simple wall-mounted handrail will be installed at one or both sides. It may be screwed directly to the wall, or it may be fixed with brackets at regular intervals.

The top ends of the balusters may simply be skew-nailed to the underside of the handrail, or they may fit in a groove and be separated by pinned-on spacers. On a closed string, a grooved capping piece is usually fixed to the top edge of the string and the ends of the balusters fit into this, again separated by spacers. On an open string, their ends are set in notches cut in the treads and are retained by a cover moulding pinned to the outer end of the tread.

A common design feature found on many staircases is a projecting bottom step, with one or both sides having a rounded shape. This is known as a bullnose step.

The underside of the staircase may be exposed, especially if the space beneath it is enclosed by an understairs cupboard. This will allow easy access to the staircase structure if repairs are necessary – for example, to cure creaking caused by movement between treads and risers, or to replace a damaged tread. In other situations the underside of the flight may be panelled in, with lath-and-plaster in older houses and with plasterboard in newer ones. The panel will generally have to be removed if any repairs are needed.

Open staircases

A variation on the standard enclosed staircase is the open variety. Here the risers are omitted and the treads are either fitted between two strings in the usual way, or they are supported on carriages so that the treads project at one or both sides.

Altering staircases

Unless a staircase has suffered physical damage or has been affected by rot or woodworm, it will generally last the life of the building. However, replacing the balustrade is a popular way of changing the look of the staircase, and kits of parts are widely available.

Routine checks

- Squeaks occur when wood rubs against wood. They can be cured by fixing reinforcing blocks to the underside of the step if the squeaks are at the top of a riser and front of the step, or by inserting shims between riser and tread if they come from the rear of the tread.

- Look for loose balusters. These can be tightened by inserting a wood shim at the loose end or by skew-nailing a baluster to its support. A damaged baluster may need to be replaced.

- If the front of a tread becomes worn, the worn section or the whole tread may need replacing.

An essential part of any house is its ability to prevent water from getting into the structure. Moisture creates unhealthy living conditions, spoils decorations and furnishings, and encourages the spread of rot – a potentially serious problem.

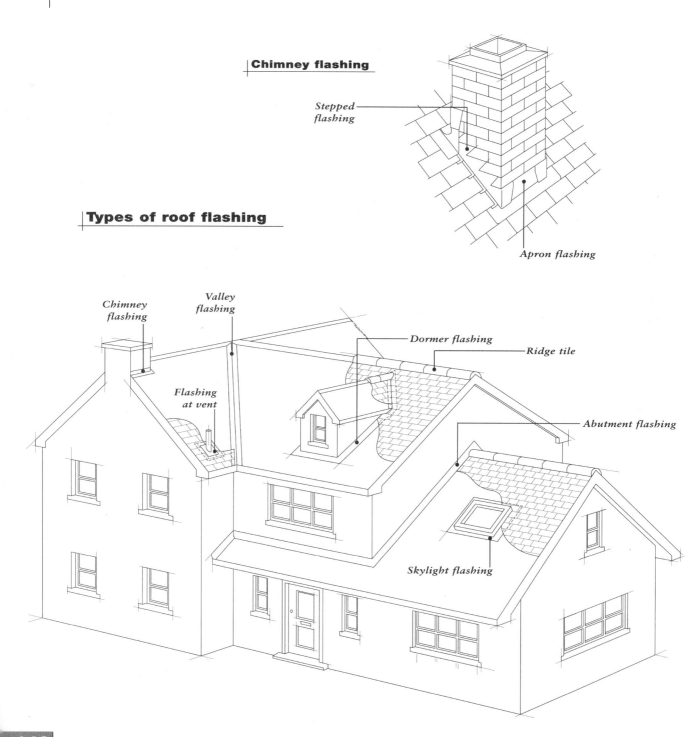

Chimney flashing

Stepped flashing

Apron flashing

Types of roof flashing

Chimney flashing

Valley flashing

Flashing at vent

Dormer flashing

Ridge tile

Abutment flashing

Skylight flashing

Damp-proof courses

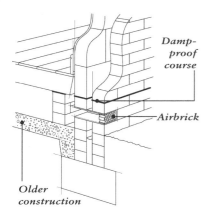

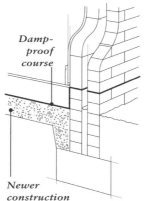

Damp-proof course

Damp-proof course

Airbrick

Older construction

Newer construction

Damp from above

The roof is the building's first line of defence against damp. Half-round or angled tiles prevent rainwater from penetrating the structure where two roof slopes meet at ridges and hips. Valleys, the internal angles between roof slopes, may be formed with specially shaped tiles, but are more commonly made waterproof by a gutter formed from lead or zinc sheet, which extends beneath the tiles at either side of the valley and runs from the roof ridge down to the eaves, where the collected rainwater is discharged into the gutters.

Chimney stacks

Where a chimney stack passes through the roof, the junction between the two is waterproofed with specially shaped one-piece sections of lead sheet called flashings. Their top edges are tucked into the mortar joints in the faces of the chimney stack, creating a stepped outline on the faces of the stack parallel to the roof slope. On the up-slope face of the stack, the flashing is tucked beneath the row of tiles or slates above it. On the other faces it lies over the tiles.

On roofs covered with flat clay tiles or slates, high winds can lift the edges of the side flashings, so another waterproofing method is used. Indivi-dual smaller pieces of lead sheet called soakers are fitted. Their top edges are tucked into the mortar joints on the stack, and their bottom edges fit beneath the roof covering. Each one overlaps the one below it to create a waterproof seal.

Windows and doors

The openings in the external walls into which window and door frames fit are a place where rainwater can penetrate. Older houses relied on little more than a good fit and some mortar infilling to keep water out, but in modern construction damp-proof courses (dpcs) are used. A vertical damp-proof course is fixed to each outer side of the frame and is sandwiched between the two skins of the cavity walls as the cavity is closed to form the door or window reveal; and a horizontal damp-proof course is fitted beneath the sill to channel water that is driven into the joint to the outer face of the wall.

Damp from below

A house also needs protection against damp rising into the structure from the ground on which it stands. Masonry walls and solid floors absorb ground water – this is known as rising damp – unless a physical barrier is incorporated to prevent it.

In older homes, the walls have a damp-proof course consisting of a strip of slates inserted between the horizontal courses of brickwork just below the internal floor level. In modern construction, a continuous strip of plastic replaces the slates. Both can be seen from outside the house unless the walls have been covered with rendering or cladding.

Houses built before the late 19th century had no damp-proof course, and they suffered from rising damp. A damp-proof course can be created by injecting the masonry with waterproofing chemicals to form a damp-proof band around the house.

Damp-proofing floors

Solid concrete floors laid directly over the ground within the building will suffer from rising damp unless a damp-proof barrier is incorporated in their structure. Until the 1930s few houses incorporated such a barrier. It then became common to cover the concrete slab with a layer of bitumen before the final floor screed was laid, and since the 1960s polyethylene sheeting has been used instead. This can be placed on top of the over-site hardcore (topped with a layer of sand to prevent sharp stones from piercing it) or sandwiched between the slab and the screed. In either case, its edges are lapped up the perimeter walls to the level of the damp-proof course and are then held in place between the courses of brickwork. This membrane and the damp-proof courses in the walls act together to prevent the incidence of rising damp and keep the structure dry and sound.

Solid walls that have suffered from rising damp can contaminate internal plaster with hydroscopic salts. These absorbs water vapour from the air and keep the wall damp even after rising damp has been cured. For this reason, specialists always remove and replace the plaster when treating rising damp.

3 Insulation

A vital part of your house is insulation. It keeps the building warm in winter, reducing heating costs, and cool in summer. It stops heat losses from hot water pipes and storage cylinders as well as central heating ducts, and it protects cold water pipes.

Insulation around a house

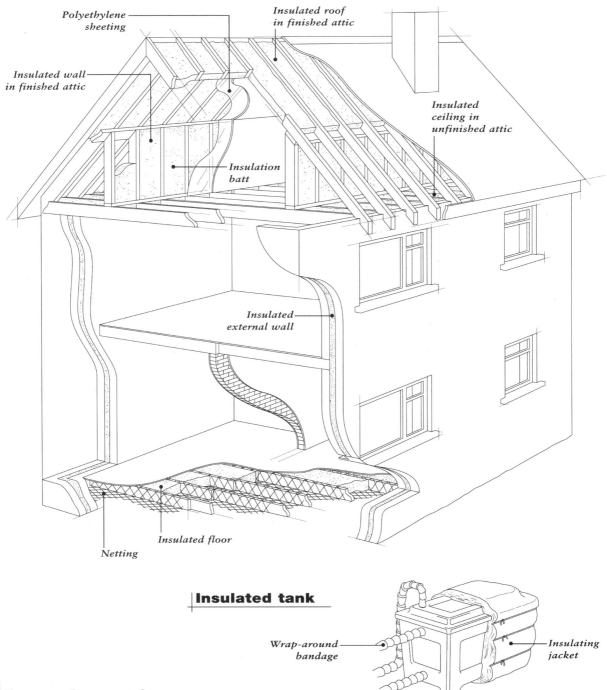

Polyethylene sheeting

Insulated roof in finished attic

Insulated wall in finished attic

Insulated ceiling in unfinished attic

Insulation batt

Insulated external wall

Insulated floor

Netting

Insulated tank

Wrap-around bandage

Insulating jacket

Roof insulation

Before the 1950s, houses had no insulation, and the first area to be addressed was the roof. Placing insulating materials between the ceiling joists in the loft greatly reduced heat losses. Mineral wool and glass fibre were generally laid as continuous strips, although mineral wool has also been used as a loose mat of fibres pressed between the joists. Polystyrene pellets, which are easily blown about in draughty lofts, are seldom used today.

All work by trapping a layer of air and stopping air from below from rising through the insulating layer. This makes the loft space much colder than before, which may result in the rising moist air condensing in the insulation, making it wet and therefore useless. Condensation can also make the roof timbers damp in a poorly ventilated loft, encouraging rot to thrive. Ceilings in new houses now incorporate a vapour barrier. In older houses, heavy-duty polyethylene sheeting can be placed beneath the insulation to serve the same purpose if condensation is a problem.

If the loft is converted to living space (see pp. 84–87), the underside of the roof slope is insulated. Semi-rigid slabs of insulation (called batts) or sheets of expanded polystyrene board are fitted between the rafters, with a gap between them and the underside of the roof slope to allow air to circulate, and are then concealed with plasterboard.

Flat roofs

Older flat roofs seldom contain any insulation and can lose heat at a high rate as a result. They can be insulated from below by putting up a new ceiling surface of insulating plasterboard – a sandwich construction of plasterboard backed by a vapour barrier and a thick layer of expanded plastic foam insulation. Alternatively, they can be insulated from above by laying a new roof decking on top of the existing one and sandwiching rigid polystyrene insulation boards between the two.

External walls

Solid walls are notoriously poor insulators, because there is nothing to stop heat from passing through them to the outside. They can only be insulated by fixing layers of insulation to their inner faces and covering them with plasterboard.

Cavity walls perform better, because the gap contains relatively still air, which acts as an insulator. The need to reduce heat losses further led to the introduction of cavity wall insulation in the mid-1960s, for both new and existing houses. The insulation was either injected into the cavity in the form of expanding foam, or insulating fibres or pellets were blown in.

Today, newly built cavity walls usually incorporate slabs of mineral wool or glass fibre insulation that are set in place on the wall ties as the walls are built up. They may fill the cavity completely, or they may be held against the outer face of the inner skin with special clips so there is a cavity between them and the outer leaf. This allows any water penetrating the outer skin to run down its inner face to ground level without saturating the insulation.

Floor insulation

Few homes built before the 1980s have any floor insulation. Recently built homes will have a layer of expanded polystyrene sandwiched between the floor slab and the final mortar screed. Older homes with suspended timber floors may have had insulation added between the joists at some time in the past, either as rigid polystyrene strips or as insulation blanket suspended in netting draped over the joists.

Pipe and tank insulation

If your house has a conventional plumbing and central heating system with cold water tanks in the loft space, these will be fitted with insulating jackets to prevent them freezing in cold weather, especially if the loft floor is insulated. Similarly, any pipe runs in the loft space will be insulated, with slip-on foam plastic sleeving or wrap-around fibre pipe bandage.

The hot water storage cylinder will either be fitted with a slip-on insulating jacket or will have a factory-applied foam outer coating. Both are essential to prevent rapid heat loss from the stored water.

Plumbing and heating pipes beneath a suspended timber ground floor should also be insulated against heat loss and freezing.

Ways to insulate an attic

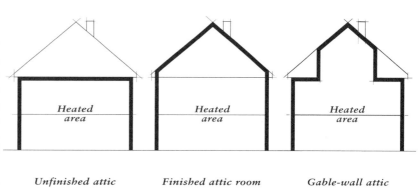

Unfinished attic   *Finished attic room*   *Gable-wall attic*

3 | Ventilation

Good ventilation ensures fresh air in the house and removes odours. It prevents condensation by allowing moist air to escape. It is vital for the safe operation of fuel-burning appliances; without it, dangerous levels of carbon monoxide can build up.

Types of roof ventilation

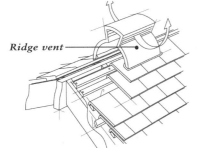

Ridge vent

Special tiles with built-in vents run along the ridge of a roof. They are used in conjunction with soffit vents.

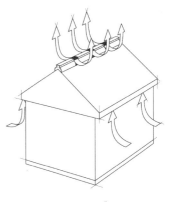

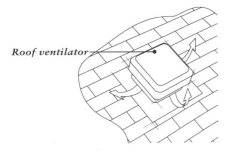

Roof ventilator

Mechanical roof ventilators work in conjunction with soffit vents.

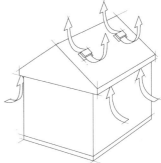

Types of soffit vents

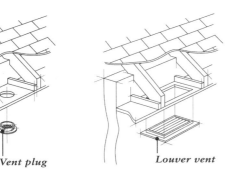

Soffit vents must be used with other vents to promote air circulation.

Ground floor ventilation

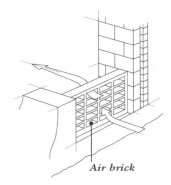

Timber floors need ventilation below.

Ventilating the structure

Two areas of the house need good ventilation to ensure that they do not suffer from condensation or damp, which could encourage rot to attack structural timbers. The first is the loft, once a fairly draughty place before under-tile felting and loft insulation became common. Insulation used to be packed into the eaves, but this reduced ventilation and allowed condensation to form on the joists and rafters. Today, eaves ventilation must be provided, usually in the form of vents or a continuous opening beneath the eaves around the house. In addition, the insulation must be kept clear of the eaves. Extra ventilation is also provided in new houses by means of special ridge tiles with vents.

The void beneath a suspended timber ground floor also requires ventilation. This is provided by air bricks built into the external walls below floor level and by openings in the dwarf brick walls that support the floor joists. In cavity walls, sleeves are installed to span the cavity and ensure that the air flow reaches the void. If these air bricks become blocked or there are not enough of them on opposite walls of the house, damp will lead to an outbreak of rot in the timbers.

Window ventilation

Most houses built before the 1960s were draughty structures. Open flues in most rooms provided natural ventilation, doors and windows were not a tight fit in their frames and gaps in suspended timber ground floors allowed continuous movement of air into and out of the house. Extra room ventilation was provided when it was needed by opening a window.

However, modern homes have doors and windows that are more effectively draughtproofed, their solid ground floors admit no draughts and many have no fireplaces and flues – they need additional ventilation. This is provided by so-called trickle ventilators, which are found along the top edge of window frames. These allow a small but continuous air flow into and out of the room, and they are required in all new homes.

Powered ventilation

In kitchens and bathrooms, activities such as cooking, washing-up and bathing create large amounts of water vapour. This can cause condensation unless it is removed from the room quickly. Smells also need dispersing if they are not to become stale and unpleasant. Opening a window is not enough to do the job, so what is needed is mechanical ventilation. This is essential in windowless bathrooms and toilets.

Extra ventilation is provided by an electric extractor fan that sucks air from the room and expels it outside. A wall-mounted fan can be fitted in an opening in window glass or in a hole cut through an external wall. A ceiling fan is connected to ducting, which discharges air via a grille in a wall or in the soffit board beneath the eaves, or through a vent in a wall. Lastly, a cooker hood is sited over the hob to extract steam and cooking smells via ducting if it is not sited on an external wall.

Fans come in various sizes, and it is important to match the extract rate to the room. Building Regulations require new houses to have a kitchen fan that can extract 216 cu m per hour of air, and a bathroom fan to extract 54 cu m per hour. Follow these requirements when fitting fans to ventilate existing rooms.

Heating appliances

Fires, other fuel-burning room or water heaters and central heating boilers need a good supply of air to burn efficiently. A fire or heater in a fireplace draws air from the room in which it is sited, and if this room is well draughtproofed, air bricks or underfloor vents may be required to give an air supply. The same applies to boilers and gas-fired water heaters. The exception is an appliance fitted with a balanced flue such as a boiler. This two-part flue draws in the air it needs through one part of the flue and expels combustion gases through the other.

Mechanical bathroom ventilation

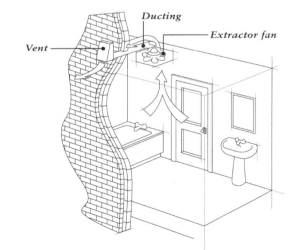

Mechanical ventilation in a bathroom helps prevent condensation.

A home's water supply may come from a mains water supply or from a private well. A mains water supply is the most common. The water is delivered around the house through a series of pipes – one for hot water and one for cold water.

Indirect water supply system

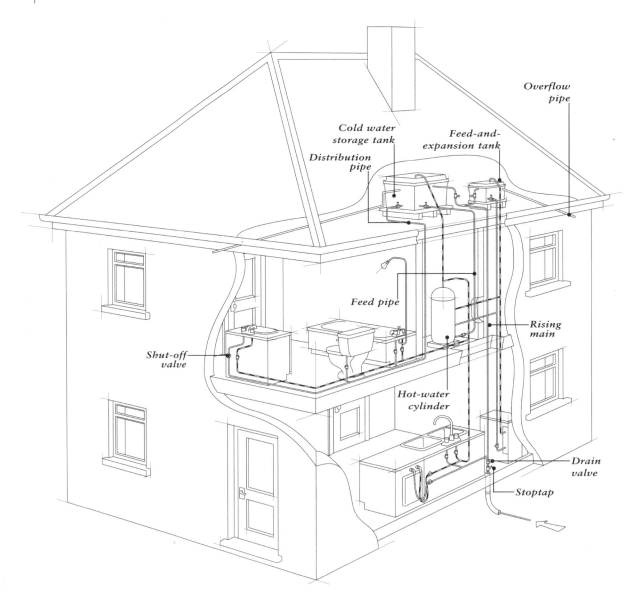

Overflow pipe

Cold water storage tank

Feed-and-expansion tank

Distribution pipe

Feed pipe

Rising main

Shut-off valve

Hot-water cylinder

Drain valve

Stoptap

Key

Hot-water pipe

Cold-water pipe

Cold water supply

A house's water supply pipe runs underground from the water main buried in the street. Old houses have lead piping, more recent ones copper and new properties blue polyethylene for the supply pipe.

There is a stoptap close to the property boundary, beneath a small cast-iron cover, to turn off the supply to the property; it needs checking regularly to ensure that it does not jam. If it does not have a handle, it may need a key to operate it. A stoptap fitted to the supply pipe as it enters the house allows the plumbing system to be isolated from the mains supply. A drain valve next to it allows the pipework beyond it to be emptied of water for repairs.

If the house has an indirect water system based on stored water, the supply pipe (known as the rising main) runs up through the house to a cold-water storage tank in the loft space or other high spot. This tank will be of galvanized iron in an old property and of plastic in a new or modernized one. A branch off the rising main feeds the kitchen cold tap, providing pure mains-pressure water for cooking and drinking. Other branches may serve a washing machine, dishwasher, outside tap, shower or water heater.

There are two feed pipes running from the base of the tank. One supplies the rest of the cold taps and the toilet cisterns, the other the hot water system. Extra pipes may supply a shower or a rising-spray bidet. Each supply pipe should be fitted with a shut-off valve called a gate-valve, allowing it to be isolated and drained for maintenance. On a newer system, in-line isolating valves are fitted on supply pipes to individual taps and water-using appliances.

Direct water systems have no cold-water storage tank, and mains-pressure water is taken directly from the rising main to supply cold taps and the hot water system.

Hot water supply

The most common hot water supply system provides hot water from a copper storage cylinder. Fed with cold water from the high-level storage tank, this cylinder may be heated by an electric immersion heater or a central heating boiler.

In older properties the cylinder may be the direct type, with water circulated from it to the boiler. The drawback with this is that fresh cold water is continuously drawn from the storage tank to replace hot water, which in hard water areas leads to a build-up of scale inside the cylinder and circuit pipework. Most houses have an indirect cylinder with an internal copper heating coil, via which heated water from the boiler is circulated by a pump. This coil heats the water without mixing with it, reducing the scale problem.

At the point where the hot water draw-off pipe emerges from the top of the cylinder, a branch pipe runs up into the loft to discharge over the storage tank. This acts as a safety valve if the cylinder overheats.

A small cold water tank near the main storage tank and known as the feed-and-expansion (or header) tank, is supplied from the rising main and connected to the pipework linking the boiler and hot water cylinder. This tank tops up any water lost from the circuit and another vent pipe runs from the circuit pipework to discharge over this tank, providing a safety valve if a fault leads to overheating in the primary circuit.

Other systems

Some houses and have an unvented hot water storage system, with a cylinder and boiler but no cold water tank. It supplies hot and cold water at mains pressure and has an expansion vessel to cater for expansion within the system. Various devices guard against overheating.

Another system employs a gas-powered multipoint heater that feeds all the hot taps with water heated on demand. Larger versions called combination boilers also run the central heating system. They eliminate the need for stored water.

Cold-water storage tank

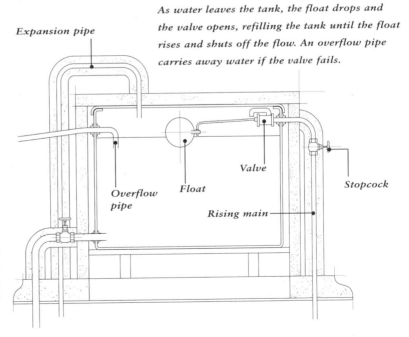

As water leaves the tank, the float drops and the valve opens, refilling the tank until the float rises and shuts off the flow. An overflow pipe carries away water if the valve fails.

Expansion pipe

Overflow pipe

Float

Valve

Stopcock

Rising main

The waste water generated within the house by bathing, flushing toilets, washing clothes and preparing food is disposed of by a drainage system, which carries used water out of the house for disposal.

Two-pipe system

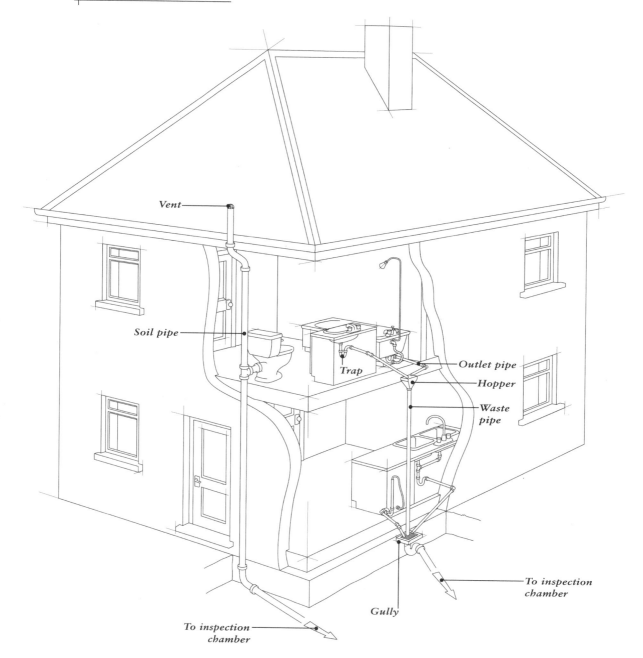

Vent

Soil pipe

Trap

Outlet pipe

Hopper

Waste pipe

To inspection chamber

Gully

To inspection chamber

Leaving the house

The soil and waste pipes, as well as any downpipes from the roof drainage system (see pp.130–131), deliver waste water through inspection chambers to the main sewer.

Inspection chamber

Interceptor chamber

Sewer

Two-pipe systems

In older and unmodernized homes you will usually find a two-pipe system, with most of the pipework on the outside walls. Waste water from water-using appliances and soil water from toilets run to the underground drains separately. At ground level, waste pipes from sinks and other appliances discharge into open gullies, which are connected to the main drains by underground pipes. Appliances on upper floors have waste pipes that run into open hoppers mounted on the outside walls, from which pipes run down to a ground-level gully. Another branch pipe links this to the main drain. Soil water from toilets flows into a large-diameter soil pipe that runs down the house wall and directly into the main drain. This pipe extends upwards to roof level to ensure that drain smells cannot enter the house. The soil pipe, hoppers and downpipes are usually of cast iron, and waste pipes of lead.

Single-stack systems

Modern homes have a so-called single-stack system. Here, a single large-diameter plastic pipe carries both waste and soil water down to the drains. Waste pipes from upstairs appliances and soil pipes from upstairs toilets are connected directly to the stack, as are pipes from downstairs appliances and toilets if these are reasonably close to it. Otherwise waste pipes run to a ground-level gully and toilets have secondary sealed soil pipes running directly to the drains. Waste pipes running to gullies discharge below the gully grating instead of above it as in old two-pipe systems, removing the risk of overflows if the grating becomes blocked with leaves.

All the pipework in a single-stack system is of PVC, and in houses built since the 1960s the stack is concealed within the building, so avoiding an unsightly rash of pipes on the house walls. Most single-stack systems have an open end at roof level, but on modern systems the stack is capped inside the building by a pressure-relief valve, so avoiding the need for a projecting vent pipe at high level.

Trapping drain smells

To prevent drain smells from entering the house through waste and soil pipes, every appliance has a U-shaped pipe called a trap fitted in its outlet pipe. Whenever the appliance is emptied, the last of the water remains in the trap, so sealing the appliance off from the drains.

Toilets (and gullies) are made with an integral trap; other appliances have a trap fitted immediately below the outlet, to which the waste pipe is then connected.

In old houses with lead waste pipes, appliance traps have a small screw-in plug at the base of the U-bend to allow access for clearing blockages. Modern waste systems run with plastic pipes have traps that can be unscrewed by hand and dismantled easily for maintenance.

The drain runs

In older homes, underground drain runs are clay pipes. The pipes from the soil stack and waste-water gullies run to a rectangular brick inspection chamber (commonly called a manhole) fitted with a metal cover. The soil pipe runs in at one end, discharging into an open half-round channel set in mortar in the base of the chamber. The other pipes from gullies are connected to the central channel as open branches, again set in the mortar. At its downstream end, the chamber discharges into an outlet pipe, running on towards the main sewer.

Other chambers are installed where the drain run changes direction, or where other branch pipes run into it. The final chamber before the main sewer is called an interceptor chamber. This has a clay trap on its outlet side to prevent sewer smells (and rats) from entering the house drains. Above this is a rodding eye with a plug that can be removed to allow drain rods to clear a blockage between the chamber and sewer if one occurs. The chamber itself is vented with a cast-iron pipe that projects above ground level close by – a sure sign that it is an interceptor type.

Modern houses have drain runs assembled from plastic components, with one-piece moulded gullies and moulded inspection chambers fitted with a round metal cover.

The electrical system is the lifeblood of the modern house, and although it is mostly concealed from view within the house structure, it is useful to understand it so that improvements and alterations can be planned sensibly and faults can be traced easily.

Household electricity system

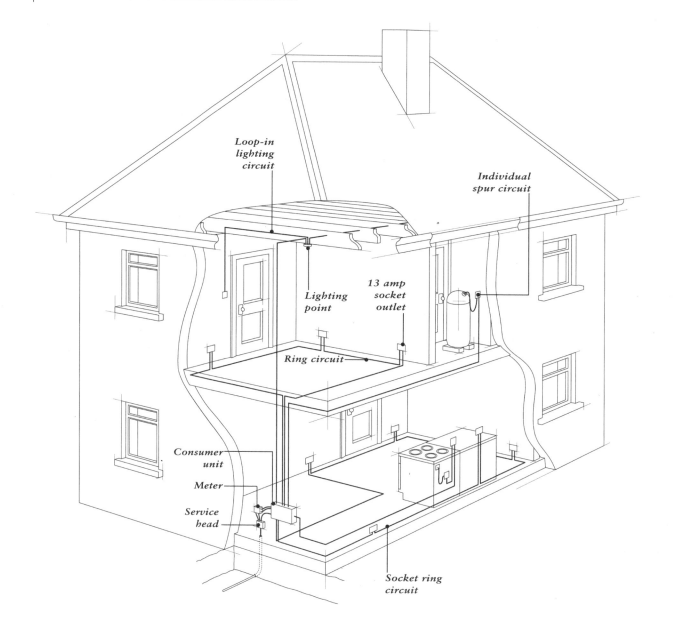

Loop-in lighting circuit

Individual spur circuit

13 amp socket outlet

Lighting point

Ring circuit

Consumer unit

Meter

Service head

Socket ring circuit

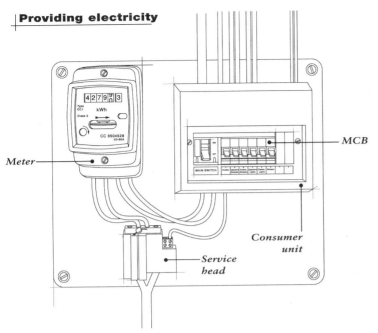

Meter

Service head

Consumer unit

MCB

system. Then the live core of the relevant circuit cable is connected to the fuse or MCB terminal. The neutral and earth cores of all the cables are connected to the main neutral and earth terminals within the fuse box or consumer unit.

Lighting circuits

Old lighting circuits are wired up as radial circuits. The cable runs from its fuse or MCB to each lighting point and terminates at the furthest point. It usually has a current rating of 5 or 6 amps. Old lighting circuits were generally not earthed, and if one is found, it will need rewiring.

New lighting circuits have loop-in wiring, with the circuit cable looping into and out of each lighting point. The cable to the light switch is wired into the lighting point itself. Older circuits have the circuit cable running into and out of a series of junction boxes – one for each lighting point. The cable to the point and to its switch is wired into the junction box.

Power circuits

Portable or free-standing appliances with power consumption of up to 3kW (3000 watts) are plugged into socket outlets, using three-pin plugs with 3 amp (small appliances) or 13 amp (more powerful items) fuses.

In a modern house, the socket circuits are usually ring circuits, with the cable starting and terminating at its fuse or MCB and running from outlet to outlet. Older houses may still have outlets taking round-pin plugs on circuits supplied as radial circuits. These circuits will almost certainly need rewiring to supply 13 amp outlets.

Large appliances that take high currents have individual spur circuits with appropriately rated fuses or MCBs in the fuse box or consumer unit. Each is controlled by a double-pole switch that allows the appliance to be isolated from the mains supply for maintenance.

The supply

The electricity supply reaches the house through an underground or overhead cable, then runs into a sealed unit called the cut-out or service head. This contains a large fuse that protects the service cable from being overloaded if the house system demands more electricity than it is designed to supply. Two double insulated cables, one live and one neutral, run from the cut-out to the electricity meter.

Two more cables connect the meter to the main on-off switch and the control panel, which distributes current around the house. In unmodernized homes the switch is in its own enclosure, and cables may run to a one-piece fuse box containing all the circuit fuses or to a series of boxes, each with just one or two fuses. In modern or rewired houses, the main switch and the circuit fuses or other protective devices are in one control panel – the consumer unit.

Safety devices

Each circuit contains a device to cut off the supply too much current is demanded. This can happen if too many appliances are plugged in, or

if a fault such as a short circuit occurs and causes a current surge. Old systems have wire or cartridge fuses, which are rated to match a circuit's maximum demand and melt if this is exceeded. Modern systems have electromagnetic devices called miniature circuit breakers (MCBs). These switch off if a fault occurs and cannot be reset until it is cured.

Each circuit cable and appliance flex contains a continuous wire that is connected to earth. This provides a safe path to earth (the ground) for any current that escapes from the circuit – due to faulty insulation, for example – and prevents users from receiving an electric shock.

Modern wiring systems contain a residual current device (RCD). This detects current leaking to earth via faulty insulation or if someone is receiving an electric shock, and it switches the power off in a fraction of a second – fast enough to save your life. One should be installed to protect circuits to socket outlets and large appliances; sometimes the main on-off switch doubles as an RCD.

Within the fuse box or consumer unit, each fuse or MCB is connected to the main live terminal of the

Most modern or modernized homes have a central heating system that delivers warmth to rooms from a single heat source, usually a boiler fueled by oil, gas or solid fuel. Others may have heating systems that run on off-peak electricity.

Wet heating system

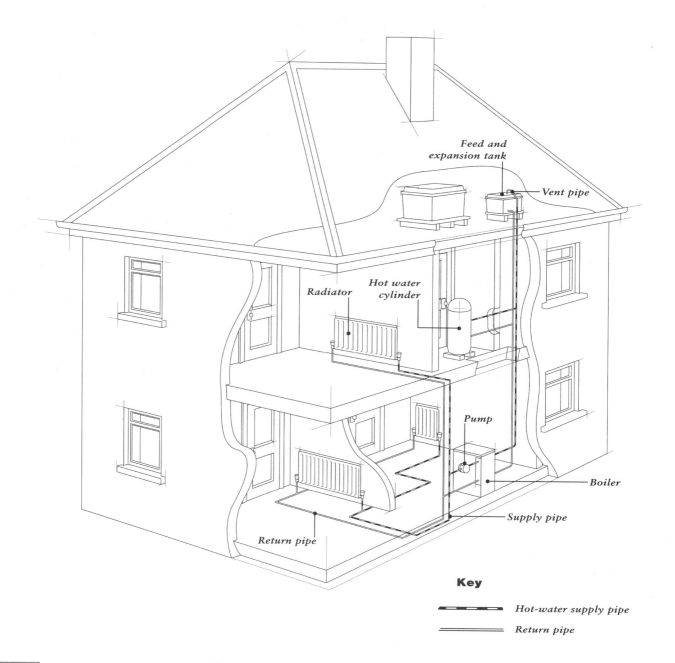

Feed and expansion tank

Vent pipe

Radiator

Hot water cylinder

Pump

Boiler

Supply pipe

Return pipe

Key

Hot-water supply pipe

Return pipe

Wet heating systems

The most common type of central heating system uses hot water to carry heat around the house. A circuit of small-diameter pipes runs from the boiler to a steel radiator in each room, and water heated in the boiler is pumped around to each one before returning to the boiler to be heated up again. The pipes are run in floor and ceiling voids or are buried in solid ground floors.

Each radiator has two valves. The inlet valve functions as an on-off control; the outlet valve is used to balance the system and ensure that each radiator reaches its design temperature. The boiler may be free-standing, wall-mounted or set in a fireplace, and may run on gas, oil or solid fuel. Boilers installed in fireplaces are gas-fired back boilers with an integral gas fire that heats the room in which the boiler is sited.

The system is controlled by a programmer, with timers and thermostats turning it on and off at preset times and as temperatures rise or fall below preset levels. Radiators may be fitted with a thermostatic valve to control room temperatures.

Most central heating boilers also provide the house's hot-water supply. A separate circuit of pipework runs from the boiler to the hot-water cylinder, and a motorized valve under the control of the programmer and the room and cylinder thermostats switches the heated water from one circuit to the other as their heat demands vary.

A combination boiler is an alternative to a conventional boiler. It supplies the heating circuit in the same way, but heats water for domestic use on demand instead of via a hot-water cylinder. It is often used in houses and flats where space is at a premium and hot- and cold-water storage is difficult to provide.

Most wet central heating systems are open-vented. They have an open tank in the loft (the feed-and-

How air circulates in a room

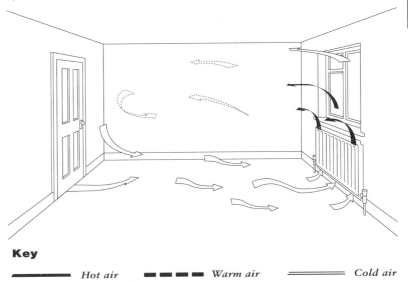

Key

———— *Hot air*   ▬ ▬ ▬ ▬ *Warm air*   ═══════ *Cold air*

Radiators are often placed under a window to allow the hot air that rises from it to mix with the cold air from the window. As the warm air cools, it lowers and returns to the radiator.

expansion tank), which feeds water into the boiler circuit to replace any losses, and it accommodates the expansion in the water content of the heating system. An open vent pipe runs from the boiler circuit back up to the feed-and-expansion tank and discharges over it via an inverted U-bend. Should the boiler malfunction and overheat, boiling water and steam would discharge through the vent pipe.

Modern heating systems may be unvented. Instead of a feed-and-expansion tank, a pressure vessel takes care of expansion within the system, and if the boiler overheats a safety valve allows the water and steam to be discharged safely.

Dry heating systems

One alternative to a wet heating system is one that uses fans to blow air heated by the boiler to individual rooms through ducts concealed in floor and ceiling voids. Dampers on the outlet grilles in the rooms can be opened or shut to control room

temperatures. This type of system can only be installed easily when a house is built, due to the disruption caused by fitting the ducting.

Other dry heating systems found in flats include underfloor or ceiling heating by electricity. Both can only be installed during construction.

Storage heaters

While not a central heating system due to the absence of a single heat source, electric night storage heaters can be used for whole-house heating by placing a heater in each room. The system runs on off-peak electricity. Each heater contains thermal blocks, which are heated by embedded elements during the night; they discharge their heat gradually during the day. The heat output can be regulated by setting the initial heat input level, then by using openable grilles to release the heat from the cabinet. The heaters are supplied by their own circuits, wired to a separate consumer unit and operated by an off-peak electricity meter.

Reference section

4

If you've had no previous home improvement
experience, talking to the professionals can be
confusing at first. To help you understand the
jargon that professionals often use, you'll find
in the following pages a glossary of common
building terms. Also included are sample budget
and contract forms and a list of resources – this
list supplies the addresses and other information
for contacting trade associations and home
improvement suppliers.

*The professionals will take time to explain the details on anything that
you are unclear about – don't be afraid to ask questions.*

Architrave
A decorative piece of moulding that covers the gaps that occur between the walls and a door frame. It is used along the sides and top of the door.

Ashlaring
A low wall, about 1 m (3 ft) high, built in the loft space to support the roof timbers in a loft conversion.

Baluster
A type of post used in a set to support a handrail along an open staircase.

Balustrade
The structure alongside an open staircase or landing, consisting of the balusters, newels and handrail, to provide support and protection from falls as people use the stairs.

Brace
A piece of timber or metal attached to a structure to provide stiffness and support to its frame. It is set diagonally at an angle less than 90 degrees.

Building Regulations
The legal requirements administered by the local authority for various aspects of building construction, with a view to safeguarding the health and safety of the public.

Casement window
A type of window in which the pane swings out when opened; there may be several glass panes in the window, side by side, or a small one above a large one. Some of the panes may be fixed.

Casing
The timber framework of a door or window opening.

Caulking compound
A material applied to surfaces, such as where ceramic tiles and a worktop meet or around the exterior of a window frame, to seal the seams or gaps. Some harden as they dry but others remain flexible.

Cavity wall
A wall made up of two independent leaves, or skins, of masonry with an air gap between, which serves to prevent moisture from penetrating through the wall.

Circuit
The path that electricity follows from the source (the power plant) to an appliance or fixture, then back to the source. There are usually several separate branch circuits within a house.

Conduit
A metal or plastic pipe that is used in electricity to protect bundles of wires.

Cripple
A part of a framing structure that is shorter than similar parts in the same structure. One example is a cripple stud, which is often used above a door or window opening.

Curing
The drying process of certain materials such as concrete, plaster and adhesive.

Damp-proof course (dpc)
A material that prevents water from penetrating into walls or

other parts of the building. The typical materials that are used as a dpc are polyethylene sheeting or leadcore.

Decking
Refers either to the exterior floor structure built for outdoor relaxation or entertaining or to the platform created by roof or floor sheathing.

Duct
Large pipes that transport air that has been heated or cooled by a furnace around the home.

Fascia
A board running under the eaves and fastened to the ends of the rafters. It may have guttering fixed to it.

Finish flooring
The top layer of a floor used mostly for decorative purposes. The materials used include ceramic floor tiles, vinyl tiles, sheet vinyl, carpet and wood strips. A concrete floor in an unused area may not be finished.

Fixture
Something that is attached to the building; for example, an overhead ceiling light is a lighting fixture and a toilet is a plumbing fixture.

Flashing
Sheets of metal, usually lead or zinc, applied in strips to weatherproof the junctions between two surfaces such as between a chimney and roof.

Footing
The concrete foundation that supports the walls.

Foundation
The base of the house, starting below ground level, that supports the whole structure.

Framing
Another term for frame or framework, it consists of the parts that give strength or shape to the object it supports such as a window or wall.

Frost heave
An upheaval of the ground or of pavement that is caused when moist ground freezes.

Furring battens
Strips of timber attached to walls or ceilings in parallel rows to provide framwork for attaching sheet materials such as plasterboard or cladding. Or they are attached to joists to make the slope for rain run-off on flat roofs.

Galvanized
Steel or other metals coated with zinc to prevent rusting; it is used in roofing and plumbing materials and in nails.

Girder
A large wooden or metal beam that helps support the structure above it. An I-section RSJ (rolled steel joist) is used over the room opening when knocking two rooms into one.

Hardwood
Wood that comes from broad-leaved trees that are usually deciduous; for example, ash, beech and oak. These usually have a characteristically hard fibrous structure.

Insulation
Materials that are used around a room or area to limit the transmission of heat or sound. Another form of insulation, which is a nonconductive material, is used around electrical wires and connections to prevent electric shock.

Jamb
The vertical side components of a door or window frame; part of the lining.

Joist
A horizontal wooden (or sometimes metal) beam; ceilings and floors are made up of parallel sets of joists.

Joist hanger
A galvanized steel bracket fastened to a masonry wall to hold the end of a joist.

Lath and plaster

A covering for an internal wall that provides a smooth finish surface. It consists of narrow wood strips, or laths, that are fixed to the wall structure; they support the plaster, which is put on in several layers. Some types use wire instead of lath.

Mastic

A type of adhesive used for setting tiles or sheet vinyl.

MDF

Medium-density fibreboard, a type of board made of compressed fine wood fibres; it is usually available in 2440 x 1220 mm (8 x 4 feet) sheets and in various thicknesses.

Mouldings

Strips of wood usually, such as skirting board or picture rail, in various profiles.

Noggings

Short lengths of timber skew-nailed between studs in a stud wall to stiffen the structure.

OSB

The abbreviation for oriented-strand board, a type of man-made board that is as strong as plywood, but can be susceptible to water damage.

Outbuilding

A building on the property that is detached from the main house; it may be a gazebo, shed or garage.

Partition wall

An internal wall that consists of a wooden frame that is covered, usually with plasterboard, to provide a smooth finish; it can be painted or decorated with wallpaper.

Plasterboard

Panels, consisting of a layer of gypsum plaster covered on both sides with paper, that are used to finish internal walls and ceilings. They are also referred to as drywall or gypsum board.

Platform framing

A technique for framing the structure of a timber house, with vertical members extending only between the floor and ceiling in each story.

Polyethylene sheeting

Or polythene, a type of plastic sheet that is used to protect surfaces, items or areas as work progresses. It may be used as a dpc (see facing page).

Primer

The base coat used to seal the surface of the work – either carpentry, such as cupboards, or walls – before applying one or more top coats of paint.

Purlin

A horizontal beam that provides support for the rafters in a roof.

Rafter

One of the sloping beams that form the main structural member of the frame supporting the roof covering.

Rebate

A step-shaped recess that forms part of a joint. The door stop of an external door that prevents the door from swinging through is a rebate.

Ridge vent

The vent that runs along the ridge, or peak, of a roof. It works in conjunction with other vents.

Run

The path of the pipework in a plumbing or heating system or the cable in an electrical system.

Runoff

The rain that drips off the roof, walls or paved areas.

Sash

A part of a window, the wood frame around a pane of glass.

Sash window

Also referred to as hung window, a type of window with

sashes, one above the other. Either both sashes or only one of them may move.

Services

A term referring to the systems in a house such as plumbing, heating, gas and electricity.

Sheathing

Panels or boards, usually 2440 x 1220 mm (8 x 4 ft) sheets, that are attached to framing timbers or girders to make roofs or walls.

Shim

A thin strip of wood that is push into a joint between two surfaces to fill the gap. It may also be used to level an object.

Shingle course

A horizontal row of shingles, either on an external wall or on a roof.

Sill

A horizontal part of a frame, such as a window frame or a partition wall.

Skirting board

A decorative wood moulding that runs along the bottom of the walls, covering the gap between the walls and floor.

Sleeper

Wood strips attached in parallel rows over a concrete floor to provide a nailing surface for a finish flooring.

Snagging

The process of checking at the end of a job for anything that has been left undone.

Softwood

Wood that comes from coniferous trees such as pine and cedar. This type of wood is characteristically soft.

Stud

One of the vertical members that make up a partition wall. They are usually spaced on 405 mm (16 in) centres.

Subsidence

The movement of a house that occurs when it is built on disturbed ground or that occurs when normally firm, stable ground has been undermined by excess moisture.

Underlay

The material laid under the finish covering for either the roof or floor; it provides a smooth surface to apply the finish. The underlay for the roof is also a waterproof barrier.

Valley

The inside corner angle formed where two sloping surfaces of a roof meet.

Weatherstripping

Narrow strips placed around windows and doors to prevent air and moisture from entering the house. The strips may be made of metal, plastic foam, fibre or some other material.

If you are employing an architect or surveyor, then they will prepare broken-down costs for you and draw up contracts. For a smaller project that you are supervising yourself, you need to be prepared to deal with these things.

The budget

Below is an example of how to compare estimates. You will need the details of what materials the professionals are going to use and their proposed work methods before you can make a comparison.

You can adapt the budget form opposite to suit your own project. It is by no means a complete form and a simple project won't need so many entries. Use it to compare estimates. Remember to look at the materials listed; the quality of the materials will affect the price given in the estimate. You may want to break down a category into subcategories to have a closer look at the expenses.

Contracts

Do not be tempted to settle for a verbal agreement – it saves both parties potential problems if you enter into a proper contract. You can still convey an air of confidence and trust even if you insist on having a written agreement that both parties sign up to.

An architect or building surveyor will be able to advise you on the most suitable form of contract. Indeed, they may recommend using a standard form issued by their own professional institute.

Comparison chart

Painter A	Painter B	Painter C
Exterior masonry	**Exterior masonry**	**Exterior masonry**
1 coat primer, 1 coat exterior-grade emulsion paint, applied with brush and roller £495.00	1 coat primer, 2 coats exterior-grade emulsion paint, sprayed on £645.00	1 coat primer, 2 coats reinforced masonry paint, applied with brush and roller £780.00
Windows (10)	**Windows** (10)	**Windows** (10)
1 coat primer, 1 coat exterior-grade gloss paint, applied with brush and roller £320.00	1 coat primer, 2 coats exterior-grade gloss paint, applied with brush £360.00	1 coat primer, 2 coats exterior-grade gloss paint, applied with brush £400.00
Doors (2)	**Doors** (2)	**Doors** (2)
1 coat primer, 1 coat exterior-grade gloss paint, applied with brush and roller £70.00	1 coat primer, 2 coats exterior-grade gloss paint, sprayed on £90.00	1 coat primer, 2 coats exterior-grade gloss paint, applied with brush £115.00
Miscellaneous trim	**Miscellaneous trim**	**Miscellaneous trim**
1 coat primer, 1 coat exterior-grade gloss paint, applied with brush and roller £400.00	1 coat primer, 2 coats exterior-grade gloss paint, applied with brush £495.00	1 coat primer, 2 coats exterior-grade gloss paint, applied with brush £650.00
Total £1,285.00	**Total** £1,590.00	**Total** £1,945.00

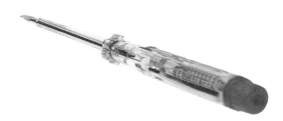

Some builders and tradespeople will have their own contract forms, which they may invite you to sign. Do not allow yourself to be pressurized into signing them until you are ready to do so. Read them carefully first. Make sure you understand what the clauses mean and the significance of them. If you feel it necessary to delete, add or amend any parts of the contract, discuss them with the contractor first, before doing so. Remember that in most cases there will be scope for negotiation over the conditions of the contract even if the price remains fixed.

Have a look at the details of the contract for small building works on the following pages and see how it compares to the one your contractor is inviting you to sign.

Homeowner's contract

The Joint Contracts Tribunal (JCT) issues contracts in various formats for differing situations – Minor works, Home Renovation Grant-aided works or Nominated Sub-Contractors. The Tribunal has also produced one specifically designed for the homeowner in simple language that is available from the JCT or from high street shops. For ambitious projects that you are supervising yourself, you are strongly recommended to use one.

However, for very small projects you can still use a simpler form of agreement and two examples are shown on pp. 166–167.

Budget form

	Expenses of renovation or extension		
	Room renovation	**Extensions**	**Exterior improvements**
Total sum available £	**Floors**	**Preparing the site**	**Roof**
	Materials £	Materials £	Materials £
Minus 10% contingency allowance £	Labour £	Labour £	Labour £
	Internal wall construction	**Foundation**	**Gutters and downspouts**
Minus building permits £	Materials £	Materials £	Materials £
	Labour £	Labour £	Labour £
Minus inspection fees £	**Internal wall decoration**	**Walls**	**External walls**
	Materials £	Materials £	Materials £
Minus living expenses during renovation £	Labour £	Labour £	Labour £
	Carpentry	**Roof**	**Deck or patio**
	Materials £	Materials £	Materials £
Remaining sum for renovation £	Labour £	Labour £	Labour £
	Curtains/upholstery	**Windows and doors**	**Fences or walls**
Minus architect fee £	Materials £	Materials £	Materials £
	Labour £	Labour £	Labour £
Minus designer fee £	**Electricity**	**Insulation**	**Landscaping**
	Materials £	Materials £	Materials £
Minus contractor fee £	Labour £	Labour £	Labour £
	Plumbing	**Ventilation**	
Minus specialist fee £	Materials £	Materials £	
	Labour £	Labour £	
	Heating	**Room decoration**	
	Materials £	See "Room renovation"	
	Labour £		

Invitation to tender/letter of agreement

<name and address of contractor>

Dear

Ref: _____*<title description of job>* _____

You are invited to submit a firm quotation for the above.

The work comprises _____

_____

_____ and shall include for incidental works necessary to complete the work to my reasonable satisfaction.

Although a formal contract will not be entered into, the JCT Agreement for Minor Building Works 1980 Edition (revised 1991 and inclusive of all amendments to date) will be deemed to apply in the event of any dispute.

Damages for non-completion; liquidated damages will be at the rate of £ _____ per day/per week during which the works remain uncompleted.

An amount equal to 2.5% of the total value of the work will be retained for a period of weeks/months after the date of practical completion.

Where applicable, all work is to comply with BS:8000, Codes of Practice and other British Standards, with materials, manufacturers' recommendations and instructions appropriate to achieve a satisfactory performance.

The Contractor is to inspect the site of the work prior to submission of the quotation. No subsequent claim arising from failure to do so will be entertained. All costs incurred in preparing the tender shall be borne by the contractor.

Include in your quotation the provisional sum of £_____ for contingent or unforeseen works as identified in the schedule of works.

This sum to be deducted in whole or part as agreed by both parties if not required.

The works are to commence on _____ and be completed by_____ .

The specification shall be fully priced and a pricing summary sheet duly completed, signed and dated with the company address. The completed quotation should be sent to :

_____*<your name and address>*_____
and must be received not later than *<date required>* _____ .

Yours faithfully,

_____

Enclosed: Schedule of Work

Contract for domestic building works

This agreement between _____ <your name>_____ of _____<your address>_____ (hereinafter referred to as "the employer") And _____<contractor's name>_____ of _____<contractor's address>_____ (hereinafter referred to as "the contractor") is made on the _____ day of _____ 20_____

Whereas

1 The employer requires the following work to be carried out _____ <description of job> _____ and has caused drawings numbered _____ and/or specification and/or schedules and/or structural design calculations and details (hereinafter referred to with the conditions annexed as "the contract documents") showing and describing the work to be done and which are attached to this agreement.

2 The contractor has stated in his quotation the sum required for carrying out the work (the sum as stated in article two of this agreement).

3 The contract documents have been signed by both parties.

4 CONDITIONS (hereinbefore referred to)

(I) Standards
The contractor shall diligently and professionally carry out the complete works as detailed within the contract documents using approved materials and workmanship standards to BS:8000 and with electrical installations installed in accordance with the IEE (Institute of Electrical Engineers) Regulations.

(II) Duration
The works may start on_____ and shall be completed by_____ or extended to a later specified date by agreement of both parties, or a reasonable extended date for reasons beyond the control of the contractor.

If the works are not completed by the completion date then the contractor shall pay or allow for, in liquidated damages to the employer at the rate of £____ per week between the contracted date of completion and the actual date of practical completion. The employer may deduct such liquidated damages from any monies due under this contract.

(III) Defects
Any defects or faults including excessive shrinkages which appear within three months of practical completion due to materials or workmanship shall be rectified and made good by the contractor at his own expense.

(IV) Variations
If any amendments or variations are required by the employer, written instructions shall be given by him within two days of the oral instruction and the price agreed for it before works are carried out. Any inconsistencies or errors in the contract documents shall be corrected and treated as a variation.

(V) Payments
Interim payments shall be made for works carried out and materials brought on to the site at intervals of not less than 4 weeks. The employer will pay to the contractor any fair amount so specified in this respect, within 14 days of the date of invoice. Retention of ____ % (not exceeding 5%) may be deducted from the final payment at practical completion to be released in two halves. The first half at 14 days after practical completion and the second half at 3 months after practical completion.

(VI) Quotation
The quotation shall be a fixed price that shall not take any account of changes to the cost of labour, materials, plant or other resources needed by the contractor to carry out the work.

(VIII) Legal Requirements and Notices
The contractor shall comply with all notices and requirements required by statute, statutory instruments, rules, regulations and bylaws. Including all necessary Notices for inspection to the Building Control Officer. If in complying with these matters of law additional works are necessary that are not shown on the contract documents he shall notify the employer immediately.

(IX) VAT
VAT shall be added to the contract sum where applicable and where it is not separately shown, the sum shall be taken as exclusive of VAT (value added tax)

(X) Insurance
The contractor shall indemnify the employer against any liability, loss, expense, claim or proceedings in respect of personal injury or death of any person, arising from the work. He shall maintain an appropriate level of insurance under the Employers Liability (Compulsory Insurance) Act 1969 as amended. The contractor shall produce evidence as required in respect of his insurance for the employer.

(XI) Determination by the employer
Should the contractor without reasonable cause default by failing to proceed diligently or suspending the works substantially, the employer may give notice of ____ days to him allowing for the default to end. A notice of determination may then be served by the employer on the contractor. If the contractor becomes bankrupt, has a professional liquidator appointed or winding-up order made the employer may by notice determine the employment of the contractor immediately by the contractor.

If the employer fails to pay any interim payments or final payment within the specified time periods or pay any VAT due on the amount, or if the employer unreasonably interrupts or disrupts the execution of the work or suspends the work for at least one month then the contractor may give notice of ____ days to the employer, allowing for the default to end. A notice of determination may then be served on the employer by the contractor.

(XII) Settling Disputes
When either party requires a dispute to be settled, they shall give written notice to the other, of the appointment of an arbitrator. The arbitration shall be conducted in accordance with the Joint Contracts Tribunal Arbitration Rules as amended.

NOW IT IS HEREBY AGREED

Article 1
For the consideration hereinafter stated the contractor will in accordance with the contract documents attached carry out and complete the work referred to, together with any changes or variations made in accordance with this contract.

Article 2.
The Employer will pay the contractor the sum of _____ for the works, exclusive of VAT.

AS WITNESS
The signatures of the parties

the employer _____

the contractor _____

in the presence of _____

name in print _____

address_____

_____

4 Resources

Associations

Association of Building Engineers

Jubilee House
Billing Brook Road
Weston Favell
Northampton
NN3 8NW
tel: 01604 404121
fax: 01604 784220
e-mail:
Buildengrs@aol.com

The Association of Building Engineers is the professional body for those specializing in the technology of building. You may telephone the ABE, which maintains a list of members in private practice.

British Bathroom Council

Federation House
Stoke on Trent
Staffordshire
ST4 2RT
tel: 01782 747074
fax: 01782 747161
e-mail:
sharon.heath@british
bathrooms.org.uk
website: www.british
bathrooms.org.uk

British Bathroom Council are representives of major manufacturers of bathroom products. It provides information on all aspects of the bathroom, and it helps to raise standards of quality and technical performance.

The British Wood Preserving and Damp Proofing Association

6, The Office Village

4 Romford Road
London
E15 4EA
tel: 020 8519 2588
fax: 020 8519 3444
e-mail:
info@bwpda.co.uk
website:
www.bwpda.co.uk

Lists members and offers advice on any aspect of timber treatment and damp-proofing. Provides leaflets on wood treatment and damp control, and provides codes of practice and specifications manual. It also has a mediation and arbitration scheme.

The British Woodworking Federation

56-64 Leonard Street
London
EC24 4JX
tel: 020 7608 5050
fax: 020 7608 5051
e-mail: bwf@bwf.org.uk
website:
bwf@bwf.org.uk

The voice of the woodworking industry, this group represents manufacturers of doors, windows, staircases, architectural joinery, timber frame buildings and engineered timber components for the construction industry.

Builders Merchants Federation

15 Soho Square
London
W1V 4LX
tel: 020 7439 1753
fax: 020 7734 2766
e-mail: info@bmf.org.uk
website:
www.bmf.org.uk

Help and advice is provided on general building materials; this federation also lists of stockers and suppliers of building materials.

Chartered Institute of Building

Englemere
Kings Ride
Ascot
Berkshire
SL5 7TB

tel: 01344 630 700
fax: 01344 630 777
e-mail:
reception@ciob.org.uk
website:
www.ciob.org.uk or
www.constructors.org

This institute represents construction managers. Members include skilled managers and professionals committed to achieving and maintaining high standards in construction. This educational charity, governed by a Royal Charter, provides a multidisciplinary technical and management-based qualification.

The Chartered Institution of Building Services Engineers

222 Balham High Road
London
SW12 9BS
tel: 020 8675 5211
fax: 020 8675 5449
e-mail: info@cibse.org

CIBSE publishes design, reference, installation and equipment data to help all who plan design or equip buildings with mechanical and electrical services. CIBSE ensures that members are trained and that they follow a code of professional conduct.

Chartered Society of Designers

32-38 Saffron Hill
London
EC1N 85G
tel: 020 7831 9777
fax: 020 7831 6277
e-mail: csd@csd.org.uk

The Chartered Society of Designers is the largest body representing professional designers in Europe. Members operate to a Code of Practice and must demonstrate a high level of professionalism to ensure membership.

CORGI

The Council for Registered Gas Installers
1 Elmwood
Chineham Business Park
Crockford Lane
Basingstoke
Hampshire
RG24 8WG
tel: 01256 372300
fax: 01256 708144
e-mail: enquiries@corgi
gas.co.uk
website: www.corgi
gas.co.uk

As the national watchdog for gas safety, CORGI is the body given the responsibility by the health and safety authorities to maintain a register of competent gas installers in Britain. By law, anyone carrying out gas-related work must be registered with CORGI. Its installers carry CORGI identification cards.

Draught Proofing Advisory Association Limited

PO Box 12
Haslemere
Surrey
GU27 3AH
tel: 01428 654 011
fax: 01428 651 401

This association represents major draughtproofing suppliers and contractors. Its aim is to promote the advantages of fitting high-quality draught excluders, together with their good installation, in the home, in industry and commerce and as original equipment by window and door manufacturers.

Health and Safety Executive

Information Centre
Broad Lane
Sheffield
S3 7HQ

tel: 0541 545 500
fax: 0114 289 2333
e-mail:
public.enquiries@hse.
gov.uk

Publishes guidance and advice to the public and the professional. Provides an information service and enforces good standards at work.

Institution of Structural Engineers

11 Upper Belgrave Street
London
SW1X 8BH
tel: 020 7235 4535
e-mail:
mail@istructe.org.uk
website:
www.istructe.org.uk

Sets and maintains standards for professional structural engineers.

Insulated Render and Cladding Association Ltd

PO Box 12
Haslemere
Surrey
GU27 3AH
tel: 01428 654 011
fax: 01428 651 401

Aims to establish and maintain technical, ethical and legal standards for the industry; to give impartial advice; and to promote insulated render and cladding designed and applied by recognized member companies.

National Federation of Roofing Contractors

24 Weymouth Street
London
W1N 4LX
tel: 020 7436 0387
fax: 020 7637 5215
e-mail: info@nfrc.co.uk
website: www.nfrc.co.uk

Britain's largest roofing trade federation, representing over 825 contractors, manufacturers and suppliers.

National Replacement Window Advisory Service

National Conservatory
Advisory Service
NRWAS
PO Box 163
Bangor
BT20 5BX
enquiries: 0800 028 5809

tel: 02981 478 779
fax: 02891 478 791
e-mail: info@nrwas.com
website:
www.nrwas.com

Aims to remove the risks in buying replacement windows, doors or conservatories; provide you the best deal; and ensure complete satisfaction with each stage of the work.

Royal Institute of British Architects

RIBA
66 Portland Place
London
W1N 4AD
tel: 020 7580 5533
e-mail: admin@insti
tute.riba.org
website: www.riba.org

Publishes guidance for clients on the appointment of an architect and the construction process. The Clients' Advisory Service (CAS) can help in finding appropriate architects for a project.

Bathrooms

Chadder & Co.

Blenheim Studio
London Road
Forest Row
East Sussex
RH18 5EZ
tel: 01342 823 243
fax: 01342 823 097
e-mail:
sales@chadder.com
website: www.chad
der.com

Antique and traditional bathroom fittings, with over 100 roll top baths in stock, many unusual basins, showers, taps and marble tops; mail order.

Max Pike Bathrooms

4 Eccleston Street
London
SW1W 9LN
tel: 020 7730 7216
fax: 020 7730 7389
e-mail: bathrooms@max
pike.com
website: www.max
pike.com

Provides bathroom fittings, including baths, basins, bidets, toilets, power showers, hydromassage systems, towel rails and mirrors and taps.

Vogue UK

Units 8–10
Strawberry Lane

Industrial Estate
Strawberry Lane
Willenhall
West Midlands
WV13 3RS
tel: 01902 637 330
fax: 01902 604 532
e-mail: sales@vogue
uk.co.uk
website: www.vogue
uk.co.uk

Manufactures heated towel rails, basin stands and shower curtain rails. Sells column radiators and offer a bespoke manufacturing service.

Bedrooms

Andrew Macintosh Furniture Ltd

462–464 Chiswick High Street
London
W4 5TT
tel: 020 8995 8333
fax: 020 8995 8999

Fitted kitchen and bedroom manufacturers and retailers. Design, make and supply furniture to fit your room.

Hammonds

Fleming Road
Harrowbrook Industrial Estate
Hinkley
Leicestershire
LE10 3DU

tel: 0800 251 505
fax: 01455 633 981

Manufacturers of individual fitted bedrooms and home office furniture.

Doors

The Designer Door Company

Bow Wharf
Grove Road
London
E3 5SN
tel: 020 8880 6739
e-mail:
desdoors@aol.com

Has a wide range of period or contemporary internal doors, front doors, room dividers and garden doors, designed and manufactured to order.

Doors Direct

Old School
School Lane
Dacre Banks
Harrogate
HG3 4ER
tel: 01423 781 728
fax: 01423 780 069
e-mail:
doorsdirect@doors
direct.co.uk
website: www.doors
direct.co.uk

Provides cabinet doors and accessories for kitchens and bedrooms in any size order, delivered anywhere in Britain. They are available in over 200 different door styles and colours, in solid wood and laminates, and they can be made to measure. A full range of accessories includes hinges, handles and knobs, drawers and runners.

Spazio Door Co

Oaklands
Tenterden
Kent
TN30 6NH
tel: 01580 763 593
fax: 01580 765 883
e-mail:
davetester@aol.co.uk
website:
www.spazio.co.uk

Supplies doors in a luxurious Italian design and quality, which are manufactured mostly in Britain to meet the customer's requirements. They produce folding doors, bi-fold doors and cassette-type sliding doors, as well as folding sliding walls.

Fireplaces

Amazing Grates

61-63 High Road
London
N2 8AB
tel: 020 8883 5556
fax: 020 8365 2053
website: www.amazing
grates.co.uk

Provides an extensive collection of fireplaces and accessories, ranging from originals to sympathetic reproductions pieces and modern contemporary designs.

Gazco Ltd
Osprey Road
Sowton Industrial Estate
Exeter
EX2 7JG
tel: 01392 444 030
fax: 01392 432 971
e-mail: info@gazco.com
website:
www.gazco.com

Gazco produce realistic living flame gas heating appliances with designs that include inset fires, convector fires and stoves as well as variants with manual, wall mounted and infrared remote controls.

Flooring
The Amtico Company Ltd
Head Office and Factory
Kingfield Road
Coventry
CV6 5AA
tel: 024 7686 1400
fax: 024 7686 1552
website:
www.amtico.com

A range of vinyls replicating the appearance of natural materials in traditional classical and contemporary styles.

Natural Materials
Crucial Trading
PO Box 11
Duke Place
Kidderminster
Worcestershire
DY10 2JR
tel: 01562 820 006
fax: 01562 820 030
e-mail: sales@crucial trading.com
website: www.crucial trading.com

Supplies handcrafted and made-to-customer specifications natural rugs and floor coverings from plant fibres such as sisal, coir, jute, seagrass, wool and paper. Free samples are available by mail order.

The Natural Wood Floor Co
20 Smugglers Way
Wandsworth
London
SW18 1EQ
tel: 020 8871 9771
fax: 020 8877 0273
website: www.natural woodfloor.co.uk

Supplies all types of wood floors, new and reclaimed, laminated, strips, block and design panels, as well as all accessories for wood floors. Also has solid wood worktops and exterior decking.

Original Seagrass Company
Shrewsbury Road
Craven Arms
Shropshire
SY7 9NW
tel: 01584 861 393
fax: 01584 861 604
e-mail:
original.seagrass@virgin.net
website: www.original-seagrass.co.uk

Supplies a range of 26 natural floorcoverings in seagrass, sisal, coir and wool.

Posners – The Floor Store
35–37 Fairfax Road
London
NW6 4EW
tel: 020 7625 8899
fax: 020 7625 8866

Offers over 900 brand of floor coverings, including Kahrs, Junckers, Tarkett and Wincanton. Will visit and quote for installations.

Stone Age Ltd
19 & 23 Filmer Road
London
SW6 7BU
tel: 0171 385 7954/5
fax: 0171 385 7956
e-mail: info@stone age.co.uk

Provides natural limestones and sandstones for internal and external flooring, bathrooms and worktops.

Home Office
Furniture Craft International
Rays House
North Circular Road
London NW10 7XP
tel: 0208 9617780
fax: 0208 9615787
website: www.furniture craft.com
e-mail:
firdaus@furn1.demon.co.uk

Supplies home office furnishings of a high quality from Europe. Contemporary and classic designer labels are available; they also have an extensive showroom.

Neville Johnson Offices Ltd
Broadoak Business Park
Ashburton Road West
Trafford Park
Manchester
M17 1RW
tel: 0161 873 8333
fax: 0161 873 8335

Designers and manufacturers of fitted furniture individually designed for home studies.

Kitchens
Camargue PLC.
Townsend Farm Road
Houghton Regis
Bedfordshire
LU5 5BA
tel: 01582 699 122
fax: 01582 609 361
e-mail: Camargue@btin ternet.com

Offers a wide range of contemporary kitchens, manufactured in Britain and available nationwide through selected kitchen specialists.

Chalon UK Limited
Hambridge Mill
Hambridge
Somerset
TA10 0BP
tel: 01458 254 600
fax: 01458 251 192
website:
www.chalon.com

Kitchen, bedroom, study and library furniture, display cabinets and plate racks, dressers, occasional furniture, available in hand painted finishes.

DuPont Corian Division
Marylands Avenue
Hemel Hempstead
Herts HP2 7DP
tel: 0800 962 116
fax: 01442 346 755
e-mail: corian@mcd cor.demon.co.uk
website:
www.corian.com

Corian ® by Dupont is a solid surface material that is sleek, nonporous and easy to maintain. Corian ® is available in over 70 colours and is ideal for worktops, sinks, basins, vanities, cladding, bath surrounds and furniture.

The Kitchen Specialists Association
P.O. Box 311
Worcester
WR1 1DR
tel: 01905 619 922
fax: 01905 726 066
e-mail: info@ksa.co.uk
website: www.ksa.co.uk

Members of the public can telephone a consumer helpline to get advice on problems concerning kitchen buying and installation or simply to find out where to buy a kitchen.

Nolte Kitchens
Mark David Enterprises Ltd
T/A Nolte Kitchens
The Clock House
43 London Road
Sawbridgeworth
Hertfordshire
CM21 9JH
tel: 01279 868 500
fax: 01279 868 802
e-mail:
nolte.kitchens@dial.pipe x.com

Combining optimal planning with the most modern technology, the new range of kitchens provided by this firm offers a choice of woods such as beech, alder and maple and laminates in a variety of exciting colours.

Plain and Simple Kitchens
Unit 1 Filmer Studios
75 Filmer Road
London
SW6 7JF
tel: 020 77731 2530
fax: 020 7834 8107
e-mail:
info@ps4kitchens
website: .
www.ps4kitchens.co.uk
Supplies a range of kitchens with handpainted finishes and contemporary styling, including Cornish maple and Shaker, using the finest materials.

Lighting
Christopher Wray Lighting
591-593 Kings Road
London
SW6 2YW
tel: 020 7736 8434
fax: 020 7731 3507
e-mail: sales@christopher-wray.com
website: www.christopher-wray.com
Sells over 6000 lights and lighting accessories in styles from traditional to contemporary – table and desk lamps, uplighters, floor lamps, spotlights and downlights, pendants and chandeliers, rise and fall lights, tension-wire track lighting systems and exterior fittings.

Materials
Kirkstone
128 Walham Green Court
Moore Park Road
Fulham
London
SW6 4DG
tel: 020 7381 0424
fax: 020 7381 0434
Manufactures and imports high quality limestones, slates and granites for use throughout the home and garden; has branches throughout Britain.

Paints
Marston & Langinger
250 A Kings Road
London
SW3 5UE
tel: 020 7823 6828
fax: 020 7881 5755
e-mail: sales@marston and-langinger.com
website: www.marston and-langinger.com
Supplies paint in a wide range of colours that are suitable for woodwork, interiors and conservatories.

Radiators
Bisque Radiators
15 Kingsmead Square
Bath
BA1 2AE
tel: 01225 469 244
fax: 01225 444 708
website: www.leonard ouk.com/
Provides classic and modern radiators in a wide variety of dimensions and finishes.

Tiles
Marlborough Tiles
Elcot Lane
Marlborough
Wiltshire
SN8 2AY
tel: 01672 512 422
fax: 01672 515 791
e-mail: admin@marlbo rough-tiles.co.uk
website: www.marlbor ough-tiles.co.uk
Makers of fine English tiles and stockists of handmade, hand painted terracotta wall and floor tiles.

Paris Ceramics
583 Kings Road
London
SW6 2EH
tel: 020 7371 7778
fax: 020 7371 8395
e-mail:
ceramics@mailhost.atla s.co.uk
website:
www.parisceramics.com
Offers handmade and painted tiles, antique limestone and terracotta tiles, as well as aeclaimed floors and newly quarried limestone. Catalogue and mail order service are available.

Stanleys Quarry
Northwick Estate
Upton Wood
Moreton-in-Marsh
Gloucestershire
GL56 9TR
tel: 01386 841 236
fax: 01386 841 845
e-mail: sales@stanleys quarry.freeserve.co.uk
website: www.stanleys quarry.freeserve.co.uk
Supplies building stone, masonry products, fireplaces and flooring at competitive prices. Free advice and estimating also available.

Wallpaper
Anna French
343 Kings Road
London
SW3 5ES
tel: 020 7351 1126
fax: 020 7351 0421
Produces printed and woven fabric, wallpaper, borders and cut-outs in distinctive styles and handmade quality.

Cole and Son
Talbot House
Rickmansworth
Hertfordshire
WD3 1DE
tel: 01923 710 041
fax: 01923 710 694
website:
www.cole.uk.com
Historic wallpaper specialist, including Art Nouveau.

de Gournay
112 Old Church Street
Chelsea
London
SW3 6EP
tel: 020 7823 7316
fax: 020 7823 7475
e-mail: info@degour nay.com
Specializes in hand-painted wallcoverings on either silk or paper, in the Chinese Export and European Classical styles, as well as specialized paint techniques.

Windows
The Original Box Sash Window Company
The Joinery
Unit 10 Bridgewater Way
Windsor
Berkshire
SL4 1RD
tel: 01753 858 196
fax: 01753 857 827
Offers original box-sash or hinged windows, front doors and French doors, crafted in timber and double glazed.

Acknowledgments

Photography credits

page 1 Camera Press/Mel Yates; 2 Houses & Interiors/Verne; 3 Elizabeth Whiting & Associates/Rodney Hyett; 4 (left) Stock Market, 4 (centre) Houses & Interiors, 4 (right) Camera Press; 5 (top left) Ikea, 5 (top centre left) Camera Press, 5 (top right) Houses & Interiors/Roger Brooks, 5 (top centre right) Elizabeth Whiting & Associates/Rodney Hyett, 5 (bottom left) International Interiors/Paul Ryan, 5 (bottom right) Houses & Interiors; 6 (top) Camera Press, 6 (centre) Mainstream/Ray Main (Behr/Mill Hill), 6 (bottom) View/Dennis Gilbert (Architects: Ingram Avenue, London); 7 (top) Corbis, 7 (centre) View/Chris Gascoigne (Architects: Gerrard Taylor Associates), 7 (bottom) Thermador Professional Series available from the American Appliance Centre, Enfield; 8–9 Elizabeth Whiting & Associates/Rodney Hyett; 10 Stock Market/Pete Salutos; 11 Corbis; 12–13 Mark Wilkinson Furniture; 15 International Interiors/Paul Ryan (Designer: J. Saladino/ S. Casdin); 16–17 The Stock Market; 19 View/Dennis Gilbert (Architects: James Melvin and Gollins Melvin Ward & Partners, refurbishment by Sauerbach Hulton); 20–21 Robert Harding Syndication/Inspirations/Russell Sadur; 22 Mainstream/Ray Main (Behr/Mill Hill); 23 Interior Archive/Henry Wilson (Owner: Florence Lim); 25 International Interiors/Paul Ryan (Designer: Jason McHoy); 27 Mainstream/Ray Main (The Maples, Adderbury); 28 Elizabeth Whiting & Associates/Rodney Hyett; 30–31 Jerry Harpur (Designer: Diane Wakelin, San Francisco); 32–33 Camera Press; 34 Houses & Interiors, 34–35 Houses & Interiors; 36 Camera Press; 37 Camera Press; 38 (top left), 38 (centre left), 38 (centre right), 38 (bottom left), 38 (bottom right) Andrew Sydenham/Marshall Editions, 38 (top right) Farrow & Ball; 39 (left) Houses & Interiors/Jake Fitzjones, 39 (centre) Arcaid Simon Kenny, 39 (right) Elizabeth Whiting & Associates/Nadia Mackenzie; 40–41 Mainstream/Ray Main (Orange Juice, Kilburn); 42 (top left) Amtico, 42 (top right) Fired Earth, 42 (centre left) William Lomas Carpets/The Chatsworth Collection, 42 (centre right) Amtico, 42 (bottom left) Kahrs (UK) Ltd, 42 (bottom right) The Original Seagrass Company; 43 (left) Elizabeth Whiting & Associates/Brian Harrison, 43 (right) Elizabeth Whiting & Associates/Tim Imrie; 44 Elizabeth Whiting & Associates; 46 Andrew Sydenham/Marshall Editions; 48 (top right) Corbis/Richard Fukuhara, 48 (top right) Kirkstone Quarries Ltd., 48(centre left and centre right) Andrew Sydenham/Marshall Editions, 48 (bottom left) Fired Earth, 48 (bottom right); Junckers, 49 (left) Interior Archive/Fritz von der Schulenberg, 49 (centre) Elizabeth Whiting & Associates/Rodney Hyett, 49 (right) Elizabeth Whiting & Associates/Tom Leighton; 50–51 View/Dennis Gilbert (Architects: Ingram Avenue, London); 52 (top) House & Interiors/Mark Bolton (Catherine Gray Bathroom), 52 (bottom) Andrew Sydenham/Marshall Editions; 53 (left) Arcaid/Richard Bryant (Designer & Architect: Spencer Fung), 53 (right) Tony Stone/David Hantzig; 54 Camera Press; 55 Elizabeth Whiting & Associates/Lu Jeffery;

56–57 Camera Press; 58 Sharps Bedrooms; 59 Robert Harding Syndication/Mike Jones; 60 Andrew Sydenham/Marshall Editions; 61 Options Fitted Furniture of Mitcham, Surrey; 62 Elizabeth Whiting & Associates; 63 Elizabeth Whiting & Associates/Rodnet Hyett; 64 CURVOFLITE STAIRS AND MILLWORK, INC.; 65 International Interiors/Paul Ryan (Architects: Hariri & Hariri); 66 View/Chris Gascoigne (Architects: Gerrard Taylor Associates); 68 Mainstream/ Ray Main (Park Road, London); 69 (left) Elizabeth Whiting & Associates/Rodney Hyett, 69 (right) Mainstream/Ray Main (Room Sets, Abbotts Langley); 70 Gazco Living Flame Gas Stores; 71 Anglia Fireplaces & Design Ltd. (01223) 234713; 73 Corbis; 75 Gen Ex Kitchen (available from the American Appliance Centre, Enfield); 77 Thermador Professional Series (available from the American Applicance Centre, Enfield); 79 Interior Archive/Andrew Wood (Designer: Leonie Lee Whittle/Snap Dragon); 80–81 View/Peter Cook (Homes for the Future, Glasgow, Kirkstone Quarries); 82 View/Peter Cook (Architect: Fiona McLean), 82–83 Mark Wilkinson Furniture; 84 Elizabeth Whiting & Associates/Rodney Hyett; 85 International Interiors/Paul Ryan (Designer: Marjolyn Wittich); 86 Andrew Sydenham/Marshall Editions; 87 House & Interiors/Roger Brooks; 88–89 View/Dennis Gilbert (Architects: Chance de Silva); 90 Ikea; 92 International Interiors/Paul Ryan (Designer: John Saladino); 95 Corbis; 96–97 Corbis; 99 Houses & Interiors/Mark Bolton; 100 Elizabeth Whiting & Associates/Rodney Hyett; 101 Elizabeth Whiting & Associates/Rodney Hyett; 102–103 Arcaid/Nicholas Kane (Architect: Shahriar Nasser, Regent's Park Glass Extension); 104–105 Houses & Interiors/Roger Brooks; 107 Jerry Harpur; 108 (left) Clive Nichols (Clive and Jane Nichols), 108–109 Houses & Interiors; 110 Elizabeth Whiting & Associates/Michael Dunne; 113 Corbis; 114–115 The Stock Market/Don Mason; 116 Jerry Harpur (Phillip Watson, Fredencksburg, VA); 117 Jerry Harpur (Design: Oehme & van Sweden Associates); 119 Elizabeth Whiting & Associates/Jerry Harpur; 120 Garden Picture Library/Brigitte Thomas; 122 Houses & Interiors; 123 Houses & Interiors/Roger Brooks; 126–125 Camera Press/Greg Waugh (Australia Brisbane); 160–161 The Stock Market/Michael Keller; 162, 163, 168, 169, 171, 172, 173, 174 Bruce Mackie/Marshall Editions; Front cover Tony Stone Images/Joe Polollio (top left), Camera Press Ltd (top centre), The Stock Market/Pete Saloutos (top right), Elizabeth Whiting & Associates (bottom)

Illustration credit

All illustrations are by Patrick Mulrey.

Acknowledgments

The publishers would like to give special thanks to Kuo Kang Chen and Alexio Farrao for assisting in the illustrations and to Su Alexander for assisting in the photography research.